A GUIDE TO THE OLD TESTAMENT

A GUIDE TO THE
OLD TESTAMENT

by

G. GILBERT YATES

LONDON
THE EPWORTH PRESS

FIRST PUBLISHED IN 1965

Book Steward
FRANK H. CUMBERS

PRINTED AND BOUND IN ENGLAND BY
HAZELL WATSON AND VINEY LTD
AYLESBURY, BUCKS

AUTHOR'S NOTE

THIS BOOK has been prepared at the request of the Local Preachers' Studies Board. The 'Passages for Study' form the syllabus for the Connexional Examination in Old Testament for Methodist Local Preachers 'On Trial'. It is a pleasure to thank the members of the Old Testament panel for their constructive criticism as the work has proceeded, and also for suggesting the Test Questions. The bibliography and the footnoes will indicate in some measure my indebtedness to the many Old Testament scholars whose writings have been a source both of information and inspiration. The book would never have been completed but for the constant encouragement of my wife, who also undertook the laborious task of reading the typescript and checking all the biblical references. A few biblical quotations are from the *Revised Standard Version of the Bible*, copyrighted 1946 and 1952.

CAMBRIDGE G. GILBERT YATES

CONTENTS

FOREWORD

THE PUBLICATION of two new Biblical textbooks is an event; and particularly when they are such notable productions as this book and its sister-volume, *A Guide to the New Testament.*

We welcome these two books with both gratitude and high expectations. Our gratitude is due to the two authors—the Rev. Arthur W. Wainwright and Mr. G. Gilbert Yates—who have devoted so much time and care to this work, and to the members of our Studies Board who collaborated with them. We are indebted also to our good friends at the Epworth Press, and their printers, who at every stage have most helpfully co-operated in the production of these two quite outstanding volumes.

We also have high expectations. These books have been prepared primarily as prescribed textbooks, to help Local Preachers 'on Trial' in their study of the Bible; and we believe that they will prove invaluable to this end. But we look for more than this; we pray that many besides those committed to this particular course of training will turn for guidance to these two books. And we dare to hope that they will find here not only new light upon God's Word, but inspiration from God Himself.

A further word is due to the student. Each of these books is *'a guide'*. They are not the only guides; nor, as they point a way forward, do they claim that theirs is the only way. As we have said before, readers will find here 'many signposts, but not a set of tram-lines'. We want to stimulate thought, not to restrict it.

Our great assurance is that beyond these and all other 'guides' there is one Guide. Travellers who desire most of all to find and follow Him will not miss their providential way. In Biblical studies as in all else He *is* the way; and His Spirit will guide us into all truth—if we are willing to receive it.

Local Preachers 'on Trial' who are using this 'Guide' in preparation for their connexional examination, will find special instructions for them on pp. 261–3.

DAVID N. FRANCIS

INTRODUCTION

THE OLD TESTAMENT is a fascinating book, pulsating with life. Yet often it fails to grip the reader because its characters seem to be unreal; puppet figures performing on a stage set with improbable scenery suggested by illustrations from a child's book of Bible stories. Nevertheless the men and women of the Old Testament were creatures of flesh and blood 'of like natures with' ourselves, having 'hands, organs, dimensions, senses, affections, passions; fed with the same food, hurt with the same weapons, subject to the same diseases, healed by the same means, warmed and cooled by the same summer and winter' as other men.

The world in which they lived, in spite of obvious superficial differences, resembled our own. The great powers of the East (Babylon or Assyria) and the West (Egypt) confronted each other, drawing the smaller Palestinian States into their respective spheres of influence. The wanderings of the Patriarchs were a part of a general migration of whole populations; the names of people and places in the early chapters of Genesis can no longer be dismissed as legend, for the spade of the archaeologist has uncovered the remains of these ancient places and has enabled us to see how these early people lived.

One aim of the 'Guide' is to point the reader to this exciting world of the Old Testament. In the 'background' sections we take a brief look at the history and culture of the ancient world. It is hoped that this will whet the reader's appetite so that he will wish to turn to fuller accounts of the story of the Ancient Near East.

It is important to realize that the Old Testament deals with real people and real situations; it is even more important to realize that basically it is not a book about men, but about God. Many years ago Karl Barth wrote: 'Within the Bible there is a strange, new world, the world of God.' He is the real 'hero' of the story, from the opening chapter of Genesis to the last chapter of Revelation. This is particularly clear in the stories of the Patriarchs and of the Exodus. It is hoped that the rather full treatment given to the Patriarchs will help the reader of Genesis to appreciate the theological significance of these stories.

The primary aim of this 'Guide' is to direct the reader to the Old Testament. With this in mind, copious references have been made to the Old Testament text, which the reader should look up, for these passages will not only illustrate the text-book, but should also stimulate further thought. It is only by reading and re-reading the Old Testament that one can truly enter this 'strange new world of the Bible'; that one can share Sarah's joy at the birth of Isaac, or suffer Abraham's anguish as he climbs Mount Moriah with Isaac, or enter into all the various experiences whether of Patriarch, or Prophet, or Psalmist.

CHAPTER ONE

THE BEGINNING

I—THE LAND OF PALESTINE

'FROM Dan to Beersheba' (2 Sam 24²) is the Hebrew equivalent of our phrase, 'from Land's End to John o' Groats', but the distance between Dan in northern or upper Galilee, and Beersheba, near the southern border of cultivable land, is only about 150 miles. This tiny country, bounded on the west by the Mediterranean Sea and on the east by the desert, was the scene of most of the events described in the Old Testament. In addition to being the home of the Israelites, Palestine also formed a land bridge between the great imperial powers of the ancient world. The road from Assyria or Babylonia, in the valley of the Tigris and Euphrates, to Egypt lay through Palestine; a road used alike by merchants or invading armies.

The land itself is divided into two unequal strips by the deep gorge of the river Jordan, which meanders for most of its course below sea-level. Already at the Sea of Galilee the Jordan is 700 feet below sea-level, and it falls a further 600 feet before emptying itself into the Dead Sea. Proceeding westwards from the Jordan valley, near Jericho, the land rises rapidly, climbing to about 3000 feet above sea-level in less than twenty miles before descending to the Mediterranean Sea a further thirty miles away. This mountainous backbone, separating the Jordan valley from the coastal plain, stretches from Sinai in the south to the Lebanon in the far north. In only one place is there an easy passage from the Jordan to the Mediterranean, where the plain of Esdraelon (the scene of Barak's triumph over Sisera; Judges 4 and 5), running south-east from Haifa along the valley of the River Kishon joins the Valley of Jezreel, which runs north-west from the Jordan about fifteen miles south of the Sea of Galilee.

To the east of the Jordan, the land again rises sharply to 2000 feet or more. This elevated land stretches from Mount Hermon in the north to Edom in the south. It is broken here and there by the valleys and gorges carved out by the tributaries of the Jordan, and by rivers flowing into the Dead Sea. The chief of these tributaries are the Yarmuk, which flows into the Jordan just south of the Sea of Galilee, and the Jabbok which joins the river farther along its course. The

Arnon flows through a deep gorge directly into the Dead Sea about half-way along its eastern shore, whilst the Zered flows in at its southern tip. These rivers formed natural frontiers between the ancient kingdoms of Bashan, Ammon, Moab, and Edom.

The geological fault which formed the valley of the Jordan reaches its greatest depth at the Dead Sea. The fault continues south of the Dead Sea to the gulf of Aqabah; the broad valley joining these is called the Arabah. This valley, which rises to 650 feet above sea-level at its highest point before descending to the sea at Ezion Geber, is about five miles wide. It is covered with sand and loose stones and carries little

Figure 1. Drawing water. Egyptian tomb painting.

vegetation apart from a few scattered trees. There are no permanent streams in the Arabah, or indeed anywhere in the Sinai Peninsula, but there are many river beds where streams run in the rainy season. This desert region was, however, important for its mineral wealth. The deposits in the Arabah were extensively exploited in the time of Solomon, when the export of the refined metal yielded an important contribution to his treasury. This was 'a land whose stones are iron and out of whose hills you can dig copper' (Deut 8^9).

When the Israelites settled in Palestine they found an environment which contrasted both with Egypt and with the wilderness. By contrast with the wilderness, which yielded a reluctant livelihood to the nomads who wandered there, Palestine was a 'goodly land, a land flowing with milk and honey'. But by contrast with Egypt it was a land which depended for its fertility upon the rain falling in due season, 'not like the land of Egypt, from which you have come, where you have sowed your seed and watered it with your feet, like a garden of vegetables' (Deut 11[10]). The annual flooding of the Nile made possible the extensive use of artificial irrigation. The arable land on the banks of the river was intersected by a network of canals from which the water was raised by means of a mechanical contrivance operated by the foot. This introduced an element of certainty into Egyptian agriculture which was lacking in Palestinian.

Palestine is 'a land of hills and valleys, which drinks water by the rain from heaven, a land which the LORD your God cares for; the eyes of the LORD your God are always upon it from the beginning of the year to the end of the year' (Deut 11[11–12]). The farmer was completely at the mercy of the climate, an abundance of rain meant abundant harvests, even a surplus which could be exported (1 K 5[11]). On the other hand drought brought famine and disaster; at such times there must have been many, like the widow of Zarephath, who watched their stock of meal dwindling away with the awful knowledge that failure of the harvest meant no prospect of replenishment (1 K 17[12], see also Jer 14[1–6]). Even in a normal year no rain falls during the summer, which extends from the middle of May to the middle of September, but the heat, which in some places is almost unbearable, is for the most part tempered by the sea breeze which blows across the land daily from the Mediterranean Sea. Each day the sun rises rapidly, quickly dispelling the light mists which form in the valleys at night (Hos 6[4], 13[3]). This is the time of harvest; first the corn is gathered, and then the fruit as it ripens.

The rainy season lasted from late October to early April. During this period rain might fall on several days each week, but the most important rains (which therefore are mentioned in the Bible) were the 'former' and the 'latter' rains. The 'former rains' fell in late October and rendered the ground, parched and cracked by the long summer, fit for ploughing and sowing. The 'latter rains' fell in March and April. These heavy showers, the last before the summer drought, were vitally necessary if a good harvest were to be secured.

In a country as varied as Palestine not all the land was capable of cultivation and the natural vegetation differed markedly from place to place. The central highlands of Judah were for the most part rough and uncultivated. They were not, however, altogether devoid of vegetation and were suitable for grazing flocks of sheep and goats. This region is called, rather inappropriately, in the English versions of the Old Testament 'the field', and it was the natural haunt of the 'beasts of the field' (i.e. 'wild beasts'). This type of country has been likened to the English moorlands with their rough grass and few stunted trees.

In Old Testament times certain regions were densely wooded. 'Cedars of Lebanon' is a well-known Old Testament phrase, the cedar being much sought-after as a timber for building purposes. Cedar wood was a valuable export commodity, which evidently brought considerable wealth to the kingdom of Tyre during the reign of Hiram. Thus in 1 Kings 5^{5-11}, there is a description of a trade treaty which was agreed between Solomon and Hiram for the supply of timber to Solomon. 2 Chronicles 2^{10} gives further details of the agreement.[1]

Less-known forest areas were Gilead, east of the Jordan, and the plain just south of Carmel. In the latter region the combination of forest and swamp which ran down to the sea made this area virtually impenetrable. The name of Gilead is usually associated with the phrase 'balm of Gilead' (Jer 8^{22}, Gen 37^{25}). This valuable substance was obtained from the mastic tree, a small evergreen bush which flourished in Gilead. There were also extensive forests of larger trees in which men might lose themselves and so perish. The battle between David's army and the rebel forces led by Absalom took place in the forest of Gilead; 'and the forest devoured more people that day than the sword' (2 Sam 18^{8}). Absalom himself was one of the victims claimed by the forest.

The cultivated land was confined to the hill-sides and the valleys. Corn was grown in the Plain of Esdraelon and the Valley of Jezreel. The ripe corn at harvest time attracted the unwelcome attention of Midianite raiders from the deserts beyond the Jordan in the time of Gideon (Jdg 6^{33}). Later, in the reign of Solomon surplus wheat from Esdraelon was one of the commodities which was exchanged for timber (1 K 5^{11}). Wheat was also grown in that part of Gilead which was watered by the river Jabbok, and on the foothills and the coastal plains to the west of the Judaean heights. This was Philistine country, though in the days of Samson the tribe of Dan also lived in the foothills overlooking the fertile valley of Sorek,[2] whose very name conjures up pictures of luscious fruit. In the revenge for the slight which he received from the Philistines, Samson fired their corn as it was being harvested (Jdg 15^{1-6}).

The steeper hill-sides which were not suited to ploughing and the

[1] In 1 Kings 5^{11} read '20,000' instead of 20, following the LXX, and supported by 2 Chronicles 2^{11} and Josephus, *Ant.* VIII.ii.9.

[2] '*Sorek*', the Hebrew name of one of the best kinds of vine.

growing of grain, were nevertheless fertile enough to justify cultivation. Here were to be found the vineyards so often mentioned in the Bible. The ground was broken up with a mattock, the stones were removed and the hill-sides carefully laid out in terraces where the vines were planted (Isa 5^{1-2}). Not infrequently fig trees were grown along with the vines, the former acting as a support for the latter, and both offering welcome shade to the farmer in the hot summer months. In the Old Testament this picture of a man sitting under his vine and fig tree is used to describe the peace which was enjoyed during the reign of Solomon (1 K 4^{25}), and it became a symbol of the peace which would be enjoyed in the Messianic Kingdom (Mic 4^{4}, Zech 3^{10}).

The grapes were used for making wine, but some were dried and used as raisins. The fig tree also yielded an abundant harvest, moreover figs could be gathered for ten months out of the twelve. The main crop of ripe figs was harvested from August to the winter. Green figs which had grown too late to ripen remained on the trees and could be plucked and used; in the spring these winter figs would ripen to yield the first-ripe fruit in June. The sycomore referred to in Amos 7^{14} was also a species of fig. The quality of the fruit was rather poor, but the crops were heavy. The fruit had to be pricked or cut to make it ripen and Amos combined the culture of these trees with sheep-farming.

Another tree cultivated throughout Palestine for its fruit was the olive. So various are the uses of the fruit that it was an ideal crop for the poorer folk. The fruit could be eaten raw or cooked, and the oil which it yielded was used for cooking, for toilet purposes, in ointments, or as fuel for lamps.

Other fruit such as apricots and pomegranates were known and cultivated. Vegetables also were used: onions, leeks, garlick, and cucumbers are named in the Bible. The well-to-do people may even have had regular vegetable gardens (AV and RV 'garden of herbs'). Ahab at any rate wished to have such a garden near his palace in Jezreel and tried to persuade Naboth to sell him his vineyard for this purpose (1 K 21).

The situation is quite different in the Jordan valley. The river follows a sinuous course along the narrow floor of the great depression which stretches from Mount Hermon to the Dead Sea. Between the Sea of Galilee and the Dead Sea the valley bottom is far below sea-level. It is about fifteen miles wide near Beth-shan in the north and also near Jericho to the south, but for the most part it is a narrow rift some three miles wide, called by the Arabs 'El Ghor', i.e. 'The Rift'.

The salty nature of the soil and humid heat of the summer have conspired to prevent any extensive cultivation of this region. The valley, filled with rank vegetation, used to be the haunt of wild beasts and particularly lions. This is the 'jungle of Jordan' (Jer 12^{5}, 49^{19}, 50^{44}), made even more repellent by the mud, shingle, and driftwood deposited annually when the Jordan floods, and spreads out over the whole valley bottom. The river itself, when not in flood, flows through a muddy course in the midst of this unhealthy jungle. It is about ninety feet wide, and its depth varies from three to ten or twelve feet. One can feel some sympathy for Naaman when he demurred at bathing in the Jordan! (2 K 5^{10-11}).

II—THE SACRED WRITINGS OF THE HEBREWS

The New Testament contains many references to 'scriptures' or 'sacred writings', with which the readers were assumed to be familiar. Thus Paul exhorts Timothy: 'Continue in what you have learned and have firmly believed, knowing from whom you have learned it, and how from childhood you have been acquainted with the sacred writings which are able to instruct you for salvation through faith in Christ Jesus' (2 Tim 3^{14-15}). In his controversy with the chief priests and elders Jesus said to them 'Have you never read in the scriptures . . .' (Mt 21^{42}). Sometimes these 'scriptures' are called more specifically 'the law and the prophets' (Mt 22^{40}), or even more fully 'the law of Moses, and the prophets, and the psalms' (Lk 24^{44}).

The 'scriptures' or 'sacred writings' mentioned in the above texts are of course the collection of books which we call the Old Testament. The longer description in Luke 24^{44} refers to the three parts into which the Hebrew Bible is divided, and for which the title in Hebrew is 'The Law, the Prophets and the Writings'. Since the Book of Psalms is the first book in the third section of the Hebrew Bible it is likely that the word 'psalms' in Luke 24^{44} is intended as a reference to the 'writings' as a whole. In the English Bible the books are arranged in the same order as in the Greek translation (the Septuagint) of the Hebrew Bible, which is slightly different from the order of the original.

The first section of the Hebrew Bible is 'the Law'. This consists of the first five books, Genesis to Deuteronomy, and was held in special veneration. It probably reached its final form in the fourth century BC but includes material of much greater antiquity. It was the first part of the Old Testament to be regarded as specially sacred, and from about the fourth century BC, if not earlier, its regulations were held to be binding upon the Jews. Since some of the regulations were very general and vague there grew up a body of scholars (the scribes), learned in the Law, who made it their business to interpret the ancient laws to suit later conditions. Unfortunately, the often humanitarian spirit of the original legislation was lost in the excessively literal and detailed interpretation given by the scribes. It was this type of interpretation which was condemned by Jesus.

'Law' is an unfortunate name for this part of the Old Testament. It is the usual translation of the Hebrew word '*Torah*', but the latter means 'instruction' as well as 'law', and so includes more than formal legislation. The laws included in the *Torah* are, of course, one means of giving instruction on what God requires of His worshippers. But the stories of the Patriarchs and the history of the Exodus show God at work guiding His servants, and these also are another way of giving instruction about the character of God.

The second section of the Hebrew Bible, the Prophets, is itself subdivided into two parts, the 'former' and the 'latter' prophets. The first subdivision contains the books of Joshua, Judges, 1 and 2 Samuel, and 1 and 2 Kings, whilst the 'latter' prophets comprises Isaiah, Jeremiah, Ezekiel, and the Twelve Minor Prophets. Daniel is not reckoned with the prophets, as in the English Bible, and this fact has some bearing on the interpretation of the book.

The Jews believed that the historical books had been written by various prophets, and so they were included in the collection of prophetic books. Though we often tend to think of them as historical works pure and simple, it soon becomes obvious that their interest is religious, rather than historical. Thus some of the kings, whose reigns would be regarded as important by a historian, are dismissed in a few verses. We are told very little about Omri, the father of Ahab, but we have reason to believe that he was a strong ruler. Ahab himself suffers by contrast with Elijah in the narrative in 1 Kings, though from records outside the Bible it appears that Ahab was the prime mover in organizing an alliance against Assyria.

The third section of the Hebrew Bible contains the rest of the books of the Old Testament. This is a varied collection, containing such extremes as the Book of Job, a profound book dealing with the problem of suffering, and the Song of Songs, a collection of love poems! This was the last section to be recognized as 'sacred scripture', and for many years the Rabbis debated whether certain books, for example the Book of Esther, should be included. Some other books which were included in the Greek translation, but were not accepted as part of Hebrew Scriptures, are to be found in the Apocrypha. Agreement on which books were to be included in the Hebrew Bible was probably reached about AD 100 by a council of Rabbis meeting in Jamnia, though most of the books had been accepted as sacred scripture long before this. The early Christians adopted the rather longer Greek version as their 'scriptures'; to this the New Testament was added later. After the Reformation the Protestant Churches followed the lead of the Reformers in accepting only the Hebrew Bible as the Old Testament, but the Roman Catholic Church still includes the Apocrypha in its Old Testament.

III—THE TRANSMISSION AND TRANSLATION OF THE OLD TESTAMENT

The Old Testament was written originally in Hebrew, the only exception being some portions of Daniel and Ezra, which were written in Aramaic. Before the advent of printing all books were copied by hand, and in spite of the great care which was taken to ensure the production of accurate copies it was almost inevitable that some mistakes would be made. By comparing ancient manuscripts it may be possible to detect and correct errors made by copyists. For this reason old manuscripts are invaluable to the scholar. Until 1948 scholars had to depend on manuscripts not older than about the seventh century AD, apart from some papyrus fragments from about the second century AD. The oldest complete Hebrew Bible dated from about the ninth century AD. The discovery of Hebrew Scrolls in caves near the Dead Sea in 1948, and since that time, has furnished us with manuscripts of many parts of the Old Testament which were in use at the beginning of the Christian era. Thus we now possess manuscripts of much of the Old Testament several centuries older than anything previously known and these new discoveries have in the main confirmed the accuracy of the text which we already possessed. The task of comparing manuscripts in order to arrive, if possible, at an accurate text is the work of the Textual Critic, and it cannot be too strongly emphasized that Textual Criticism is *not* destructive criticism, rather it is an arduous task aimed at the vital and constructive purpose of reproducing as faithfully as possible, the very words of the ancient scriptures.

After 721 BC Israel ceased to be an independent kingdom, and in 586 BC her smaller sister Judah was also overrun by the powerful Babylonian army. In accordance with the practice of the times many of the Jews were deported to Babylonia, and others fled to Egypt. Thus from this time onwards there were Jewish colonies to be found scattered about the ancient world. After 330 BC when Alexander the Great, by his conquests, spread Greek language and culture throughout the Near East, many of the Jews began to use Greek as their native tongue, and it was natural that they should require a translation of their scriptures into the language with which they were most familiar. Tradition has it that a translation of the Law into Greek was made in Egypt during the reign of Ptolemy II (285–247 BC) by a group of seventy scholars who, working independently, produced identical versions. Hence this Greek translation of the Old Testament is always known as the Septuagint (LXX or the version of the seventy). Whilst we may regard some of the details of this tradition as fanciful, it seems certain that the translation of the Pentateuch dates from about 250 BC. The remaining books of the Old Testament were translated during the next 150 years, so that at the beginning of the Christian Era the whole of the Old Testament was available in Greek, and in this form was known and used by the New Testament writers.

By the first century AD, Hebrew had been displaced by Aramaic as the spoken language in Palestine, and during the first two centuries AD, translations of the Hebrew scriptures were made into Aramaic. These were rather free translations called '*Targums*', an Aramaic word meaning 'interpretations'.

Another language, rather similar to Aramaic, which was spoken in Palestine, was Syriac; a translation was made into this language probably about AD 200.

During the fourth century AD, St Jerome made a Latin version of the Old Testament. This translation, which was made directly from the Hebrew, was intended to replace an earlier one which had been made from the Septuagint. Jerome's Bible, known as the Vulgate, became the official Bible of the Church, a position which it still enjoys in the Roman Catholic Church.

IV—INTRODUCTION TO THE PENTATEUCH

The first section of the Hebrew Bible, the Law or *Torah*, is divided into five books, Genesis to Deuteronomy, as in the English Bible. This subdivision is indicated in the alternative title 'Pentateuch', which is often given to these five books. 'Pentateuch' is derived from a Greek word which means 'five volumes'. Traditionally these books were ascribed to Moses, in spite of the fact that Deuteronomy 34^{5-6} records the death, and burial of Moses. This is only one of the more obvious pointers to the non-Mosaic authorship of the 'Pentateuch'. Careful study of these books reveals variation in style, duplication of narratives, and even discrepancies between various parts of the same narrative. Thus the story of creation in Genesis 1 and 2 falls into two distinct sections: 1^{1}–2^{4a}, and 2^{4b-25}; these are distinguished not only because the manner of creation is portrayed differently in the two parts, but also by totally different literary styles. Again Genesis 12^{10-20}, 20^{1-18}, and 26^{1-11} appear to be variant recitals of the same story. (Some scholars believe that the Isaac story is the original one. This version assumes that there were Philistines in Canaan in the Patriarchal period —Genesis $26^{1, 8}$ etc. In fact the Philistines did not enter Canaan until about 1200 B C, i.e. long after the Patriarchal times. We conclude that this story was written some centuries after the Philistines came into the land, and hence long after the death of Moses.) In Genesis 37 there seems to be a union of two slightly different accounts of the sale of Joseph by his brothers. In one account the Midianites buy Joseph, in the other, the Ishmaelites.

These and similar facts may be explained by supposing that the stories were originally handed down separately, and orally, then later, collections of stories and other material, particularly codes of laws, were made and finally the complete Pentateuch came into being. Working from the books as we now have them, it has been possible to analyse them into four main strands, and with a fair degree of confidence to assign probable dates to their composition.

The earliest of the four collections of material is usually called the 'J' source or document, after one of its most easily recognized characteristics, namely, the use of the proper name 'Yahweh' ('LORD' in the English versions) as the name of God, whereas throughout Genesis the other sources prefer to use the general term, 'God' (in Hebrew, 'Elohim'). In fact there is a very good reason for this preference, as we read in Exodus 6^{2-3}. 'And God said to Moses, I am Yahweh (the LORD); I appeared to Abraham, to Isaac, and to Jacob, as El Shaddai (God Almighty); but by my name Yahweh (the LORD) I did not make myself known to them.' This is to be contrasted with Genesis 4^{26b} which suggests that the name Yahweh was used from very early times. Views so diametrically opposite could hardly be attributed to the same author. The 'J' collection is believed to have been made in Judah during the early monarchy, say about 950–900 B C.

The stories connected with Hebron, the great sanctuary in southern Palestine, are found in this source.

The next oldest collection is denoted by the letter E, since this source uses the Divine name 'Elohim' ('God') in Genesis. E and J are not always easy to distinguish, especially in the later books of the Pentateuch, when both sources use the name 'Yahweh'. There are, however, other differences of vocabulary and style which help to separate out the two sources. The E collection was probably made in the Northern Kingdom of Israel about 750 B C; stories referring to the northern sanctuaries of Bethel, and Shechem, are a feature of this source. Copies of E were probably taken to Judah by refugees from Israel after the fall of that kingdom in 721 B C. J and E would then be combined into a single narrative, giving an account of the origins of the Hebrew people up to the time of the conquest of Canaan.

The third source of the Pentateuch is distinguished from the other three in that it is confined in the main to the Book of Deuteronomy, and conversely the bulk of that book is thought to belong to this one source, which is therefore denoted by the letter D. D is generally identified with the Book of the Law which was found in the Temple during the reign of Josiah about 621 B C (2 K 22[8]). The teaching of Deuteronomy shows the influence of the eighth-century prophets, and it also expressly forbids sacrificial ceremonies at the high places, requiring such solemn observances to be performed at one central sanctuary. Such a regulation was unknown before the time of Josiah's reform which was influenced by the law book discovered in the Temple.[3] Thus it is held by many scholars that this book was compiled, on the basis of ancient legislation, during the reign of Josiah's grandfather Manasseh. As his reign was characterized by the encouragement of all manner of idolatrous worship in imitation of the Assyrians, the book was probably written secretly and concealed.

The latest collection of material, which was ultimately included in the Pentateuch, appears to have been made by the priests during, or shortly after, the Babylonian exile. Though the actual compilation was late, this does not preclude the inclusion of material which had been handed down for many centuries. The particular interest of the priests in ritual, and religious ceremonies is evident in this source, which is usually called P, or the Priestly Code. Included in this document is the second part of Exodus, Leviticus, and the bulk of Numbers, as well as shorter passages in Genesis, and in the rest of Exodus. The formal

[3] See p. 173, *infra*.

style of writing, which is prominent in Genesis 1, is characteristic of this source as a whole.

We have attempted to give in the above paragraphs an outline of a widely held view of the process by which the Pentateuch grew. Ultimately, probably about the time of Ezra (*c.* 400 BC), these four traditions were woven into a single work, dealing with Israelite origins and history up to the time of the conquest of Canaan. It is probable that the J and E sources also contained material which was eventually incorporated into the books of Joshua and Judges and perhaps even Samuel.

Though it is possible, with a fair degree of success, to analyse the Pentateuch into its constituent sources it should not be forgotten, that as we now have it in the Bible, it is intended to be seen as a unity. Its focal point is the Exodus interpreted as a saving act of God and summed up in the opening words of the Ten Commandments: 'I am Yahweh your God, who brought you out of the land of Egypt, out of the house of bondage' (Ex 20[2]).

NOTE. It is not possible in a few paragraphs to present, in detail, evidence justifying the separation of the Pentateuch into four primary sources J, E, D, and P. The reader who desires further information should consult a full-scale introduction to the Pentateuch, e.g. *A Critical Introduction to the Old Testament,* by G. W. Anderson.

THE NAMES OF GOD IN THE OLD TESTAMENT

The Hebrew word for 'God' (or 'god') is 'Elohim'. This is actually plural in form, and must occasionally be translated 'gods' when the word is used of the gods of the heathen. The usual meaning and translation is 'God'.

God also has a personal name in the Old Testament, this is the name 'Yahweh', once abbreviated to 'Yah' (or 'Jah') in Psalm 68[4]. This abbreviation is commonly used as a part of proper names, e.g. Isa-iah, Jerem-iah, etc., and it occurs in the familiar exclamation 'Hallelu-iah'. From motives of reverence the Jews ceased to use the name 'Yahweh', and substituted the word 'Adonay' ('My Lord') in the public reading of the scriptures. Thus in the Hebrew Bible we find a composite word made up of the consonants of 'Yahweh' and the vowels of 'Adonay' which appears in English as 'Jehovah'. (J, Y, and I are all used to represent the same Hebrew letter; also the short 'a' at the beginning of Adonay becomes 'e' in the composite word 'Jehovah'.) The English versions usually translate 'Yahweh' by 'LORD'.

V—PASSAGES FOR STUDY

Genesis 1[1]–2[4a] (P)—*The Creation of the World*

In order to appreciate the description of the creation given in Genesis 1 the reader should be familiar with the ancient ideas of the structure of the universe. The sky was thought to be a solid hemisphere (the 'firmament'), directly below the highest point of this inverted bowl was the dry land which rested upon water and was surrounded by water (the seas). Above the firmament was the vast upper ocean from which the rain fell upon the earth when the 'windows of heaven' were opened.

Verse 1 is a title to the creation story and a summary of its contents. The subject of this chapter is the creation of the world, and this opening verse gives us a picture of a spontaneous action on the part of the self-existent God. The particular Hebrew word here translated 'created' is only used in the Hebrew Bible of the divine creative activity, and it implies effortless creation, without any thought of the material from which the universe is made. We find it difficult, perhaps impossible, to think of creation out of nothing; so did the Hebrews, the nearest they could get was the conception of a primitive, formless, watery chaos in total darkness (verse 2), out of which the heavens and the earth were created. T. S. Eliot uses words from Genesis 1[2] with great dramatic effect:

> *'waste and void, waste and void,*
> *and darkness on the face of the deep.'*

Each element in this description contrasts with the final state of creation which is characterized by order instead of chaos, light instead of darkness, and life instead of a dead waste. The fundamental idea of Genesis 1 is not so much the creation of the world out of nothing, as the bringing of form and orderliness out of chaos, harmony out of discord. By the will of God the forces of chaos are held in check, by the word of God the ordered universe rises out of the formless void.

The creation is described schematically as taking place in eight stages, each of which is inaugurated by a divine command, and thus the primeval chaos is duly reduced to order. First the darkness gives place to light. Then the waters are confined to their appointed place, some above the solid inverted hemispherical bowl (the firmament), and the rest underneath forming the seas. These surround the dry land which is situated in the centre of the bowl.

The scene is prepared for the appearance of life, and in successive utterances of the creative word the various forms of life appear. First the lowliest—vegetation and trees, then the animals of the seas and the air, and finally the denizens of the earth. In the middle of this description of the appearance of living things occurs, apparently incongruously, the account of the creation of the Sun, Moon, and stars. The comparatively subordinate place assigned to the creation of the heavenly bodies is probably deliberate, and designed to counteract the

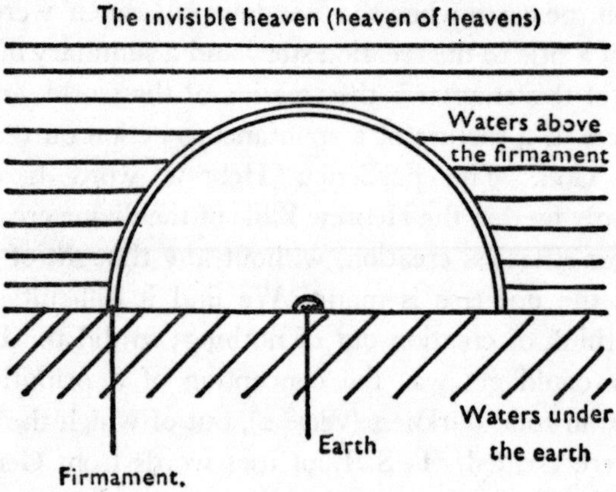

Figure 2. The universe according to early ideas.

current heathen beliefs in which the Sun, Moon, and stars were worshipped as gods. In Genesis the heavenly bodies are placed firmly among the rest of creation.

The eighth work is the creation of mankind. Although in the six-day scheme which forms the framework of Genesis 1 this act of creation takes place on the same day as the creation of the land animals, yet it is evident that the creation of man is clearly distinguished from all the previous creative acts. All other living things, whether vegetable or animal, are described as being each 'after its kind', i.e. not modelled on anything else. Of man alone it is said: 'Let us make man in our image, after our likeness.' Before the act of creation is described in verse 27, we are permitted a glimpse into the court of heaven as God deliberates with the heavenly hosts—this is the probable meaning of the plural form, 'Let *us* make . . .'. This imagery appears elsewhere in the Old

Testament, e.g. 1 Kings $22^{19\,ff}$, Job $1^{6\,ff}$, and seems to be implied here. The purpose of man's creation is that he should exercise dominion over the earth. But he exercises this dominion as God's 'image'. 'Just as powerful earthly kings, to indicate their claim to dominion, erect an image of themselves in the provinces of their empire where they do not personally appear, so man is placed on earth in God's image as God's sovereign emblem.'[4] It is clear that even in this opening chapter of the Bible we are taught that man is both privileged (as God's representative on earth), and responsible to God in whose Name he exercises dominion.

The conclusion of the whole matter is that creation as it came from the hand of God is 'very good'. This does not mean that the editor of Genesis was either ignorant of, or chose to ignore, the imperfection and evil in the world as we know it, but it does mean that he was convinced of the goodness of the Ultimate Power behind the created world. The fact of evil is faced in the succeeding chapters, whilst redemption from it is the theme of the Bible.

According to the priestly scheme of Genesis 1 the work of creation occupies seven days, but on the seventh day the work was finished (Gen 2^2) and God rested.

Genesis 2^{4b-25} (J)—*The Garden of Paradise*

The compiler of Genesis included two accounts of the creation in his final composition. There are obvious differences between them, but these did not trouble him. The second narrative is included to explain the tremendous attraction between the sexes which overrides even the ties binding children to parents. Thus the narrative opens with the creation of man who is the focal point of the description.

This Yahwist account begins with the second part of verse 4: 'In the day that the LORD God made the earth and the heavens, . . . then the LORD God formed man of dust from the ground, and breathed into his nostrils the breath of life. . . .' The Yahwist (as we may call the writer of J) works on a more modest canvas than the Priestly writer; his conception of the universe barely extends beyond the earth. His starting-point is not the primeval watery chaos of Genesis 1^2, but rather a barren infertile earth which cannot support even the sparsest vegetation because, as yet, it has not received from God the gift of life-giving water. The contrast in the mind of the writer is clearly that between the inhospitable desert, and the cultivated land.

[4] G. von Rad, *Genesis* (ET), p. 58.

Yahweh's first act is to make man. Even less than P is the Yahwist able to imagine creation out of nothing so he pictures God as a master craftsman moulding a man out of 'dust of the ground', but the form receives life from God Himself.

As in Chapter 1, man is the one for whom the world is created, though in the present chapter this truth is set forth differently. Thus God plants 'a garden' for the man. This should rather be understood as an extensive park of the kind which were occasionally laid out by the great Oriental monarchs. Thus everything is provided for man's well-being. (Verses 10–14 interrupt the sequence of the narrative which is resumed at verse 15.) At the same time there is laid upon man the responsibility of tending and guarding the garden, which will provide all that he needs for sustenance. He has complete freedom to use all that Yahweh so bountifully provides, only the tree of knowledge is forbidden to him.

The Yahwist sees the creation of the animals as further evidence of God's gracious care for man. It is 'not good' for man to be alone; the animals are created to be his companions. In naming the animals the man asserts his authority over them; this thought of the dominion which man should, under God, exercise over nature is also prominent in the Priestly narrative of Chapter 1. But the man did not find the desired companion among the animals, they were not 'after his kind'. So the scene is set for the final act of creation in the Yahwist narrative.

A supernatural sleep falls on the man (cf. Gen 15^{12}) during which God fashions (literally, 'builds') the woman from one of his ribs. 'The narrative is moved by the thought that God's miraculous creating permits no watching. Man cannot perceive God "in the act", cannot observe His miracles in their genesis; he can revere God's creativity only as an accomplished fact.'[5] Yahweh brings the woman to the man who greets her in an ecstasy of joy. 'Then the man said, This time this one is bone of my bone, and flesh of my flesh; this one shall be called Woman for this one was taken from Man' (Gen 2^{23}).

On this note, which in its own way implies the goodness and harmony of the creation as it leaves the hands of the Creator (cf. Gen 1^{31}), the Yahwist brings his narrative to a close. Verse 25 reflects the idyllic perfection of the original creation, and also prepares the way for the story of the Fall. 'It is a transition verse, leading over to the main theme to which all that goes before is but prelude.'[6]

[5] G. von Rad, *Genesis* (ET), p. 81.

[6] J. Skinner, 'Genesis', *ICC*, p. 71.

Genesis 3 (J)—*The Fall*

Of Man's first disobedience and the fruit
Of that forbidden tree....
Milton—*Paradise Lost*

Both the Priestly and Yahwist writers agree that the world and all its creatures owe their origin to the one God who is supreme. Both writers agree that the result of God's creative activity was 'very good'. It is a fact of experience, however, that we do not know the life of Paradisical perfection and harmony. Instead we experience imperfection and disharmony; not only is there enmity between men, but man's dominion over nature is imperfect; so the problem of evil forces itself upon our attention. If creation came perfect from the hand of God, and if Yahweh alone is God, how did this evil arise? This problem forms the subject of Genesis 3.

The writer makes use of primitive legends to convey his teaching. There seems little doubt that serpents were once worshipped as demons, nevertheless the writer of Genesis 3 is at pains to stress the fact that even the serpent, in spite of its reputation for craftiness, was only a 'wild creature', owing its existence to Yahweh like any other creature. Although in the narrative the serpent plays its part in directing the woman to the Tree of Knowledge, yet it is made plain that the root of all evil is the disobedience of man.

It is worth considering the story in some detail. The serpent accosts the woman, 'Did God say . . . ?' which is as much a statement as a question, and asked sneeringly. Of the opening word of the question, translated 'Yea' in the Revised Version, Luther commented: 'I cannot translate the Hebrew either in German or Latin; the serpent uses the word *aph-ki* as though to turn up its nose and jeer and scoff at one.'[7] The sneer produces the desired effect; the woman is quick to reply that all the trees except one are for their use. The serpent is now completely master of the direction which the conversation will take. It is easy to point to the prize to be secured for eating the forbidden fruit—'You shall become divine beings'—with perfect knowledge. Man covets that which belongs to God alone.

Even as they grasp the prize it turns to dust; for the knowledge which they secure is knowledge of their guilt. The serpent now virtually disappears from the story. The man and woman are left to

[7] G. von Rad, *Genesis* (ET), p. 83.

confront Yahweh whose approaching footsteps they already hear. They have aspired to divinity, and now they hide, trembling, among the trees. Their action condemns them before ever the man makes his self-betraying reply to Yahweh's question. The terrible aftermath of man's attempt to overstep the limits assigned to him by Yahweh is graphically described. The idyllic life, where the work of caring for the garden, which yields the food necessary for his welfare, was congenial, gives place to the hard unrewarding toil of the peasant farmer, whose life is a constant struggle against the thorn and thistle which the ground now bears. The perfect state of blissful communion between man and woman hinted at in Genesis 2^{24} is now distorted almost beyond recognition, in the unenviable lot of woman in ancient society, groaning in childbirth and in complete subjection to her husband.

Yet in spite of this harrowing description of the fruits of disobedience, the writer refrains from saying that man is cursed by God. The serpent is cursed for its part in the tragedy; the ground is cursed for man's sake, and under the shadow of this curse man must live. But though punished and expelled from Eden lest further presumption should evoke further disobedience, he is not forsaken by God. For Yahweh Himself intervenes to cover the shame which is the result of the ill-gotten knowledge (3^{21}). 'That means, he accepts men as those who are fallen. He does not compromise them in their nakedness before each other, but he himself covers them. God's activity keeps pace with man.' [8]

NOTE. Genesis 3^{5}. The RVm reading is to be preferred. The Hebrew 'Elohim' generally means 'God'. It is, however, a plural word and occasionally its primitive significance 'divine beings' is intended. It is unlikely that a biblical writer would equate (even in the mouth of the serpent) man and God, but he could say: 'You will become divine beings.'

SOME PSALMS IN PRAISE OF GOD THE CREATOR

The splendour of the universe, reflecting the glory of its Creator, not unnaturally forms the subject of some of the poetry of the Old Testament. The creation stories of Genesis are retold in poetry in Psalms 8 and 104, whilst in Psalm 29 there is a vivid description of a violent thunderstorm sweeping across Palestine.

[8] Bonhoeffer, *Schoepfung und Fall*, quoted by von Rad in *Genesis*, p. 94.

Psalm 8—*Genesis* 1 *in Poetry*

The psalm begins with an ascription of praise to Yahweh. The English version somewhat blunts the effect of the opening words by retaining the rendering 'LORD' for the personal name 'Yahweh'. The psalmist is proclaiming that Yahweh 'our Lord' is not only God of Israel, but the Creator of the universe. 'The God who makes himself known to Israel by his name Jehovah, as their Redeemer (cf. Ex 3^4), is the God who created the heavens and laid the foundations of the earth.'[9]

The psalm then raises the perennial question of man's place in the universe. This was evidently as much a problem to some of the ancients as it is today. There were those who were so impressed by the immensity and splendour of the heavens, that they were ready to write off man as an insignificant speck. The question which the psalmist asks in verse 4 would seem to demand the answer 'nothing'. Instead he recalls the teaching of the creation stories. Man is made in the image of God, and so can be described as 'little less than God' and crowned with glory and honour. The true perspective has been restored; all nature in its varied forms is intended to be in subjection to man.

Verse 2. Translate 'children' rather than 'babes'. There is a climax in the verse: 'Out of the mouths of children, yea even sucklings Thou hast founded strength. . . .' The verse is probably contrasting the unquestioning faith of a child with the scepticism of the adult.

Verse 4. 'son of man'—The phrase means quite simply 'man'. This verse furnishes a good example of the parallelism so characteristic of Hebrew poetry, in which the second half of a verse repeats in slightly different language the meaning of the first half.

> What-is-man that-Thou-art-mindful-of-him,
> And-the-son-of-man that-Thou-dost-care-for-him?

The original consists of four word groups as indicated by the hyphens, the second group is almost identical with the first in meaning.

The Title of the Psalm: 'The Gittith'. The meaning of this word is uncertain. It appears to be an adjective derived from the name of the town Gath, and so has been explained (*a*) as the name of an instrument which came originally from Gath, or (*b*) as a melody originating there.

Psalm 104—*In Praise of the Creator*

'This Psalm painting for us in the frame of the world, and the order of

[9] J. J. S. Perowne, *Psalms*, I.157.

nature, the living image of God's wisdom, power, and goodness, exhorts us to praise Him, because in this our frail mortal life He manifests Himself to us as a Father' (Calvin).[10]

The psalm begins and ends on a note of praise: 'Bless the LORD, O my soul!' The grounds of the psalmist's praise are the wonders of the creation, which bear witness to the might of the Creator, and also to His continued activity in replenishing the earth and in caring for man and animal alike (verses 10–23). Twice in the psalm the author breaks out in a pean of praise.

> 'O LORD how manifold are thy works!
> In wisdom hast Thou made them all;' (verse 24);
> 'I will sing to the LORD as long as I live;
> I will sing my praise to my God while I have being' (verse 33).

(cf. Isaac Watts's hymn, 'I'll praise my Maker while I've breath'—*MHB*428.)

The psalm should be read in conjunction with Genesis 1. Verses 2–9 of the psalm recall the first three acts of creation in Genesis 1$^{1-10}$; verses 10–23 of the psalm emphasize the dependence of man and beast alike on the life-giving rain. There is nothing outside God's care; even the sea and the great monsters of the deep, so often thought of as objects of terror, are here shown in their dependence on God, not only for food, but equally with all other creatures for life itself (verse 29).

Psalm 29—*The Storm*

This remarkable psalm wonderfully conjures up the impression of a violent storm sweeping across Palestine from the Lebanon in the north to Kadesh in the south. It falls into five parts:

(i) The Prelude: verses 1–2. The psalmist conveys us to the court of heaven where we hear the heavenly beings praising God.

(ii) The first rumblings of the storm: verses 3–4. Thunder ('the voice of the LORD') is heard re-echoing among the distant storm-clouds. The repetition in verse 4 imitates the growing violence of the storm, which is unleashed in all its fury on Lebanon and Hermon (Sirion is another name for Hermon).

(iii) The storm at its height: verses 5–7. When the storm reaches its climax, the cedars are struck down and the mountains themselves seem to rock (verse 6) as the jagged forks of lightning shoot out from the storm clouds.

[10] Quoted by Perowne, *Psalms*, II.232.

(iv) The storm dies away: verses 8–9. The storm clouds sweep southwards, and at last the fury of the storm is spent in the final outburst over Kadesh, stripping the forests bare, and causing the hinds to calve prematurely in their terror.

(v) The conclusion: verses 10–11. These verses beautifully reproduce the atmosphere of calm after the storm. (The musical reader will be reminded of the similar impression created by the final movement of Beethoven's 6th symphony.)

The storm, which spoke of God's power, is also the source of life-giving rain. After the fury the psalmist can say: 'May the LORD bless His people with peace.' 'This closing word *with peace* is like a rainbow arch over the Psalm. The beginning of the Psalm shows us heaven open, and the throne of God in the midst of the angelic songs of praise; while its close shows us His victorious people upon earth, blessed with peace in the midst of the terrible utterance of His wrath. "*Gloria in excelsis*" (Glory in the Highest) is the beginning, and "*Pax in terris*" (Peace on earth) is the end.' [11]

[11] Delitzsch, quoted by Kirkpatrick in *Psalms*, p. 151.

CHAPTER TWO

THE PATRIARCHS (1)

'ABRAHAM IS OUR FATHER'

A PERIOD of almost two thousand years separates Abraham from the New Testament, yet even in New Testament times the Jewish people still remembered with pride their descent from the Patriarch. The early traditions of the ancestors of the Hebrew people were recited at the annual religious festivals, and so remembered until eventually they were committed to writing. Joshua 24 describes such a religious ceremony at Shechem which must have been typical of the ceremonies where the people reaffirmed their faith in God, and heard again the stories of their origins (cf. also Deut 26^{1-11}).

But it seems that it was, above all, in the dark days of the Babylonian exile and the disheartening period that followed, that the faithful were encouraged as they recalled God's dealings with Abraham. He had been called from 'beyond the River' (i.e. the Euphrates, Josh 24^{3}), and had received the promise that he would be the father of a great nation and the source of blessing for 'all the families of the earth' (Gen 12^{2-3}). As later generations pondered the stories of Abraham, so he became for them the great example of the man of faith and hope (cf. especially Heb $11^{8-12, 17-19}$), for the promise made to him and fulfilled in Isaac became a symbol of hope to the Jews in exile—'Look to Abraham your father, and to Sarah who bore you, for when he was but one I called him, and I blessed him and made him many' (Isa 51^{2}). Again his communion with God seemed to be so intimate that 'he was called the friend of God' (Jas 2^{23}; cf. also 2 Chr 20^{7}, Isa 41^{8}).

By New Testament times, however, the Jewish opponents of Jesus and Paul had come to believe that the physical descent from Abraham, in which they boasted, was a sufficient guarantee of their acceptance with God. This is very clear in the controversy between Jesus and the Jews recorded in John 8. The true descendant of Abraham, however, must emulate the Patriarch in whom they show so much pride (Jn 8^{39-40}, Rom 9^{7-8}).

The story of Abraham is related in Genesis 12–25. We have already learnt how the Pentateuch was ultimately compiled from the traditions and laws which had at first been handed down orally from one generation to another. We have also seen that it was particularly at the sanctuaries, such as Shechem, that these stories were remembered and retold as a part of the religious celebrations. The worshippers themselves were encouraged to remember and recite some of the ancient traditions. It is clear that the purpose of telling and retelling these stories was more than entertainment, but rather that each succeeding generation should learn that Yahweh, the God of Israel, had made Himself known by His activity in history, and particularly by His dealings with Israel. This same instructional purpose was served when the stories were collected together and committed to writing, for the writers were conscious that they were drawing back the curtains on the opening scenes of the great drama of Redemption. The Old Testament writers were primarily theologians and not historians, though much of their work is also of first importance for the historian. Thus even the earliest collector of ancient stories, the unknown author whom we have called 'J', already understood that in the wanderings of the Patriarchs the Divine purpose was being fulfilled. In this he is at one with the latest compiler 'P', who equally understood the theological significance of the tradition that in the call of Abraham there was also the promise of blessing for all mankind. All the Abraham stories are linked by one dominant theme : the promise and its fulfilment through Isaac.

But Abraham was also a historical figure, and the Bible preserves memories of the migration of his clan from Mesopotamia to Canaan, though it gives very little information about the land and the people among whom they moved. Indeed some Old Testament scholars of a previous generation had begun to doubt whether there was much, or even any, historical value in these chapters of Genesis. Archaeological discoveries over the past few decades have completely altered the picture. Whilst it is too much to claim that these discoveries have 'proved' the existence of the Patriarchs, they have shown that the migrations hinted at in Genesis fit into the general pattern of the movement of peoples in the period 2200–1500 BC. Furthermore the Creation and Flood stories of the early chapters of Genesis, as well as much of the Pentateuchal legislation, are of Mesopotamian origin and could have been carried by the migrants as they made their way to Canaan. An account is given at the end of this chapter of the fascinating civilization of the Near East during the Patriarchal period, which has been recovered for us by recent archaeological research.

PASSAGES FOR STUDY

Genesis 11^{28}–12^{9} (Mainly J)—*The Call of Abraham*

This passage describes the migration of Abraham and his clan from Ur to Canaan, which was accomplished in two stages. First the larger clan headed by Terah, Abraham's father, made the journey to Haran. It has sometimes been supposed that Terah left Ur to get away from the cult of the Moon god, Sin, but this can hardly have been the motive as Haran was also an important centre of this worship. We shall see below that the Habiru, among whom were Abraham and his clan, were by nature a wandering people. Some of the clan settled in Haran (Gen 27^{43}, 28^{10}, 29^{4}) whilst Abraham with his nephew Lot and their clan moved southward into Palestine (Canaan). In their wanderings they avoided the well-populated valleys with their fortified cities and kept to the highlands, camping in turn near Shechem and then near Bethel before making their way to the southern wilderness, the Negeb. Subsequently a famine drove them to seek food in Egypt. If the migration of Abraham from Haran took place at the time when the Hyksos were invading, or in possession of Egypt, we can understand why the Habiru wanderers were able to find refuge in the land. In the present state of our knowledge it is impossible to give precise dates for the Patriarchs. Various dates have been suggested for Abraham and reasons have been given both in support of and against each suggested date! The present writer believes that the period of the Hyksos invasion of Egypt (*c.* 1730 BC) is as likely as any. For further information about the Hyksos invasion of Egypt see the section on the historical background to the Patriarchs at the end of this chapter.

NOTES

Genesis 11^{30}. 'Now Sarai was barren; she had no child.' The fact that Sarai was childless is noted thus early in the narrative; its significance becomes increasingly clear as the story unfolds.

Genesis 12^{1}. 'There is intentional pathos in the lingering description of the things he is to leave: *thy land, thy kindred,* and *thy father's house*; and a corresponding significance in the vagueness with which the goal is indicated: *to a land which I will show thee.*'[1]

Genesis 12^{6}. 'the *place* of Shechem' is not the town or city of Shechem but an ancient sanctuary near Shechem marked by a single

[1] J. Skinner, 'Genesis', *ICC*, p. 243

tree. Near this place Abraham receives Yahweh's promise (verse 7) and so learns the reason for the command of verse 1.

Genesis 13 (J)—*The Separation of Abraham and Lot*

This chapter gives another glimpse of nomadic life. The wealth of a nomadic clan and its prosperity depended on the possession and welfare of the herd of small cattle, sheep, and goats, for which they must find grazing grounds. This necessitated constant change of pasture, but each clan had its own circuit of grazing-grounds and would not normally trespass beyond it. Also by arrangement with the settled population, the nomads were permitted to graze their flocks on the stubble of the cultivated fields after the harvest had been taken off. Abraham and his clan evidently moved between the Negeb and the region adjacent to Bethel. They were probably to be found in the latter regions after harvest time, returning again to the Negeb for winter and spring before the sparse vegetation had been scorched by the high summer.

The difficulty of finding adequate pasture for the ever-increasing herds led to friction within the clan. Abraham, magnanimously forgoing his rights as chief of the clan, allowed Lot to choose grazing-grounds for his herds. Lot looked eastwards over the valley of Jordan, and coveted the well-watered plain with its ample pasturage which seemed like the Garden of Eden. So he made his choice and departed. Abraham must now make the best of what is left to him, but it is in this situation, childless, deprived of the best land, that the divine promise is renewed. The real climax of the passage is reached in verses 14–17. 'Abraham is now alone, but Yahweh comes to him; and while Lot took the land that pleased him, God says, "I will give it to you".'[2] So Abraham journeyed south again and settled near Hebron.

NOTE. Genesis 13^{13}. This comment is interjected here in anticipation of Chapter 19.

Genesis 15 (E)—*Promise and Covenant*

The opening words of the chapter, 'After these things', denote an indefinite, but possibly rather long, passage of time. The fulfilment of the promise that Abraham should have heirs who would possess the land of Canaan seems to be increasingly unlikely. Then 'the word of Yahweh' came to Abraham in a dream. (Verse 1 mentions a vision whilst verse 5 makes it clear that this occurred during the night.) This word carries the promise of a great reward (verse 1), but to Abraham

2 G. von Rad, *Genesis* (ET), p. 168.

this is no compensation for the lack of an heir (verse 2). So he concludes that he must adopt one of his trusted slaves as his legal heir. It was supremely important that there should be an heir; the estate and the possessions must be kept within the family and clan. Thus adoption was a common practice if a couple were childless. Many of the tablets found at the ancient city of Nuzu (see map 'The Ancient World') refer to legal adoptions which were often of advantage to both parties. The childless person secured an 'heir' who would care for him (or her!) in his old age and finally give him a proper burial. The 'heir' enjoyed security during the life of his 'parent' and inherited the estate on the death of the latter. This, however, is not the meaning of Yahweh's promise for in due time Abraham will have a natural son—'and he believed Yahweh' (verse 6).

The remainder of the chapter describes a solemn and mysterious ceremony associated with the making of a covenant. Jeremiah 34^{18-19} refers to a similar ceremony, and from the description in this passage it is evident that those entering into the covenant walked between the pieces of the slain animals. The mysterious solemnity of the present ceremony is vividly portrayed. As the sun sets, the lonely Patriarch keeps his watch, beating off the birds of prey. Then he is overcome by a deep and supernatural sleep[3] during which Yahweh, represented by the flaming torch, passes between the pieces. But in *this* ceremony Yahweh alone passes between the pieces, Abraham is the passive recipient both of the promise, 'To your descendants I give this land' (verse 18), and of the guarantee—the covenant. For this covenant with Abraham has its origin in the will of Yahweh, and He alone contracts the obligation to fulfil His promise.

Notes

Genesis 15^2. The latter part of this verse, 'and the heir of my house, etc.', is untranslatable; none of the attempts, ancient or modern, to get a meaning for, or from, the Hebrew original of this phrase are convincing. Fortunately the absence of this phrase does not affect the general sense of the passage.

Genesis 15^6. Translate 'and he trusted in Yahweh'; this trust was the basis and condition of a right relation to Yahweh.

Genesis 17^{1-22} (P)—*The Sign of God's Covenant*

The story of Abraham is moving steadily toward its climax. God again speaks of the covenant which is being established with Abraham, who

[3] This is the significance of the Hebrew.

on his part is required to 'walk before' God (i.e. to live consciously in God's presence) and to be 'perfect'. The Hebrew word translated 'perfect' (RV) or 'blameless' (*RSV*) also means 'spotless' or 'without blemish', and is used to describe the animals which were fit for sacrifice. Here it signifies surrender to God's will. There is now a fuller statement of the benefits of the covenant, which looks beyond the birth of an heir to the future generations with whom the covenant is also made. These future generations will receive the land of Canaan as their possession, and God will be their God also. As a sign that he has accepted the terms of the covenant Abraham is required to circumcise all the males of his household. The promise of an heir is again repeated, and with each repetition the promise becomes more explicit. First Abraham has learnt that his heir would not be an adopted slave (15^{4}), now he learns that Ishmael, his son by the slave woman, is not the chosen heir (17^{19}), but Isaac, whom Sarah will bear in due time, and with whom the covenant will be established. The introduction of the story of Ishmael into the narrative spotlights another custom, common in ancient times, whereby the continuity of the family could be ensured. The childless wife would give one of her personal maids to her husband in the hope that a son might be born of their union. The son would then be reckoned as the child of the wife and would succeed as heir. So Sarah had hoped to secure an heir by giving Hagar to Abraham, but though Ishmael was to be the ancestor of a nation (17^{20}), he was not the one concerning whom the promises had been made. God's hand will not be forced; 'the story of Hagar shows us to some extent a faint-hearted faith that cannot leave things with God and believes it necessary to help things along' [4]

Genesis 18^{16-22} (J)—*Abraham's Intercession*

This is one of the great chapters of the Old Testament. Abraham has entertained three strangers at his encampment near Hebron, and one of them has revealed himself to be Yahweh. When the heat of the midday is past, Abraham goes with his guests a little way from Hebron towards Sodom. Two of the guests continue on their way, but Yahweh stays with Abraham, for He has decided to unfold to him His purpose in visiting Sodom. He is about to investigate the complaints concerning the sinfulness of the city and to punish it.

Then on one of the heights east of Hebron, overlooking the Dead Sea and in view of the sinful city, Abraham engages in a remarkable

[4] G. von Rad, *Genesis* (ET), p. 168.

conversation. He does not question the validity of the complaint concerning the sinfulness of Sodom. This is assumed to be established beyond doubt, but guilty and innocent are inextricably mixed up in a community, so Abraham asks: 'Wilt Thou indeed destroy the righteous with the wicked' (18^{23}). 'The meaning of his question then is: "What determines God's judgement on Sodom the wickedness of the many or the innocence of the few?"'[5] Abraham was well aware that, according to the ethics of his day, the crime of an individual might involve the punishment of his family. The new insight which he has gained suggests to him that the innocence of the few might save the many. As the astonishing conversation proceeds he learns that even ten righteous men are sufficient to avert the judgement. Abraham stops at ten; is this the limit of God's grace? This seems to have been so in Abraham's view, but though *he* stops short yet the finger is already pointing towards the Suffering Servant of Isaiah 53 and beyond towards the 'Son of Man' who 'came to give His life as a ransom for many' (Mt 20^{28}).

Genesis 19^{1-29} (J)—*The Destruction of Sodom and Lot's Deliverance*

The scene changes to Sodom, it is evening and the two messengers have just arrived at the city. Lot alone offers them hospitality for the night, though as the city gate was the place where the inhabitants gathered to exchange news, we must presume that other men of Sodom were also present. The latter indeed spread the news abroad that the strangers were lodging with Lot, and by their subsequent actions gave abundant proof that 'their sin is very grave' (18^{20}). Lot's attempt to protect his guests seemed to be doomed to failure, then, when quite at the end of his own resources and in danger of being overwhelmed, the protector becomes the protected. In his extremity Lot discovers a power sufficient for the need. None but his own family heed the warning to flee from the city, others whom he warned received his words with incredulity (19^{14}). Even Lot hesitated and might have perished with Sodom but 'the LORD, being merciful to him' (19^{16}), constrained him to flee from the doomed city. As the sun rose the cataclysm fell on the city; away on the heights east of Hebron, overlooking the valley, stood Abraham. By *his* intercession Lot had been saved, but the prosperity he had enjoyed by choosing 'all the Jordan valley' (13^{11}) was at that moment disappearing with the smoke of Sodom. But Abraham's hope lay in God's promise drawing ever nearer to its fulfilment.

[5] G. von Rad, *Genesis* (ET), p. 208.

NOTES

Genesis 19^{11}. 'blindness.' The Hebrew probably indicates not total blindness so much as being dazzled so that the men were no longer able to see distinctly, but groped about trying to find their way.

Genesis 19^{24}. The catastrophe may have been caused by an earthquake which released inflammable vapours, engulfing the region in 'brimstone and fire'. The writer of Genesis 19 is however primarily concerned with sin and its consequences.

Genesis 21^{1-8} (J, E, P)—*The Birth of Isaac*

At last the promise of an heir to Abraham is fulfilled. Sarah's joy is unbounded. The barren woman was an object of pity and even contempt (see for example Gen 16^{4}), but now Sarah's reproach has been taken away and she cries: 'God has made laughter for me.' There is a play on words here which is lost in English; the Hebrew word for 'laughter' closely resembles the name 'Isaac'. But Sarah's joy is perhaps tinged with a slight embarrassment as she recalls her sceptical laughter of twelve months previously (18^{12}) for now 'every one who hears will laugh over (i.e. 'at') me' (21^{6}) (N.B. not 'with me' as in the RV). Some two to three years later according to the custom of the times Isaac was weaned, and this was the occasion of a great family celebration.

Genesis 22^{1-19} (E)—*Abraham's Gethsemane*

Several years have passed since the joyous festival which celebrated the weaning of Isaac (21^{8}), for Isaac is now old enough to understand what things are necessary for a sacrifice and to carry a load of wood as he and Abraham climbed to the mountain-top (22^{6}).

Abraham's camp is now located at the oasis of Beersheba, in the Negeb, twenty-eight miles south-west of Hebron. There had been some conflict with his Canaanite neighbours (21^{22-4}) which had been settled amicably. Abraham and Abimelech concluded a formal treaty (covenant) of friendship ($21^{27\,ff}$) so that 'Abraham sojourned many days in the land of the Philistines' (21^{34}). This outward peace was rudely shattered by the peremptory command which came to Abraham one night. The narrator tells us that God was seeking to test Abraham (22^{1}). 'The story which is the literary masterpiece of the Elohistic collection, is told with exquisite simplicity; every sentence vibrates with restrained emotion, which shows how fully the author realizes the tragic horror of the situation.'[6] The enormity of God's demand is emphasized by the long-drawn-out description of Isaac: 'Take your son, your only son Isaac, whom you love, and go to the land of Moriah, and offer him there as a burnt offering' (22^{2}). The situation in which Abraham finds himself is just that kind of situation envisaged by our Lord when he bids us pray: 'Do not bring us to the test' ('Lead us not into temptation') (Lk 11^{4}). This is Abraham's Gethsemane, he has been brought to the test, and while *we* know what the outcome will be, we must, nevertheless, walk with him along this terrible road.

In this narrative, conversation is cut to a minimum. The old man, burdened with his thoughts, the young lad as yet unaware of the full significance of the journey, and the two servants set out early in the morning, while it is still cool, for their distant objective. The journey itself was a part of the test to which Abraham submitted; during the three days his obedience to the divine command did not waver. The final stage of the journey was undertaken by Abraham and Isaac alone; each thinking his own thoughts. Isaac pondered on the lack of the sacrificial lamb, Abraham on the deeper mystery of God's strange, incomprehensible demand. For Isaac was the son through whom the promise made to Abraham was to be fulfilled; every hope for the future was pinned upon him and his loss seemed to be God's denial of His own promise. So this road which Abraham must tread has been described as 'a road out into Godforsakenness on which Abraham does not know that God is only testing him'.[7]

The silence is broken by Isaac's question and Abraham's evasive and yet strangely prophetic answer. The drama moves on to its terrible climax as Abraham raises the sacrificial knife to perform the final dreadful act that absolute obedience demands. It is enough. The angel of Yahweh can now say: 'I know that you fear God.' The tension eases, Abraham sacrifices the ram instead of his son, whom he has received back as it were from the dead (Heb 11^{17-19}). Now the promise can be renewed that through Abraham all the nations of the earth shall be blessed.

Notes

(*a*) Genesis 22^{1-19} is the appointed Old Testament lesson for the service of Matins on Good Friday.

(*b*) Genesis 22^{2}. 'The land of Moriah.' The name Moriah occurs

6 J. Skinner, 'Genesis', *ICC*, p. 328. 7 G. von Rad, *Genesis* (ET), p. 239.

again only in 2 Chronicles 3[1], where it refers to the mountain in Jerusalem on which the Temple stood. It seems improbable that this was the scene of Abraham's sacrifice. The latter place is unknown, and seems to have been unknown to very early translators of the Old Testament, some of whom translated the phrase as 'the land of the Amorites'.

(*c*) Many scholars hold that the story in its earliest form was told to explain how human sacrifice came to be replaced by animal sacrifice at a certain shrine the name of which is now lost from the story. The Elohist's motive in including the story in his collection was to show how Abraham's faith was equal to the test put upon it.[8]

Psalm 105—*A Song of Thanksgiving*

Israel not only remembered her history through the stories which were handed down, probably at the sanctuaries, from one generation to another, and which were ultimately collected into the sacred scriptures, but also in the hymns which were used at the great festivals. God's choice of Israel, His covenant first made with the Patriarchs, and the great event of the Exodus form the subject matter of many of the psalms. According to his mood the psalmist might work these historical themes into a hymn of praise as he meditates on God's goodness, or a hymn of penitence as he contrasts Israel's faithlessness with God's mercy.

Psalm 105 is a psalm of praise and thanksgiving. Throughout the psalm the worshipper's attention is directed towards God, and there is no mention of Israel's sin. It has been suggested that this psalm may have been used in a ceremony of covenant renewal. In the opening section, verses 1–6, the people are summoned to praise God, and to remember 'his wonderful works'. The long central section, verses 7–42, recalls God's gracious dealings with their forefathers as exemplified in the covenant with the Patriarchs, the redemption of Israel from Egypt, and their preservation in the wilderness. These are the grounds for joyous thanksgiving and for wholehearted obedience (verses 43–5).

HISTORICAL BACKGROUND

The Fertile Crescent

Although we naturally and rightly associate the events and personalities of the Old Testament with the land of Palestine, for a fuller understanding of the Book it is desirable to take note of the nations and happenings beyond the confines of the Holy Land. The story of the

[8] J. Skinner, 'Genesis', *ICC*, p. 332; G. von Rad, *Genesis* (ET), p. 238–9.

migration of the family of Abraham from Ur, a city in southern Mesopotamia, shows that the ancestors of the Hebrews had come into Palestine from farther east. Again the fortunes and misfortunes of the Israelites were closely connected with the rise and decline of the empires of the Ancient Near East.

Men could only establish permanent settlements for themselves where there was an adequate supply of water, and so the earliest settlements have been in the great river valleys. The story of the garden of Eden illustrates this fact, and rightly directs our attention to the valley of the Tigris and the Euphrates as one of the early homes of mankind (Gen 2[14]). Remains of villages and towns which abound in this fertile valley show that already in 5000 B C men were living in organized communities in this region. From the same early period men were also settling in that other fertile valley of the Near East—the Nile Valley, and these two valleys were destined to become the homes of some of the great imperial powers of the ancient world. Palestine forms the bridge between these two river valleys; a fertile strip connecting two fertile valleys, the whole forming a 'Fertile Crescent' of land bordered by desert, sea, or mountains. Within the crescent lay the Syrian Desert, and beyond, a mountainous region separating Mesopotamia from the Steppes of Russia and the Caspian Sea.

Sumer and Egypt

We pointed out above (p. 33) that Abraham's migration from Ur was a part of large-scale movements of people early in the second millennium B C. But before describing these migrations which disturbed and ultimately brought to an end civilizations which had long been established both in Mesopotamia and Egypt, we must look first at these earlier civilizations. A confused memory of one of them (the Sumerian) is preserved in the story of the Tower of Babel (Gen 11[1–9]), and in the names of some of the cities such as Babel (i.e. Babylon) and Erech (or Uruk) (Gen 10[10]). The Sumerians were building these cities, a score or more of them, in southern Mesopotamia (Shinar) almost 2000 years before Abraham (*c.* 3500 B C). They had already learnt how to make bricks from a fine clay which abounds in this region. They had also learnt how to write by making signs on wet clay tablets which were subsequently baked. Such inscribed clay tablets, many of which have now been deciphered, are an invaluable source of information to historians.

The most striking feature of these ancient Mesopotamian cities was the tower or Ziggurat. These were artificial mountains surmounted by a small temple (or house of the god). The Sumerians, who had originally come from a mountainous region, believed that their gods dwelt on the mountain peaks, and since there were no mountains in southern Mesopotamia they provided these towers as substitutes. In biblical times the Ziggurat of Babylon was a well-known feature of this city, but much of our information about the construction of these towers has been obtained by the investigation of the rather well-preserved Ziggurat of Ur.[9] The residential parts of the cities give an impression of wealth and affluence. The private houses of the wealthy people at any rate 'bespoke comfort and even luxury'[10]; they were two-storey buildings with a dozen or more rooms arranged around a central court-yard, and they were equipped with drainage, sanitation, and toilet facilities. The literary and scientific attainments were hardly less sophisticated than the architectural ones. Inscribed tablets containing subjects as various as hymns and mathematical tables bear silent testimony to the cultural achievements of this long-dead civilization.

At the other end of the Fertile Crescent, in the Nile Valley, the first period of Egyptian splendour (the Old Kingdom 2660–2180 B C) had reached its zenith and had passed away long before Abraham visited the land of the Pharaohs (Gen 12[10 ff]). The great pyramids at Giza, perhaps the best known of the Egyptian monuments and a lasting tribute to the skill of the ancient engineers, were built about 2600 B C. The pyramids impress by their very size and symmetry, but these great buildings and the temples, which were associated with them, were beautified yet further by the work of the artist and sculptor. The Pharaohs and their wives and sometimes their children, as well as great officers of State, have been preserved in life-like, and often more than life-size statues sculptured in stone. Scenes from everyday life were depicted in relief, and often brilliantly coloured, on the walls of the temples or tombs. The art of writing had been practised probably from about 3200 B C and medical science was sufficiently advanced for a treatise on surgery to be written about 3000 B C.

The Amorite Invasions

This first period of Egyptian Imperial splendour came to an end with the reign of the Pharaoh Pepi II, then for about 160 years there seems to have been little effective central government in Egypt. It is probable

[9] Sir L. Woolley, *Ur of the Chaldees*, p. 130. [10] Ibid., p. 130.

that a part of the country was overrun by Asiatic invaders, whilst some of the provinces temporarily became independent kingdoms under local Egyptian princes. This invasion of Egypt was part of a great upheaval affecting the Near East generally, and marking the end of a well-defined phase of civilization and culture in that area—The Early Bronze Age.

The invaders who had spread through Syria and Palestine were the Amorites, a people of Semitic stock, nomads from the Syrian desert who overran the old cities, destroying as they went. Ancient centres of civilization such as Jericho and Megiddo were completely devastated, and rebuilding was not undertaken for many decades, in fact the chief material remains of this period are cemeteries! Evidently these nomads were careful to secure permanent sites for their tribal burial-grounds. In this connection we recall that Abraham purchased such a burial-ground for his clan from the Hittites (Gen 23[3 ff]). About this time other elements of the great Amorite migration were sweeping into the Tigris-Euphrates valley, eventually bringing to an end the age-old civilization of Sumer.

The Recovery of Egypt—The Middle Kingdom

Some 160 years after the death of Pepi II, one of the provincial rulers in southern Egypt was able to extend his authority over the whole land and assume the role and title of Pharaoh. In 1991 B C, the first king of the twelfth dynasty came to the throne, and under this new dynasty Egyptian power and influence began to increase. The grouping of the reigns of the Pharaohs into dynasties was due to the Egyptian priest Manetho, who compiled a history of Egypt in the third century B C in which he gave a list of the Pharaohs who had reigned from about 3000 B C. These names he divided into thirty groups or dynasties. Later historians have used Manetho's system as a matter of convenience. Monuments of the twelfth-dynasty Pharaohs have been found as far north as Ugarit on the coast of Syria (see map 'The Ancient World'), and it is evident that by 1900 B C the whole of Palestine and Syria was under Egyptian control. In Palestine, under the influence of stable conditions in Egypt, urban civilization reappeared. The nomads were settling down, building new cities on the ruins left by their predecessors, and a civilization destined to last about 700 years was developing. This was true not only of Palestine, but of the whole Fertile Crescent, where a number of city States ruled by Semitic (Amorite) princes had developed.

The Middle Bronze Age

Excavation of the royal palace at Mari, one of these Amoritic city States (see map 'The Ancient World'), has brought to light some 20,000 inscribed clay tablets. These proved to be letters in the Assyrian language written in cuneiform script. They were composed during the eighteenth century B C and give considerable insight into the complex civilization of the Middle Bronze Age. Some of the letters deal with affairs of State, and it appears that the various rulers had their accredited ambassadors at foreign courts who sent regular reports to their Governments. Other letters give details of military operations from which we

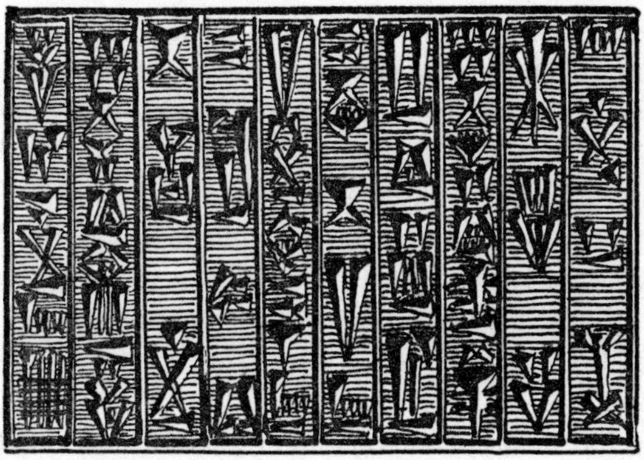

Figure 3. Syllabic cuneiform writing (Code of Hammurabi).

learn, among other things, that Assyrian engineers could build a ramp of earth against a city wall in six days, thus enabling a city to be taken by storm in a comparatively short time. Another correspondent complains of the lack of competent builders in a provincial town, and yet another that the carpenters of Mari were superior to the Assyrian ones! Significantly, nowhere in this vast correspondence do we find Egypt or the Hittites mentioned. It is clear that the influence of Egypt was waning. The vast empire, stretching as far as the Euphrates, carved out in the twentieth century B C by the Pharaohs of the twelfth dynasty, had collapsed. Even their monuments in Ugarit had been defaced. On the other hand, the Hittites were not yet a threat to the Mesopotamian States. It was a period of small States and fluctuating alliances in which Hammurabi of Babylon would ultimately emerge as the most powerful ruler. An agent of Zimri-lin, king of Mari, sent this report to his master: 'There is no king really powerful in himself. Some ten or fifteen kings go with Hammurabi of Babylon, as many with Rim Lin of Larsa, as many with Ibal-pi-el of Eshnunna, as many with Amut-pi-el of Watanum, and twenty with Yarim-Lim of Yamkhad' (i.e. Allepo).

The Hurrian and Hittite Migrations

The Amorites who had overrun Mesopotamia and Palestine from about 2300 B C were a Semitic people. Sometime in the third millennium B C, people of Indo-European origin, the Hurrians, began to migrate westwards from their home near the Caspian Sea. By 2000 B C they had taken possession of the city of Nuzu (see map 'The Ancient World'), which became an important centre of Hurrian culture. Excavation of this city has yielded valuable information about the life and particularly the laws of these people, throwing welcome light on some of the practices of the Patriarchs. During the next two centuries the Hurrians gradually pressed westwards into Upper Mesopotamia where they met the Amorites. 'At Chagar Bazar, in the heart of Upper Mesopotamia where the two streams meet it is the Hurrians who came off best. On the other hand, to the south, at Mari, on the edge of the desert, the Amorites are completely triumphant.[11] Having secured control of the region to the north of Mari, the Hurrians carved out for themselves a kingdom, Mitanni, which was to become a powerful State in the fifteenth century.

Yet other Indo-European wanderers, the Hittites, eventually found their way into Asia Minor. It is as yet uncertain what route they took, but early in the second millennium they had begun to build up the nucleus of a strong kingdom in Asia Minor and the power politics of the fifteenth century was to centre around the three empires, Egyptian, Hittite, and Mitannian.

The Habiru

Early in the second millennium B C another name, the Habiru, also begins to appear in the records. The first references to these people were discovered in the cuneiform tablets which were recovered from the ruins of Akhetaton, near to the modern village of Tell el-Amarna (see map 'The Ancient World'). This was the capital city of the Pharaoh Akhnaten (*c.* 1379–1362 B C). During his reign the city States of Palestine, which were nominally subject to Egypt, were being attacked by raiders from the desert, and the rulers of these city States appealed to Pharaoh for military assistance. These communications, inscribed on

[11] J-R. Kupper, *Northern Mesopotamia and Syria*, p. 26.

clay tablets, were carefully filed away in the archives at Akhetaton, though it seems very doubtful whether any aid was despatched to Palestine.

The raiders are called 'Habiru' on the tablets. When these tablets were first discovered it was believed by many scholars that here was a clear reference to the invasion of Palestine by the Hebrews under Joshua. Further discoveries have made this view extremely unlikely, but they have given us a clearer picture of the Habiru.

We now know that people called by this name were to be found in Nuzu about 2000 B C, where they often served as voluntary slaves. Somewhat later the name occurs in the Mari letters, but here the Habiru are free-booters who lived by making lightning raids on the flocks of sheep which they drove off, killing or capturing the shepherds. There are various references in Egyptian texts from which it appears that some Habiru (Apiru in the Egyptian texts) served as slaves in Egypt. These may have been captured in battle, for one Pharaoh recounts how 2600 Habiru were taken prisoner after a battle in Palestine. The general picture which emerges is that of a people who had no fixed roots, living as free-booters, or as slaves, or as mercenary soldiers according to circumstances. Thus the name Habiru did not apply to a particular race of people, but rather to folk of a somewhat dubious social status. The name Hebrew as used in the Old Testament carries something of this stigma too, for example Potiphar's wife says contemptuously of Joseph: 'See, he has brought among us a Hebrew to insult us . . .' (Gen 39[14]).

It is clear that these Habiru, most of whom were probably Semites, were also involved in the migrations which we have seen to be a feature of the Middle Bronze Age, and it is among them that we should look for the Abrahamic clan of 'wandering Arameans'. For unlike the Amorites and Hurrians who developed the highly complex Middle Bronze Age civilization on the ruins of the Early Bronze Age cities, the Habiru, and among them the Hebrews of the Bible, remained throughout this period wanderers on the fringe of this civilization. For the most part they coexisted peacefully with their settled neighbours, though occasionally there was violent conflict as when the clans of Levi and Simeon sacked the Canaanite city of Shechem (Gen 34).

The Epistle to the Hebrews portrays the situation in miniature: 'By faith Abraham obeyed the call to go out to a land destined for himself and his heirs, and left home without knowing where he was to go.

By faith he settled as an alien in the land promised him, living in tents, as did Isaac and Jacob' (Heb 11$^{8-9}$ *NEB*).

The Hyksos

We have already seen that in the twentieth and nineteenth centuries BC Egyptian power was paramount in Palestine, and in the stable conditions which then existed the Middle Bronze Age civilization began to develop. From about 1800 BC, however, Egyptian influence in Palestine began to wane, and a new military ruling class seized control of many of the Amorite city States. The newcomers seem to have consisted of small, but well-organized, groups of Hurrians who had been joined by some of the Habiru. Their military superiority lay in their possession of a formidable new weapon, the war chariot. By force of arms they took possession of the Palestinian city States, without however changing or influencing the now well-established civilization. During the eighteenth century BC they penetrated into Egypt and in 1730 BC finally conquered it. The Egyptians called these foreign rulers 'Hyksos', a name of rather uncertain meaning. The historian Manetho understood the name to mean 'Shepherd', and so these rulers are often referred to as the 'Shepherd Kings'. Many Egyptologists now prefer to translate the word as 'rulers of foreign lands'. When the Hyksos had secured control over Egypt they established their capital at Avaris on the Nile Delta and for a time ruled over an empire stretching from Nubia to the Euphrates.

Hyksos rule in Egypt came to an end when a Theban prince headed a successful nationalist rising about 1580 BC. The foreigners were driven out of Egypt by his son, Pharaoh Aahmes I. They held on grimly in Palestine for many years and were a constant menace to Egypt until Tuthmosis I, the grandson of Aahmes I, made a great raid through Palestine and Syria as far as the Euphrates, securing another era of peace for Egypt.

TABLE I

From the Patriarchs to David

BC	*Egypt*	*Palestine*	*Mesopotamia and Asia Minor*
2270	End of Old Kingdom		Hurians in Nuzu
2220–2210	Amorite migrations from Arabian desert into Fertile Crescent and Egypt		
2000–1800	Middle Kingdom		
1730–1570	Hyksos in Egypt	Abraham	Rise of Hittite and Mitannian Empires
1379–1362	Akhnaten	Israelites go into Egypt. Habiru raids in Palestine	
1301–1234	Rameses II		
1234–1222	Merenptah	Exodus	
1210		Israelite invasion of Canaan	
		Period of the Judges	
1000		Saul (*c.* 1000 BC)	
		David (1000–961 BC)	
		Solomon (961–922 BC)	

NOTE.—These dates are approximate.

CHAPTER THREE

THE PATRIARCHS (2)

THE HISTORICAL BACKGROUND: FROM THE EXPULSION OF THE HYKSOS TO THE EXODUS

IN THIS introductory section we continue the study of the historical background to the Patriarchal stories. In the last chapter we suggested that Abraham and his clan migrated to Palestine during the time of the Hyksos invasion of Egypt. In this chapter we take up the stories of Jacob and Joseph, and find an appropriate setting in the reign of the Pharaoh Akhnaten (1379–1362 B C).

The Expulsion of the Hyksos

During the Hyksos period it appears that the Theban princes continued to exercise authority over Upper Egypt, whilst acknowledging the overlordship of the Hyksos rulers in Avaris. In this small semi-independent kingdom of Upper Egypt the Thebans endeavoured to keep alive the traditions and customs of the earlier centuries. 'Above all, we find in this small Upper Egyptian kingdom evidence of the indomitable spirit which had already in the eleventh Dynasty lifted Egypt out of a state of depression and disorder and which was again destined, within the next hundred years, to bring her to new heights of prosperity and power.' [1]

The struggle, which ended with the triumph of the Theban rulers and the expulsion of the Hyksos from Egypt, began with the revolt of the Theban prince Seqenenre II, 'the Brave', against his overlord Apophis. Seqenenre met a violent end; his mummy shows that he died as a result of terrible head wounds which he may well have received in battle against the Hyksos. The war of liberation was carried on by his son. Eventually Aahmes, another of his sons, reduced the Hyksos capital city of Avaris, drove the foreigners out of Egypt and assumed the throne himself.

The Rise of the New Kingdom in Egypt

The reign of Aahmes marks the beginning of the period of Egyptian Imperialism, a period which lasted from about 1570 B C to 1070 B C.

[1] W. C. Hayes, *Egypt: From the Death of Ammenemes III to Seqenenre II*, p. 27.

This 'New kingdom', as it is usually called by historians, attained the peak of its power in the reign of the Pharaoh Tuthmosis III, *c.* 1470 BC. This ruler undertook systematic campaigns to reduce Syria-Palestine to subjection, though his predecessors had already made raids into Palestine and Syria. His grandfather, Tuthmosis I, had penetrated into Asia as far as the Euphrates.

Palestine was at this time divided into a number of small city States, which were often at war with one another, though on occasion several such States might combine, temporarily, against a common enemy. Opposition to Tuthmosis III was headed by the King of Kadesh, a city on the Orontes (see map 'The Ancient World'). The two armies met at the pass of Megiddo; the Egyptians routed the Canaanite forces and eventually captured the fortified city of Megiddo after a siege lasting seven months. In a series of seventeen campaigns spread over a period of twenty years Tuthmosis finally broke the power of his inveterate enemy, the King of Kadesh, and also contained the Mitanni beyond the Euphrates. It was during his campaigns against the Mitanni that for the first time an Egyptian ruler crossed the Euphrates, erecting a monument there to commemorate his achievement. The Euphrates was in fact to serve as the northern frontier of this new Egyptian Empire. A settlement was made with the Mitanni, and friendly relations, which lasted for the next hundred years, were established.

The campaigns of Tuthmosis III and his predecessors brought much wealth by way of material booty and prisoners into Egypt. A great proportion of this was dedicated to the use of the god Amun, in whose name the Pharaoh reigned. The priesthood of Amun became all-powerful in Egypt and probably exercised considerable authority, indirectly, over the Pharaoh himself.

The Reign of Akhnaten

About a century after the reign of Tuthmosis III a remarkable revolution took place in Egypt. In 1379 BC Amenophis IV came to the throne, though he had already been acting as co-ruler with his father, Amenophis III, for some years before his accession. Early in his reign he challenged the power of the priests of Amun by instituting the worship of Aten, the solar disc, as the sole deity. The Pharaoh changed his name to Akhnaten and had a new capital city built at Tell el-Amarna. The worship of Amun was forbidden. The significance of this revolution for the student of the Old Testament is not, as some have asserted, that in this new worship are to be found the seeds of Hebrew monotheism, but that Pharaoh Akhnaten neglected his Asiatic dominions. Akhnaten's indifference to the fate of his Asiatic Empire and of his ally, the Mitanni, was exploited to the full by the shrewd and scheming ruler of the Hittites. He attacked and defeated the Mitanni and at the same time stirred up the petty kinglets of Palestine to throw off the Egyptian yoke. Appeals for help, charges and counter-charges of treason were sent by the rulers of the various city States to the Pharaoh. This vast correspondence was carefully filed away in the archives of the new capital city, and apparently was ignored by the Pharaoh, if indeed the contents of the communications were ever revealed to him by his foreign-office staff.

This was the period of the Habiru raids, which form the subject of some of the correspondence. Probably the Hebrew account of one such (from the Hebrew point of view) successful raid is to be found in the description of the attack by Levi and Simeon on Shechem in Genesis 34. Somewhat later, during a time of famine, Jacob migrated with his family to Egypt where Joseph had already risen to the office of Prime Minister.[2] The following inscription from the tomb of Horem-heb, who was Army Commander during the reign of Akhnaten, and who later seized the throne, reminds us of the situation in Palestine described in Genesis 42[5]: 'Their countries (i.e. Palestine) are starving, and they live like the beasts of the desert', 'Certain of the foreigners who do not know how they may live have come begging the breath of life of Pharaoh, after the manner of their fathers' fathers since the first time ... so Pharaoh gives them into your hands to guard their boundaries'.[3]

The reign of Akhnaten was perhaps the only one when a foreigner, such as Joseph, might rise to high office. The Pharaoh's quarrel with the priests of Amun would have deprived him of his civil service so that an astute person such as Joseph would be welcomed into his employment. In this period also it would be a high honour to be given a daughter of the priest of On (On was the centre of solar worship) as wife, furthermore Akhnaten is known to have employed Semites in high positions in his civil service.[4] We may also wonder whether Joseph withheld news of the Habiru raids from his royal master.

Towards the end of Akhnaten's reign the priests of Amun were able gradually to reassert their power. It is probable that during the

2 H. H. Rowley, *From Joseph to Joshua*; where arguments are presented placing the descent into Egypt during the reign of Akhnaten.

3 J. A. Wilson, *The Burden of Egypt*, pp. 236–7.

4 J. Skinner, 'Genesis', *ICC*, p. 501.

latter part of his reign, disease prevented him from exercising effective control, and his younger brother, Smenkha-Re, ruled as co-regent, succeeding to the throne on Akhnaten's death. With the death of Akhnaten most traces of the short-lived revolution rapidly disappeared, but another forty years were to elapse before any attempt was made to recover Egypt's lost dominions. The expulsion of foreign officials from the Government service, which followed the reinstatement of the priesthood of Amun, may be reflected in the statement in Exodus 1^{8} about the 'new king who did not know Joseph'.

The Rise of the Nineteenth Dynasty

In 1319 BC the throne of Egypt passed to Rameses I, who had been vizier of Upper Egypt, but after a year he was succeeded by his son Seti I. Most of the kings of the next two hundred years (the nineteenth and twentieth dynasties) bore the name Rameses after the founder of the nineteenth dynasty. One of the first acts of the new ruling house was to remove the capital from Thebes to Tanis in the Nile Delta. This latter city was rebuilt by slave labour and renamed Raameses or Pi-Raameses—there is a reference to this building-work in Exodus 1^{11}. This was but a prelude to military operations designed to restore Palestine to the Egyptian Empire. In the first years of his reign Seti I marched into Palestine and secured a victory over the local forces in the Jordan Valley just south of the Sea of Galilee, and later established his northern frontier near to Kadesh.

Rameses II (1301–1234 BC), who succeeded Seti I, was almost certainly the Pharaoh of the 'Oppression' (Ex $1^{8\,\mathrm{ff}}$), though the Exodus probably occurred in the reign of his successor Merenptah (1234–1222 BC). Rameses II evidently hoped to extend the Empire to its former limits on the Euphrates, and in the fifth year of his reign he met the Hittite forces in battle at Kadesh. Although Rameses claimed to have secured a great victory, the truth seems to be that he narrowly missed a resounding defeat. The forces were well matched and not long after this indecisive battle Rameses concluded an alliance with the Hittites in an effort to meet a new threat from the Sea Peoples. Between 1400 and 1100 BC there had been a steady migration of Indo-Europeans from the north-east. These people were seeking living space on the Mediterranean coastlands, and were menacing the Hittite Empire in Asia Minor, and the coasts of Palestine and of North Africa. In the Bible we meet these people as the Philistines, who had settled in the coastal plain of Palestine at about the same time that the Israelites were entering the land from the east.

The Sea Peoples were repulsed by the Egyptians when they attempted to invade Egypt. They probably contributed to the collapse of the Hittite Empire. In the general confusion on the borders of Egypt and Palestine caused by this new menace, some of the Hebrews who had been enslaved by the Egyptians made their escape and began that long journey which would eventually bring them to their Promised Land.

PASSAGES FOR STUDY

JACOB

Genesis 25^{19-34} (J, E, P)—*The Birth of Esau and Jacob*

The divine promise to make of Abraham a great nation is focused in the special promise that Abraham should have as his heir a son born of Sarah. Isaac is the heir of promise (Gal 4^{23}), but Isaac stories do not bulk largely in Genesis. After recounting the death of Abraham in Genesis 25^{11}, the writer proceeds almost immediately to describe the birth of Jacob and Esau. There is little of the suspense in the account of the birth of Jacob which is so marked in the story of the long-awaited birth of Isaac. But even in the present verses there is a hint of the same kind of suspense which had been engendered by the long delay before the divine promise was fulfilled in the birth of Isaac, for from verses 20 and 26 we learn that Isaac and Rebekah had been married for twenty years before the sons were born, and this event occurred only after Isaac had 'prayed to the LORD' (verse 21).

Twins were born to Rebekah, but only the younger was destined to be the ancestor of the chosen people. Verse 23 also summarizes the actual historical situation at the time when the J source was being compiled. Edom, which counted Esau to be its ancestor and which had arrived at nationhood earlier than Israel, had been subjugated by David; thus the elder served the younger. The first half of verse 27 is the only note of the boys' childhood, the remainder of the narrative is concerned with their adult life. The brief account in verses 27 and 28, describing the way of life of Esau and Jacob, and the attitudes of the parents to the sons, prepares the reader for the story of the great deception which will be told in Chapter 27.

Jacob is described in verse 27 as a 'quiet man, dwelling in tents'. The word translated 'quiet' can mean 'perfect' or 'blameless', and must be given this meaning sometimes. Here it describes the orderly, respectable life of the farmer, contrasted with the rougher and more precarious life of the hunter (Esau). But Jacob's manner of life did not make him 'soft' as is sometimes asserted, rather some of the exploits related of him force us to the conclusion that he was a man of considerable physical strength.

The remainder of the chapter (verses 29–34) illustrates vividly the precarious nature of the life of the huntsman. Esau arrived back from the chase, faint with hunger, to find Jacob preparing a stew. 'Let me eat some of that red pottage, for I am famished!' (verse 31). When Jacob demanded his brother's birthright in exchange Esau agreed. Jacob clinched the bargain by requiring Esau to swear a solemn oath thus legally transferring the birthright. So Esau relinquished his valued rights as the firstborn in exchange for the cheapest of meals—lentil soup! The writer comments devastatingly, 'thus Esau despised his birthright'; he at any rate has no sympathy for Esau!

NOTES

Verse 30. There is a play on words in the original; the Hebrew for 'red' is ''*adom*' which is virtually identical with ''edom'.

'*Birthright*'. This 'denotes the advantages and rights enjoyed by the eldest son, including such things as (*a*) natural vigour of body and character, (*b*) a position of honour as head of the family, and (*c*) a double share of the inheritance'.[5]

Genesis 27^{1-45} (JE)—*The Great Deception: Jacob secures Isaac's Blessing*

The story of Jacob and Esau which was begun in Genesis 25 and interrupted by Chapter 26, is resumed in Chapter 27. The tension within the family, hinted at in 25^{28}, increases to breaking-point as Isaac realizes that his long life is drawing to its close. Isaac intends to give his blessing to Esau. Rebekah determines to frustrate this plan. This dramatic situation is unfolded in five scenes. The tension in the situation arises from the ancient belief that a blessing (or a curse) when once uttered cannot be revoked. The recipient of the blessing, even if he should not be the one intended by the giver of the blessing, will nevertheless receive all its benefits. Once the words had been spoken, they were believed to have an independent existence, the blessing could not be revoked. Thus 'a blessing is the *effective* utterance of a good wish'.[6]

[5] J. Skinner, 'Genesis', *ICC*, p. 362. [6] Ibid., p. 38.

Scene 1—27^{1-4}

Isaac, blind and frail, believing that he is nearing the end of his life, wishes to give his blessing to Esau. He asks his son to prepare a meal, and although the dish of 'savoury food' is described as a dish which Isaac 'loved', it is probable that the meal was also an essential part of the ceremony of giving the blessing. Isaac only pronounces the blessing *after* he has eaten ($27^{27\,ff}$).

Scene 2—27^{5-17}

Rebekah is quite determined that her favourite, Jacob, shall receive the blessing and is even prepared to bear the curse which would result if the deception were discovered. She dresses him up as Esau, even using the latter's festal raiment ('the best garments'); a garment only to be used on solemn religious occasions.

Scene 3—27^{18-29}

Jacob confronts Isaac and, in spite of the latter's suspicion, which is roused by what seems to him to be the unexpectedly early return of Esau, the deception succeeds. Nevertheless Jacob's treachery brings its own punishment as he will have to live an exile from his homeland for twenty years.

The first part of the blessing (verse 28) has reference to the fertility of the land. The second part describes the situation when Israel exercised dominion over Edom (cf. verse 37).

Scene 4—27^{30-40}

Scarcely has Jacob left his father than Esau arrives, soon to discover that he has been deprived of his blessing. In spite of his heart-rending entreaties Isaac is impotent to do anything for him. Significantly, verse 39 simply reads, 'Then Isaac his father answered him: . . .' and his words cannot be read as a blessing (as the AV and RV may suggest); the *RSV* translates correctly:

> 'Behold away from the fatness of the earth shall your dwelling be,
> and away from the dew of heaven on high. . . .'

Jacob has been given the fertile land, there remains only the arid wilderness of Edom for Esau.

Scene 5—27^{41-5}

Jacob's deception earns Esau's hatred, now Rebekah fears that she has overreached herself. If Esau killed Jacob this would in turn lead to the death of Esau, and Rebekah would be bereaved indeed. Even so she was too optimistic when she thought that Esau's anger would evaporate in a short time. The 'few days' (27^{44}, RV) were twenty years, and when Jacob returned, Rebekah was already dead.

The divine promise to make of Abraham a great nation was to be fulfilled through Jacob, but this does not absolve him from responsibility for his actions. Jacob must suffer banishment for twenty years and in his turn be deceived by Laban. Nevertheless God's purpose is not to be frustrated either by Rebekah's and Jacob's deception, or by Esau's hatred, or by Jacob's unworthiness.

Genesis 28^{10-22} (JE)—*Bethel*

Genesis 27^{46} to 28^{9} belongs to the P strand. It interrupts the older narrative and gives a rather different reason for Jacob's journey to Haran. The JE story continues at Genesis 28^{10}.

Of Jacob's long journey from Beersheba to Haran the writer has little to say, the only incident which he relates is Jacob's encounter with Yahweh at Bethel. This chapter should be compared with Genesis 15. In both cases Yahweh appears to a Patriarch in a dream, in both cases Yahweh makes a solemn promise that the land of Canaan is his gift to the Patriarch's descendants, in both cases the writer has succeeded in conveying the feeling of awe and creatureliness experienced by the Patriarch (Gen 15^{12-17}; 28^{16-17}).

Jacob is making his way northwards from Beersheba and arrives in the vicinity of Bethel at sunset. The place where he makes his camp for the night was, though Jacob was unaware of the fact, a sacred place of Bethel. (In 28^{11} the 'place' means 'a holy place'.) The details of the story preserve several very primitive religious ideas. Thus Jacob selects a stone at random to serve as a head-rest, but the dream which he has in the night convinces him that this particular stone is a sacred one and so he sets it up as God's house (28^{22}). Again 'the ladder' is rather a stairway or even a sloping ramp along which messengers (angels) could walk, the width being ample for two-way traffic, for in the Old Testament, 'angels' are wingless creatures. In Jacob's dream the stone is the 'house of God', i.e. the place where God appears, and the top of the stairway is the 'gate of heaven', heaven being the permanent dwelling of God. Such ideas serve to explain the significance of the Babylonian ziggurats. The temple at the foot of the structure is the place where the god appears; the small chamber at the top is his dwelling-place. The latter is reached by means of a sloping ramp.

Jacob has stumbled unawares on the 'house of God', so Yahweh stands 'beside him' (28^{13} *RSV*m). With verse 14 we reach the climax of the passage which is the reiteration of the promise made first to Abraham. Verses 13 and 14 should be compared with Genesis 12^{3} and 13^{14-17}. But once again it seems doubtful that the promise could be fulfilled. Jacob is fleeing for his life to Haran, leaving far behind the promised land. So to the general promise there is added in verse 15 the specific assurance matched to Jacob's condition: 'I will not leave you, until I have done that of which I have spoken to you.'

On waking, Jacob is seized with dread: 'The underlying feeling is not joy, but fear, because in ignorance he had treated the holy place as common ground.'[7] Early in the morning he sets up the stone as a sacred pillar anointing it with oil. Such pillars have been found in many places in the Near East. They are generally massive stones some six or seven feet high, only a man of colossal strength could have raised such a monument. Jacob was no weakling!

When Jacob realizes the significance of God's promise, with His offer to be with him, then out of gratitude he makes his vow. It is doubtful whether this should be regarded as a bargain. The offer had already been made, there was no need for Jacob to drive any bargain. Rather verses 20–1 express his amazement at God's gracious dealings with him, and his own thankful response.

Genesis 29—*Jacob's Marriage*

After describing Jacob's encounter with Yahweh at Bethel, the writer goes on immediately to describe a very different encounter at the end of his long journey. With the change of scene there is also a change of atmosphere. No longer do we share with Jacob the feeling of awe as he stands in the presence of Yahweh, instead we share his rapture as he meets Rachel for the first time. He is nearing the end of his journey and encounters three flocks of sheep with their shepherds gathered near to a well, the mouth of which was covered by a great stone. The shepherds were waiting to water their flocks, but apparently it was the custom to wait until all the flocks had gathered before watering them. Either the stone was too heavy to be moved single-handed, or else there

7 J. Skinner, 'Genesis', *ICC*, p. 377.

may have been the fear that the first-comer might take too great a share of the precious water (29^{8}).

With the arrival of Rachel, Jacob takes matters into his own hands, and rolls the stone away from the mouth of the well. The introduction to Laban follows, and Jacob enters the household where he will spend not merely 'a while' as Rebekah supposed (27^{44}) but twenty years.

The remainder of the chapter (29^{15-35}) is concerned primarily with Jacob's marriage to Laban's daughters. It is clear from the outset that Jacob loves Rachel, and Laban is ready to take advantage of this. Jacob, the penniless refugee (cf. Gen 32^{10}), is unable to pay the bride price for Rachel, and so offers seven years' service, an offer which Laban accepts with a deliberately evasive reply (29^{19}). Laban's duplicity becomes clear when ultimately, at the marriage ceremony, Leah is given to Jacob instead of Rachel. The custom of bringing the bride heavily veiled to the bridegroom made the substitution possible. Laban is ready with his excuses as soon as the deception has been discovered. Even if it were the local custom (29^{26}) not to give the younger in marriage before the elder, Jacob had been kept in ignorance of it. There is little that Jacob can do but accept Laban's new and more onerous terms for Rachel, whom he married a week later, not seven years later as has often been asserted but immediately that the wedding festivities for Leah were over. But although Jacob then receives the bride he desires, he is now committed to a further seven years' service to Laban.

Genesis 32^{3-21} (JE)—*The Road Back*

In all, Jacob served Laban for twenty years, for after serving fourteen years for Leah and Rachel, he had to serve yet another six in exchange for flocks and herds which he obtained (not without some shrewd management) from Laban. His increasing prosperity excited the jealousy of Laban's sons, so that relations between uncle and nephew became very strained. At this juncture, and in response to the command of God received in a vision (31^{13}) Jacob determined to return to Canaan. The quarrel with Laban was evidently settled and a covenant made between them (31^{44-5}). But now Jacob must prepare for the possibility of an encounter with Esau, who may still regard him with hostility. Jacob, with large flocks and accompanied by his family and servants, moved slowly towards Canaan, and when he arrived at the river Jabbok he sent out messengers to try to discover the whereabouts of Esau, and to determine his attitude towards his brother. The report was far from reassuring (32^{6-7}), so Jacob divided his party into two companies in the hope that at least one might escape in the event of a hostile encounter with Esau. He further endeavoured to win Esau's favour by sending on ahead a series of lavish presents.

But the climax of this passage is in verses 9–12: Jacob's prayer to Yahweh. Jacob was realizing at last that his craft and guile would not always deliver him, and that his ultimate dependence was on Yahweh. Face to face with a crisis he first confessed himself to be unworthy of Yahweh's steadfast love (mercy and truth), and then recalled with gratitude Yahweh's care for one who had fled over the Jordan a fugitive and was now returning a great company. His natural, human fear expressed in verse 11 is matched by the expression of confidence in verse 12 with which the prayer ends.

Genesis 32^{22-32} (JE)—*Peniel*

Jacob completed the preparation for the next stage of his journey by getting his family and flocks over the Jabbok by night. But before he himself made the crossing he underwent a strange experience. As in the Bethel story, we have here also some very primitive religious ideas. It is likely that when the story was first told, long before it was incorporated into the J collection, it described a struggle between Jacob and a 'man', who was in fact believed to be the god of the river. Verse 26 hints at such a primitive idea, for according to these early notions the supernatural being must vanish at dawn. Once again this part of the story speaks of Jacob's great strength, so that he almost overcame his adversary.

Though the story retains these primitive features, the later writer used it 'to represent Yahweh's work with Israel's ancestor'.[8] For this encounter at Peniel, not indeed with the demon of the river, but with Yahweh Himself, concluded the work of grace whose beginning was marked by Jacob's prayer (32^{9-12}).

In answer to Yahweh's question 'What is your name?'—which really means 'What is your nature?'—Jacob must confess 'It is Jacob—the deceiver.' For 'in giving his name, Jacob at the same time had to reveal his whole nature. The name "Jacob" actually designates its bearer as a cheat.'[9] But Jacob's confession, for such it was, called forth Yahweh's blessing which was granted with the giving of the new name 'Israel'. The new name implies the reception of a new nature. Whatever might be the interpretation of the rather difficult verse 28, the

[8] G. von Rad, *Genesis* (ET), page 319. [9] Ibid., p. 316.

blessing implied by the giving of the name means at least that Jacob has now found favour with God. 'I have seen God face to face, and yet (in spite of this) my life is preserved' (verse 30). But to know God completely is not man's prerogative, and so Yahweh preserves the secret of His Name (and Nature) (verse 29).

The night passed and this moving encounter was over. As the sun rose over Penuel Jacob limped away to follow after his family. Has he learnt now that it is better to enter into life maimed?

NOTE. Genesis 32^{32}. The story of Jacob's wrestling and his subsequent injury was used to explain the Israelite custom of not eating that portion of the animal containing the sciatic nerve.

JOSEPH

Genesis 37–47 (omitting Chapter 38)

The accounts of the lives of Abraham, Isaac, and Jacob consist of a number of isolated stories only rather loosely joined together. The story of Joseph differs in that we are presented with a brief, but continuous, account of the life and adventures of the hero from his youth to his old age and death. The story should be read through as a continuous tale, omitting Chapter 38 which is not part of the Joseph story. This story has been described as 'the first example of the "novelistic" type of literary composition in the Old Testament',[10] and it may be read merely as a fascinating story. The writer, however, had a theological motive in telling the story of Joseph. The promise made to Abraham of a land for his descendants still awaited fulfilment, and this story takes its place in the unfolding of the fulfilment of that promise. Thus Joseph, through whom the family of Jacob has been preserved from starvation, looks forward at the close of his life to the eventual settlement of Israel in a land of her own. 'And Joseph said to his brothers, "I am about to die; but God will visit you, and bring you up out of this land which he swore to Abraham, to Isaac, and to Jacob"' (Gen 50^{24}).

Whilst the theme of the promise and its fulfilment underlies the story of Joseph, the writer also uses the story to illustrate God's providential care of Joseph, and His way of bringing good out of the evil intentions of men. Joseph recognizes this when he allays the fears which his brothers entertained after the death of Jacob. 'And as for you, you meant evil against me; but God meant it for good, to bring it

[10] C. T. Fritsch, 'Genesis', *LBC*, p. 100.

about that many people should be kept alive, as they are today' (Gen 50^{20}, cf. Gen 45^{7-8}).

The story as it has been handed down to us, has been compiled from material taken from the J, E, and P strands, though the P material is confined to a few verses. Both the J and E sources appear to have had a Joseph story, and slight differences between the originals may still be detected in the combined narrative. Thus in Chapter 37 one account probably told of the sale of Joseph to the Ishmaelites (J), whilst the other relates that he was kidnapped by Midianites (E). A rough attempt is made in verse 28 to harmonize the two stories, but this in turn contradicts verse 36. Such minor discrepancies, however, in no way detract from the purpose of the story.

Genesis 37—*The Dreamer*

When the story opens, Joseph is seventeen years old (37^{2}). This is one of the few notices in the story which enable us to realize its temporal development. The son of Jacob's favourite wife, Rachel, had been singled out for special favour by his father. The 'coat of many colours' was a type of garment worn only by those who did not have to work. It reached down to the ankles, and had sleeves coming down to the wrists. Such a garment is mentioned in one other place in the Old Testament, viz. 2 Samuel $13^{18\,ff}$, where it is a garment worn by a royal princess. It was clearly a type of clothing unsuited to the work of a nomadic shepherd. 'Thus the picture of the spoiled and preferred prince, Joseph, is painted with very few strokes.'[11] The envy, which Jacob's treatment of Joseph has aroused in his brothers, is further increased when Joseph relates to them his dreams. There is perhaps an element of foreboding in the brothers' hatred, for in ancient times the dream was believed to be a prophecy of future events, and 'the double dream indicates the certainty of fulfilment'.[12] The brothers are incensed by the thought that this spoilt younger brother would one day be their lord and master, and so they plan to get rid of him when he seems to be entirely at their mercy (37^{18}). The fear of shedding blood restrains them from their first violent intention, and the appearance of a caravan of traders bound for Egypt suggests a neater plan for getting rid of the unwelcome upstart.

This introductory chapter closes on a tragic note. Jacob, the deceiver, has been bitterly deceived by his own sons, and deprived of his favourite son. He will go down to the grave mourning his loss, and

[11] G. von Rad, *Genesis* (ET), p. 346. [12] C. T. Fritsch, 'Genesis', *LBC*, p. 102

he has no resurrection hope. Joseph is sold into slavery in Egypt. Would he share the usual fate of a slave, toiling and dying a mere cipher in a foreign land?

Genesis 39–40—*Humiliation*

These two chapters give us a glimpse of the first twelve or thirteen years which Joseph spent in Egypt (see Gen 37^{2}, 41^{1}, 41^{46}). It is necessary that Joseph be brought to the lowest position, a prisoner in the State prison, before he can become second only to Pharaoh himself. Yet there is no thought in these chapters that Joseph's humiliation is a punishment, rather it is insisted that in all his trials 'the LORD was with him' ($39^{2, 23}$). These chapters are straightforward and need no further detailed comment.

Genesis 41—*Prime Minister of Egypt*

This chapter describes Joseph's elevation from a common prisoner to the highest position in Egypt. Pharaoh's double dream had convinced him that it presaged some event of great importance, Joseph's interpretation confirmed his forebodings, whilst his suggestions for dealing with the situation convinced him that here was a man eminently fitted to organize the resources of the land to withstand a prolonged famine.

Thus Joseph rose to the position of supreme authority in Egypt, and was further honoured by being given the daughter of the high priest of On in marriage. 'The remark about the birth of two sons completes the picture of the mighty turn of fate in Joseph's life: grand vizier of Egypt, married to the daughter of the high priest of the land, and now two sons from the marriage.'[13] The years of plenty give way to the years of famine, but the Egyptian granaries are full (Gen $41^{47\,ff}$), so that 'all the earth came to Egypt to Joseph to buy grain, because the famine was severe over all the earth' (Gen 41^{57}). So the way is prepared for the preservation of the family of Jacob.

Genesis 42–44—*'Corn in Egypt'*

The closing verses of Chapter 41 prepare the reader for the next phase of the story. Jealousy had driven Joseph's brothers to get rid of him when he was in their power, now famine brings them face to face again after a lapse of twenty years or more. But in the all-powerful prime minister of Egypt they do not recognize the one whom they had sold into slavery.

13 G. von Rad, *Genesis* (ET), p. 373.

By adroit question and suggestion Joseph learns that his father is still alive, and then, by threatening to withhold the precious corn from them in future, he ensures that his younger brother Benjamin will accompany the brothers on their second visit to Egypt. Joseph has already decided what he will ultimately do, but he conceals his intentions from his brothers, treating them with reserve and suspicion. Finally, by a trick, he ensures that Benjamin shall be found 'guilty' of the 'theft' of his divining cup, a 'theft' which might be punished by death and certainly by life-long slavery. Then as if to atone, all unwittingly, for the evil which he and his brothers had brought on Joseph twenty years previously, Judah offers, in a speech of great pathos (Gen 44^{18-34}), to take the place of Benjamin. To hear the one who had originally sold him into slavery (Gen $37^{26\,f}$) plead, 'Now therefore, let your servant, I pray you, remain instead of the lad as a slave to my lord' (verse 33), was too much for Joseph, who had throughout exercised an iron control over his emotions. The moment had come when the true identity of the prime minister of Egypt could no longer be concealed from the suppliants.

NOTE. Genesis $44^{2,5}$. The silver cup. 'Joseph's ordinary drinking vessel, but at the same time an implement of divination; therefore his most precious possession.' [14]

Genesis $45–47^{12}$, 47^{27-30}—*'Israel in Egypt'*

Judah's impassioned plea for Benjamin finds an answering chord in Joseph's revelation of his identity. Overcharged with emotion he can only utter the bare words: 'I am Joseph; is my father still alive?' This revelation, however, troubles rather consoles the brothers who naturally are apprehensive lest Joseph should seek revenge for the ill which he had long ago received at their hands. The latter, however, proceeds to set his life in the larger setting of God's promise to Abraham and his descendants. 'Here in the scene of recognition the narrator indicates clearly for the first time what is of paramount importance to him in the entire Joseph story: God's hand which in all the confusion of human guilt directs everything to a gracious goal.' [15] 'God sent me before you to preserve life' (Gen 45^5; cf. verses 7–8 and 50^{20}). The climax of the story has been reached, and it now moves forward to its inevitable conclusion. At Pharaoh's command the tribe of Jacob is moved into Egypt, and Joseph arranges an interview between Jacob and Pharaoh, which the narrator graphically portrays (Gen. 47^{7-10}).

[14] J. Skinner, 'Genesis', *ICC*, p. 483. [15] G. von Rad, *Genesis* (ET), p. 393.

The aged Patriarch stands before the Pharaoh (was it the young Pharaoh Akhnaten?) and blesses him.

The Israelites are allowed to settle in the land of Goshen, another stage on the long journey to the Promised Land has been reached. Jacob indeed recognizes that he will die in Egypt (Gen $47^{29\,ff}$), but makes Joseph promise that he will be buried in the family sepulchre near Hebron (cf. Gen 50^{13}).

NOTES

Genesis 45^{8}. 'A father to Pharaoh.' This was the title of one of the important court officials.

Goshen. Probably the modern Wadi Tumilat, a narrow valley leading in an easterly direction from the Nile Delta to the head of the Gulf of Suez. It is recorded that about 1220 BC the Pharaoh Merenptah permitted Edomite Bedouin to settle in this region, as the Israelites had been permitted to do.

Genesis 47^{13-26}—*Joseph's Agrarian Policy*

These verses stand rather apart from the rest of the chapter. The narrator makes the peculiar system of land tenure which prevailed in Egypt a direct consequence of the famine. In order to procure corn the peasants were eventually driven to selling their possessions, including land, to the Pharaoh. 'The land became Pharaoh's; and as for the people he made slaves of them from one end of Egypt to the other' (Gen $47^{20\,ff}$). When the famine ceased the farmers paid a 'rent' of one-fifth of their harvest to the Pharaoh for the land. Only the priests and the temple lands were exempt from this taxation.

It is known that some such system of land tenure became general in Egypt sometime after the expulsion of the Hyksos.

Psalm 139—*'And the* LORD *was with him'*

One of the features of the Joseph story is the writer's confidence that whatever the circumstances in which Joseph found himself 'the LORD was with him' (Gen $39^{3,\,21}$).

The omnipresence of God is one of the truths expressed in this psalm, which is a meditation on the omniscience, omnipresence, and omnipotence of Yahweh. 'Nowhere is there a more overwhelming sense of the fact that man is beset and compassed about by God, pervaded by His Spirit, unable to take a step without His control.' [16]

[16] J. J. S. Perowne, *The Psalms*, II.438.

(1) Verses 1–6—*Yahweh knows all about the psalmist*

The psalmist realizes that his whole life, whether he is resting or active, lies open before God; even his inmost thoughts are known before they have been formed into words. God has laid siege to him and holds him in His hand. This section concludes with an expression of wonder as the psalmist meditates on Yahweh's intimate knowledge of himself.

(2) Verses 7–12—*It is impossible to escape from God*

If this psalm belongs, as it may, to the exilic period, when some Jews believed that they had been removed beyond Yahweh's care and influence, then the conviction that Yahweh was present everywhere would be a source of strength and comfort. But the psalmist also knows that some would like to escape from God's presence, for such folk this truth would be unpalatable. Neither the darkness of night, nor the fearful recesses of Sheol would serve to hide a man from God. But the psalmist at any rate can rejoice that wherever he is God is also present, that even 'the night is bright as the day'.

(3) Verses 13–18—*'Wonderful are Thy works'*

The element of wonder pervades this whole section, as the psalmist reflects on the marvel of human birth. He is even more overawed by the thought that this marvel, though hid from human eyes, is followed in all its details by the all-seeing eye of God, for indeed it is by the will of God that each human life begins (cf. Jer 1^5). As he contemplates the wonder of all God's works (verse 14) the psalmist's mind is overwhelmed; he realizes that he cannot understand God's mind fully, much must remain a mystery. 'How precious to me'—better, how hard to understand—'are Thy thoughts, O God' (verse 17). This 'great God of wonders' is the subject of his continual meditation, 'as often as he awakes from sleep, he finds that he is again in the presence of God, again occupied with thoughts of God, again meditating afresh with new wonder and admiration on His wisdom and goodness'.[17]

(4) Verses 19–24—*'O that Thou wouldst slay the wicked, O God'*

The harsh opening words and the sustained expression of anger which dominates this section come as a shock to the reader whose thoughts have been directed Godward by the moving meditation of the previous verses. Before condemning the psalmist for this sub-Christian attitude

[17] J. J. S. Perowne, *The Psalms*, II.442.

towards the wicked, we should remember that it is his passionate devotion to God which leads him to condemn those who regard God lightly and even slightingly.

At the end the psalmist turns again to God with the anxious prayer that he might be found righteous in God's sight. Verses 23 and 24 are a prayer, and not an assertion of self-righteousness, so he dares to invite God's scrutiny in order that 'any wicked way' which had hitherto gone undetected and unheeded in his own life might be corrected. Finally he can pray with assurance to the All-powerful, All-seeing, and All-wise God : 'and lead me in the way everlasting'.

CHAPTER FOUR

MOSES AND THE EXODUS

THE FLIGHT FROM EGYPT

IN THE previous chapter we traced the history of Egypt from the expulsion of the Hyksos to the reign of Merenptah. The change of dynasty after the death of Akhnaten had brought a change in the fortunes of the Israelites who were resident in Egypt. The favoured kinsfolk of Joseph, or their descendants, had been reduced to the status of slaves, employed in strengthening the frontier defences of Egypt in the very region where they had been settled.

For the reconstruction of the history of the Exodus and the nomadic period we are dependent almost entirely on the biblical records with little illumination from other sources. Hope has sometimes been expressed [1] that support for the veracity of the biblical record from extra-biblical sources might be discovered. This appears to be unlikely. The escape of a few hundred slaves and the loss of a small contingent of chariotry is not likely to have been chosen as a subject for an inscription on a temple wall or other monument! It is evident that the Pharaoh himself was undecided as to the best way of dealing with the Hebrew slaves, whether to drive them out, or to attempt to break their spirit by ever more oppressive treatment (cf. Ex 12^{33}, 14^{5}). Though valuable as a source of cheap labour, they could prejudice the security of the State in the event of war. Perhaps their flight was not altogether unwelcome to the Egyptian authorities, though prestige demanded that some military action be taken against the fugitives.

Whilst it seems unlikely that any Egyptian record of the Exodus ever existed, some indirect confirmation of the general reliability of the biblical account of the nomadic period given in Exodus and Numbers comes from archaeological work in the Transjordan. Archaeological surveys, which have been carried out there, have demonstrated that the region to the east of the Jordan was unoccupied during the greater part of the second millennium B C, and it was only during and after the thirteenth century B C that this area was inhabited by settled populations.[2] About this time the kingdoms of Edom and Moab were

[1] W. H. Bennett, 'Exodus', *Century Bible*, p. 6.

[2] See Nelson Glueck, *The Other Side of the Jordan*.

established to the south and east of the Dead Sea,[3] whilst the two Amorite kingdoms of Heshbon and Bashan occupied the region eastward of the Jordan. These latter kingdoms were in fact overthrown by the Israelites as they made their way towards Canaan.

The details of the nomadic wanderings of the Israelites are scattered through the Books of Exodus and Numbers, so that it will be convenient and make for clarity if a continuous account based on the biblical material is presented here. For the same reasons the work of Moses, which will form the subject of a later section, will only receive a passing mention, though it is necessary to emphasize at the outset that Israel owed her existence as a nation to his leadership during the critical years following the escape from Egypt.

As a result of Moses' pleading on their behalf, and a series of disasters in the land of Egypt, the Israelites won a grudging permission from the Egyptian authorities to leave the land. Realizing that this decision might quickly be reversed, as indeed was the case, the Israelite slaves, joined by others ('a mixed multitude'—Ex 12^{38}), fled from Raamses where many of them had laboured on the great building programmes. They made their way towards the northern tip of the gulf of Suez, presumably avoiding the Egyptian frontier posts in this region, only to find their way blocked by an expanse of water.

In this situation their worst fears were realized as they saw an Egyptian chariot force approaching. Moses endeavoured to calm the panic that seemed likely to sweep through the horde of refugees, whilst the rising of a strong wind made their passage through the water possible. The Egyptian chariots, attempting to follow the fleeing Israelites, were bogged down in the soft sand and in the ensuing confusion many of the Egyptians perished. The Israelites' ultimate destination was Canaan, but their immediate objective was Mount Sinai, where Moses had received his commission to lead Israel out of Egypt. The exact location of Mount Sinai is somewhat uncertain, but there seems to be no compelling reason to abandon the traditional view that it was the mountain still known among the Arabs as Jebel Musa (i.e. the mountain of Moses), near the southern tip of the Sinai Peninsula.

The Journey to Sinai

After crossing the Red Sea the Israelites turned southward, and for upwards of sixty miles their way, through the Wilderness of Shur, ran parallel with the coast on the west and a range of barren, mountainous

[3] Millar Burrows, *What Mean These Stones?*, p. 75.

country to the east. Their first taste of wilderness life was not to their liking, water was scarce and the limited supplies were sometimes barely fit to drink, as at Marah which they reached after three days' march. But the nearby oasis of Elim afforded a welcome resting-place where the wanderers encamped for several weeks. When the march was resumed Moses led the people through the wilderness of Sin, a barren, rocky, mountainous region toward Sinai. The summary of the wilderness wanderings given in Numbers 33 names Dophkah, Alush, and Rephidim as places where the Israelites camped between Elim and Sinai. Unfortunately these places have not been identified, and so do not help in fixing the exact location of the route followed by the Israelites.

Whilst encamped at Rephidim, the Israelites were attacked by Amalekites, possibly a band of raiders, as the regular Amalekite settlements were to the north of the Sinai Peninsula, in the neighbourhood of Kadesh-barnea. By this time Moses must have established some sort of order among the Israelites, as it was possible to raise a regular fighting-force under Joshua to meet, and defeat, the Amalekite aggressors. A further stage brought Israel to her immediate goal, and when 'they came into the wilderness of Sinai, they encamped in the wilderness; and there Israel encamped before the mountain' (Ex 19[2]).

An Unsuccessful Attempt to enter Canaan

The Israelites remained in the neighbourhood of Sinai about a year before resuming the journeyings towards Canaan. Moses' intention appears to have been to enter the land from the south. With this in view the Israelites moved northwards into the wilderness of Paran, whence spies were sent into Canaan to gather all possible information about the land before a full-scale attack was mounted. The report of the majority of the spies was so discouraging that Moses called off the attempt. An irregular force of Israelites, stung into action by Moses' scorn, made an abortive attack on Amalekite territory, but they were utterly routed.

The attempt to enter Canaan was abandoned; the Israelites turned westwards, making their way to the oasis of Kadesh-barnea, which was to be the centre of their nomadic wanderings for the next thirty-eight years. Little is known of this period, though we may assume that during this time some form of national organization was developed, but the primary allegiance of the people was to their individual tribes. The record of one incident belonging to this period has survived. The authority of Moses, as spiritual and temporal leader, did not go unchallenged, and there is an account in Numbers 16 of an unsuccessful revolt led by Dathan and Abiram, of the tribe of Reuben, against Moses' civil authority, and also of a protest by Korah and his followers against the claim that Moses and Aaron enjoyed the special favour of Yahweh.

The Defeat of Sihon and Og, and the Settlement in Canaan

The story of the migration of Israel is resumed in Numbers 20, where the death of Miriam is reported, and the account is given of the unsuccessful attempt by the Israelites to gain permission from the Edomites to pass through their land. Evidently the Israelites did not feel strong enough to force a passage across the well-fortified frontiers of Edom, and so they followed a circuitous route, skirting the frontiers of Edom and also the eastern frontier of Moab, until at length they came to the frontiers of the Amorite kingdom of Heshbon. During this part of the journey Aaron died and was buried in Mount Hor (Num 20^{22-9}).

Heshbon lay between the Israelites and the Jordan Valley, but a request that Israel might be allowed to pass over this Amorite territory in peace was refused. This time Moses mounted an offensive against the kingdom which stood in his way. In the subsequent war the two Amorite kingdoms, Heshbon and Bashan, were overthrown. Thus Israel began the settlement of the Transjordan, taking over the fertile land of Gilead.

An Israelite encampment was established in the plains of Moab opposite Jericho, but no further move was undertaken against Canaan during the remainder of Moses' lifetime. The Israelites seem to have enjoyed peaceful, though perhaps rather strained relations with Moab, who feared that the fate of the Amorites might overtake them. The power of the Midianites, who had been a source of trouble to Israel (Num $25^{16\,ff}$), was destroyed in a war which Israel waged against them. Having thus secured themselves on the east, the Israelites were now ready to advance into Canaan.

PASSAGES FOR STUDY

Exodus 1 (J, E, P)—*The Oppression*

An introductory paragraph (verses 1–7) forms a connecting link with the book of Genesis. The death of Joseph is noted (verse 6) whilst verse 7, which marks the passage of a rather indefinite length of time, also indicates the measure of prosperity enjoyed by the Israelites under a friendly Egyptian rule. This in turn paves the way for the description of the sudden change of fortune which these now unwelcome guests are about to suffer.

If Joseph is correctly identified as one of Akhnaten's ministers of State, then not only did a 'new king' arise over Egypt, but a new dynasty determined to obliterate all traces of the former reign. Although we may identify the 'new king' of Exodus 1^{8} with Rameses II, under whose harsh rule the Hebrews were employed as slaves, working on the Pharaoh's building-projects, and as agricultural labourers (1^{14}), no doubt the lot of the Israelites had been steadily deteriorating under Rameses' predecessors of the nineteenth dynasty. An attempt was also made to exterminate the Hebrew population by trying to kill off the male children in infancy, though the non-co-operation of the midwives and the vigilance of the Hebrew mothers nullified the effects of this brutal policy. 'The midwives' fear of God proves to be a real factor in history. . . . Thus God helps Israel in Egypt invisibly yet effectively by means of the midwives'.[4]

The writer notes (verse 20) that 'the people multiplied, and grew very strong'; even in oppression and bondage he can trace, like a golden thread, the overruling providence of God.

Notes

Exodus 1^{21}. The interpretation of this verse is rather difficult; it appears to mean that Yahweh 'gave them a husband, children, and descendants'.[5]

Exodus 1^{11}. *Pithom and Raamses:* for the location of these cities see map 'Egypt and the Sinai Peninsula'. Raamses was built by Rameses II, and was the Nile Delta residence of the Pharaohs.

Exodus 2^{1-10} (J)—*The Birth of Moses*

The description of the increasing oppression and misery of the Israelites in Exodus 1 forms a natural prelude to the story of the great deliverance, which is itself the beginning of the fulfilment of the divine promise that Israel should possess the land of Canaan. Thus the narrative proceeds to recount the story of the birth of the one who is destined to be the human agent in that deliverance. When it was no longer possible to hide the child Moses from those who might destroy him (cf.

[4] M. Noth, *Exodus* (ET), p. 24.
[5] W. H. Bennett, 'Exodus', *Century Bible*, p. 46.

Ex 1^{22}), the mother placed him in a basket among the reeds on the bank of the Nile. 'Perhaps someone will find it and take it home without realizing that it is a Hebrew Child. In any case it seemed better to expose the healthy, "goodly" child to an uncertain fate than to leave him to a quite certain death. The "uncertain fate"—as the story with all its later developments intends us to understand—in fact means Yahweh.'[6] The faith of the mother was quite unexpectedly rewarded when she was employed to nurse her own son for Pharaoh's daughter.

NOTE. Exodus 2^{10}. Moses: the Hebrew writer offers an explanation of the name 'Moses' based on its similarity to the Hebrew verb '*mashah*'. It is, however, much more likely that 'Moses' is an Egyptian name; one would in any case expect an Egyptian princess to choose an Egyptian name for her adopted son. The form 'Moses' occurs in such Egyptian names as 'Ah*mose*', 'Thut*mose*', etc.

Exodus 2^{11}–4^{23} (J, E, P)—*Moses in Midian*

Exodus 2^{11-22}. The compilers of the Pentateuch show no interest in the early life and career of Moses at the court of Pharaoh, though in New Testament times traditions concerning this period of his life were current. According to Acts 7^{22}, 'Moses was instructed in all the wisdom of the Egyptians', and Josephus, the Jewish historian, relates that Moses served as an army commander and conducted a successful campaign in Ethiopia. But all this was irrelevant to the theme of Exodus, so the narrative jumps from the infancy of Moses to the eve of his flight into Midian. Between Exodus 2^{10} and 2^{11} a period of some thirty or forty years must have elapsed (cf. Acts 7^{23}). As yet, Moses is unaware of the crucial part he is to play in the life of his people. Indeed the kernel of this section of Exodus is Moses' encounter with Yahweh, and his commission to act as Yahweh's agent in leading Israel out of Egypt.

Without offering any explanation, the writer assumes that Moses has learnt of his kinship with the Hebrews. The brutality of the 'Oppression' is brought home to him when he catches an Egyptian overseer in the act of killing a Hebrew slave, presumably for some trivial or even imagined offence. The demoralizing effect of slavery is revealed when some time later Moses catches one slave in the act of murdering another. Moses does not yet appear as a champion and deliverer of the slaves, and indeed he has to flee for his own safety to Midian before the rumour of his actions reaches the ear of Pharaoh.

[6] M. Noth, *Exodus* (ET), p. 26.

But the flight to Midian will be the means of bringing him face to face with Yahweh. Until his call comes, however, Moses is 'content to dwell' with the priest of Midian (Ex 2^{21}), to whom he had been introduced after championing his daughters, who were watering the priest's flock at a well. Moses is received into the priest's family, and marries one of his daughters. Far from Egypt, Moses is no longer in danger and apparently the trials and sufferings of his kinsfolk, which had indeed excited his compassion, and had provoked him to violent action, were forgotten. This section closes (2^{21-2}) on a note which suggests that Moses would be quite content to pass the remainder of his days among the Midianites.

Exodus 2^{23-5}—*Egypt*

The years roll by; the passage of time being indicated in the text by the usual kind of vague comment, 'in the course of those many days'. Rameses II had been succeeded by Merenptah, but this brought no relief to the burdened Israelites. Nevertheless, as he prepares the reader for the crucial encounter between Yahweh and Moses, the writer also hints that the day of redemption is beginning to dawn. Even as the cries of enslaved Israel rose to heaven so 'God heard their groaning, and God remembered his covenant with Abraham, with Isaac, and with Jacob. And God saw the people of Israel, and God knew their condition' (2^{24-5}).

Exodus 3^{1}–4^{23}—*The Call of Moses*

The scene switches back to Midian again, where Moses peacefully pursuing his vocation of shepherd, stumbles, like Jacob at Bethel, all unawares into the presence of God. A strange phenomenon of a desert thorn-bush, which appeared to be ablaze and yet was not burning away, had attracted Moses' attention. But this external event is quickly forgotten as the writer proceeds to describe in the form of a dialogue, the encounter between Yahweh and Moses. This encounter was to change once again the course of Moses' life. The one, whose life in Pharaoh's court had fitted him for the leadership of the Israelites, was being challenged to throw in his lot with his oppressed brethren. The theme of the promise and its fulfilment, which we have already seen to be the theological 'motif' of the Patriarchal stories, is also evident in Exodus. The God who calls Moses is 'the God of Abraham, the God of Isaac, and the God of Jacob'. The divine purpose is not only to deliver Israel from Egypt, but 'to bring them up out of that land to a good and broad land, a land flowing with milk and honey; to the place of the Canaanites. . . .' (3^{8}). But Moses has a part to play in the outworking of this divine plan. 'Come, I will send you to Pharaoh that you may bring forth my people, the sons of Israel, out of Egypt' (3^{10}). He feels unequal to the task but is assured that God will be with him, and he also receives some token confirming and authenticating his call (3^{12}). What this sign was we do not know, for the latter part of verse 12, where we should expect a description of it, is actually a continuation of verse 10.

The Israelites will also require to be convinced that Moses is God's messenger and will ask him the name of the One who sent him. According to Exodus 3^{14} Moses is told that the 'name' of God is 'I am that I am' though the more direct answer to his question is given in verse 15, namely: 'Yahweh, the God of your fathers . . . has sent me to you.' It is possible that verse 14 was interpolated in an attempt to explain the meaning of the name 'Yahweh'.

The remainder of Chapter 3 anticipates in summary form the events which will be described in greater detail in later chapters of Exodus. Moses, who still fears that he will not be able to convince the Israelites of the authenticity of his commission, is given a series of signs by which he can support his claim to be speaking and acting for Yahweh. Even then Moses objects that he is not suited to the task assigned to him (4^{10}). He 'objects with an excuse which conceals the anxiety of man before a task given by God . . . (cf. Jer 1^{6}). Moses is taught by Yahweh that He, Yahweh, is the Creator and thus the real Lord over man and his faculties for perception and expression (4^{11}), that He can therefore let man serve Him with his natural aptitudes and will give him whatever is necessary to fulfil the task in hand.'[7] In spite of this assurance Moses still tries to evade the task. 'Oh, my LORD, send I pray, some other person' (4^{13}). Yahweh will brook no refusal, but promises that Aaron will be Moses' spokesman and companion. 'Yahweh, who means to do a great work in which Moses is to serve as His messenger, shows considerable forbearance towards Moses' human weakness.'[8]

NOTE. Exodus 3^{14}. This verse is so important that it merits rather more detailed consideration. The various possible translations which are given in the margin of the text indicate the difficulty of ascertaining the real meaning of the verse. It seems probable that the name

[7] M. Noth, *Exodus* (ET), p. 46. [8] Ibid.

'Yahweh' is connected linguistically with the Hebrew verb *'hayah'* meaning 'to be'. Some scholars have thought that the phrase 'I am that I am' means that the God whose name is Yahweh is the supreme reality, the One who was, and is, and is to be. Others have thought that the phrase does not so much interpret the name Yahweh, as indicate that the God Yahweh is the One who will be found trustworthy in every time of crisis. It is not necessary that Israel should know the name of her God, i.e. that she should fully comprehend God, which is indeed impossible. But it is vital that Israel should know that the One who says of Himself 'I am' should be found faithful.

Exodus 4^{27}–6^{1} (J, E)—*The Return of Moses*

After taking leave of Jethro (4^{18}), Moses made his way back to Egypt. On his journey through the wilderness he was met by Aaron and the two of them brought a report of Moses' commission to the elders of Israel. The latter received the news with awe and wonder so that 'they bowed their heads and worshipped' (4^{31}).

However, the hopes, which the return of Moses to his people had raised, were soon dashed. Moses, Aaron, and the elders sought Pharaoh's permission for the Israelites to make a pilgrimage into the wilderness to worship Yahweh. This request was not only refused, but the conditions of labour were made even more oppressive. The release from bondage appeared to be even farther from realization, so that the Israelite foremen who had complained to Pharaoh of their increased burdens now roundly condemned Moses for the evils which his actions had brought upon them. Thus we are led to understand from the outset that the redemption of Israel from Egypt will mean for Moses a path of loneliness and suffering. At every set-back Moses will be blamed (cf. 5^{21}); but he will plead, as a true mediator, for his people (5^{22-3}), and will be sustained by Yahweh's promise (6^{1}). This pattern will be repeated many times throughout Moses' life.

NOTE. Exodus 5^{7}. 'Bricks were made by trampling clay or clayey soil in which straw was mixed to bind it.'[9]

Exodus 11^{1-8} (J, E)—*The Last Plague*

In this section we reach one of the climaxes of Exodus. The earlier chapters (7–10) have given an account of the plagues, and whatever the natural events, which are recalled in the narrative, may have been,

[9] W. Corswant, *Dictionary of Life in Bible Times* (ET), p. 57.

the biblical writers interpret them as manifestations of the power ('the mighty hand') of Yahweh. But these demonstrations of power have not been sufficient to compel Pharaoh to release the Israelites, though they form a prelude to the ultimate demonstration of divine power now to be related. 'Yet one plague more will I bring upon Pharaoh and upon Egypt; afterwards he will let you go hence' (11^{1}). Moses then presents what is in effect Yahweh's ultimatum to Pharaoh: 'About midnight I will go forth in the midst of Egypt; and all the first-born in the land of Egypt shall die . . .' (11^{4-5}). The dramatic effect of this tremendous scene involving Moses, as Yahweh's plenipotentiary, and Pharaoh is heightened by the narrator's final comment: 'And he went out from Pharaoh in hot anger' (11^{8}).

Exodus 12^{21-42} (J, E)—*The Passover Night and the Exodus*

The main narrative is resumed at Exodus 12^{21}. The Israelites are to remain in their houses during the night, when the fearful power of Yahweh will be displayed. Their houses will be distinguished from those of the Egyptians by the blood of the lamb which has been sprinkled on the lintels and the door-posts. But when the fatal blow has fallen on the Egyptian households events move rapidly; Pharaoh calls for Moses before daybreak, giving permission for the departure of the Israelites and even urging them to depart lest a still greater evil fall upon the land. Pharaoh 'even asks that Israel will procure for him the blessing of the God of Israel at the feast which they purpose in the wilderness. . . . Now he can no longer say, as he had in 5^{2}, that he does not know Yahweh; he has come to know him in all his fearful reality.' [10]

This section closes with a statement of the route which the Israelites took in their journey out of Egypt.

NOTE. Exodus 12^{37}. 'Succoth.' This the Hebrew form of an Egyptian town name. The town has been identified with ruins on Tell el-Maskhuta in the Wadi Tumilat east of Pithom.

Exodus $12^{1-20, 43-51}$; 13^{1-16} (P)—*'Remember this Day'*

These two sections, which break the natural sequence of the narrative of the flight from Egypt, give regulations for the proper observance of the Passover and the Feast of Unleavened Bread (Mazzoth). The sections belong to the latest strand of the Pentateuch, and describe

10 M. Noth, *Exodus* (ET), p. 98.

festivals which had for centuries been observed as memorials of Israel's deliverance from Egypt (cf. 12^{14}; $13^{8-10, 14-16}$).

Passover and Mazzoth were originally distinct festivals, the former being pastoral and nomadic in origin, the latter an agricultural feast. The feast of Unleavened Bread may well have been a festival which the Israelites adopted from the Canaanites when they settled in Canaan. The feast was celebrated at the beginning of the barley harvest, which was the first crop to be gathered. It was a thanksgiving in which an offering was made from the first of all the harvests, and in addition the use of unleavened bread, made from the new grain, represented a new beginning.

The passover sacrifice seems to have been an extremely ancient institution which may have been known amongst the Israelites even before they went into Egypt. The sacrifice was made at full moon in the spring-time, when the nomads were preparing to move from the winter to the summer grazing-grounds. The manner in which the sacrifice was made is described in Exodus 12^{3-14}. This was a spring ritual and it also involved the use of unleavened bread (Ex 12^{8}) which probably accounts for the fact that eventually Passover and Mazzoth were celebrated together. These celebrations also took place at that period of the year when Israel departed from Egypt and hence they served as a lasting memorial of that historic deliverance. 'There was a feast called the Passover, probably even before Israel became a people; there was also a feast of Unleavened Bread, adopted perhaps from the Canaanites; . . . and the two feasts were celebrated in spring-time. One spring-time there had been a startling intervention of God; He had brought Israel out of Egypt, and this divine intervention marked the beginning of Israel's history as a people, as God's Chosen People: this period of liberation reached its consummation when they settled in the Promised Land. The feasts of Passover and of Unleavened Bread commemorated this event which dominated the history of salvation.'[11]

NOTE. Exodus 13^{4}. 'the month of Abib.' This was the ancient name of a month in the spring, falling in the period March to April. This month was later, i.e. after the exile and in New Testament times, called Nisan.

Exodus 13^{17}–14^{31}(J, E, P)—*'by a mighty hand'*

The story of the departure from Egypt is resumed at Exodus 13^{17}. The

[11] R. de Vaux, *Ancient Israel* (ET), p. 493.

Israelites made their way slowly eastwards towards the Sinai Peninsula. After meandering in the wilderness region near to the Egyptian frontier, they arrived at a stretch of water which seemed to present a formidable obstacle to their further progress. Meanwhile Pharaoh, having regretted his decision to set the Israelites free, despatched a chariot force in pursuit.

Once again we are confronted with a situation in which hopes of the fulfilment of the divine promise to establish Israel in the land promised to them are dashed to the ground. But the writer of Exodus has understood that history is a means of revealing the living God. When Moses was pleading before Pharaoh for his people, Pharaoh had said: 'Who is Yahweh, that I should heed his voice to let Israel go? I do not know Yahweh' (Ex 5^{2}). But now at this moment when Israel seems to be in Pharaoh's hand once more, Yahweh will demonstrate to him that He, Yahweh, is Lord both of nature and of history. So we read twice in Chapter 14 that 'the Egyptians shall know that I am the LORD' (verses 4, 18).

So at this moment when Israel in her fear complains both to and about Moses, as she will time and again in her future journeyings, at this moment when Israel feels utterly helpless, Moses bids her 'stand still and see the salvation of the LORD'. A way is opened for her across the 'sea', but the Egyptian chariots are bogged down in the soft sand.

It is not possible to recover the details of this great event. Which stretch of water is intended by the name 'Red Sea' (Ex 13^{18}) is not known. The Hebrew name is *'yam suph'* which means 'sea of reeds', and so more probably indicates a lake than the open sea. Again it is no longer clear how 'a strong east wind' could operate either so as to drive back the waters or to divide them. But these questions which interest us did not interest the writer of Exodus. What mattered most for him was that in the hour of crisis Yahweh had delivered His people.

Exodus 19 (J, E)—*Sinai*

The first stage in the journey towards Canaan nears completion. The Israelites have made their way rather slowly across the wilderness region of the Sinai Peninsula. After ten or twelve weeks they reached the mountain where Moses had been surprised and challenged by the experience of the 'Burning Bush', and they pitched camp at the foot of the mountain. Here they will stay for more than a year, and here they will begin to learn what it means to be a people with whom God has established a covenant.

But the commandments which will set out Israel's obligations under the covenant must first be received by Moses alone, acting as mediator between God and His people. The encounter between God and Moses is graphically suggested in this chapter. The overwhelming majesty of this God, who had nevertheless chosen Israel as His own 'unique' treasure (19^5), and had delivered them as a mighty eagle protects her young (19^4), is dramatically portrayed by the mounting tension of the chapter. The 'sanctification' would consist primarily in the performance of certain purification rituals such as the washing of the person and his garments, though we would do well not to underestimate the inward preparation which could accompany the ceremonial. Even after this preparation the people must not attempt to ascend the holy mountain lest the near presence of such divine power should destroy them. Only Moses is chosen to stand face to face with God on behalf of the people. As he climbs the mountain alone, all nature conspires to enhance the awesome splendour and terror of the occasion. The lonely man of God disappears from sight into the thick cloud, which is torn now and again by forks of lightning, whilst the mountain reverberates with the crashing thunder (20^{21}).

Exodus 20^{1-17}, Deuteronomy 5^{6-21}—*The Ten Commandments*

It is convenient to study Deuteronomy 5^{6-21} along with the passage from Exodus. The two passages are in all essentials identical, the only difference being in the reasons assigned for keeping the sabbath. The original form of all the commandments may have been short, easily remembered sentences such as 'you shall not kill'. The ten commandments would then read:

You shall have no other gods before me.
You shall not make for yourself a graven image.
You shall not take the name of Yahweh your god in vain.
Remember (Observe) the sabbath day.
Honour your father and your mother.
You shall not kill.
You shall not commit adultery.
You shall not steal.
You shall not bear false witness.
You shall not covet.

Laws of this form are known to have been included in treaties which the oriental kings, particularly the Hittite kings, made with their vassals.

The following provision occurs in one such treaty: 'You shall keep the land which I have given you, and shall not covet any territory of the land of Hatti' (i.e. the land of the Hittites).[12] The covenant or compact between the king and his vassal was sealed by a treaty, and 'the decalogue is the deed of the Sinaitic covenant, inscribed on large stones entrusted by God to Moses'.[13] The Mosaic origin of the Decalogue may be regarded as probable. We may note in passing that Nathan's rebuke of David for his conduct with Bathsheba presupposes the injunction, 'You shall not commit adultery'; whist Hosea 4^2 recalls the whole of the ethical teaching of the Decalogue.

The laws are prefaced by an introductory statement (Ex 20^2; Deut 5^6) which expresses in the most concise form Israel's relation to Yahweh. Israel is His people because by His own freedom and by the exercise of His sovereign power He redeemed them from bondage. God is known as Saviour in the Old Testament as well as in the New; the theme of the 'bringing out of Egypt' recurs time and again in the Prophets and in the Psalms. If Israel truly recognizes Yahweh as her God who chose her freely and who redeemed her by a 'mighty hand', then her attitude to Him will be one of thankful worship, and to each other one of mercy. These attitudes receive formal expression in the Ten Commandments, but it should be emphasized that these only become an irksome requirement when the motive of thankfulness is no longer present.

'You shall have no other gods before (beside) me.'

Yahweh alone is to be worshipped; if the existence of 'other gods' is not expressly denied in this statement, nevertheless they are to be disregarded. This attitude will pave the way for the ultimate denial of the existence of these other gods.

'You shall not make for yourself a graven image.'

This prohibition reflects the ancient idea that by means of an image a man might exercise power over the being represented by the image, just as according to primitive ideas a man would make an image (a wax or clay model) of his enemy, which he would then proceed to 'kill' in the belief that he would thereby bring about the destruction of his foe. But Yahweh is the Absolute Sovereign and 'Israel is forbidden any image so that the people cannot even make the attempt to gain power over God'.[14]

[12] R. de Vaux, *Ancient Israel*, p. 147. [13] Ibid., p. 147.
[14] M. Noth, *Exodus* (ET), p. 163

The exclusive claim which Yahweh makes on the loyalty of His worshippers is expressed in the phrase 'for I am a jealous God', where in this context 'jealous' 'means that claim for utterly exclusive loyalty which is alone worthy of God'.[15] The penalty for disloyalty to Yahweh ('them that hate me') seems harsh, but it does underline the obvious truth that the actions of an individual often have undesirable consequences for others, even though this teaching required and received at the hands of Jeremiah and Ezekiel a corrective in their doctrine of individual responsibility. Even here (Ex 20^{6}, Deut 5^{10}), however, the final emphasis is on God's mercy, for if His wrath extended to four generations His mercy extends to a thousand! (Deut 7^{9}). 'The visitation of punishment lasts for only a fraction of the time of His loving grace. God is much more a God of grace than a God of judgement.'[16]

'You shall not take the name of the LORD *your God in vain.'*

This prohibition is rather similar in intention to the previous one. To know a person's name was to have power over him (cf. Gen 32^{29}, Jdg 13^{18}). God had revealed His name to Israel, but this knowledge must not be misused. Originally this prohibition would be a warning against attempting to use the divine Name to make blessings or curses effective. Jesus expressed the positive side of this commandment in the prayer, 'Hallowed be Thy Name'.

'Remember the Sabbath Day.'

The first three commandments are concerned with defining the proper attitude of reverence towards God. The fourth one singles out one day in seven to be kept as a 'holy' (i.e. separate) day, a day of rest from the normal secular occupations. The humanitarian spirit of Deuteronomy is evident in the instruction to allow the household slaves to enjoy the benefits of a day of rest. Deuteronomy thus regards the sabbath as a perpetual memorial of the deliverance of Israel from Egypt. Exodus 20^{11} connects sabbath observance with the Creation Story.

'Honour your father and your mother.'

As the commandments were addressed to the adult, male population, it is clear that the real emphasis is on showing honour (i.e. obedience, service, and respect) to ageing parents.

[15] H. Cunliffe-Jones, *Deuteronomy*, p. 53.
[16] L. Koehler, *Old Testament Theology*, p. 162.

The remaining five commandments deal specifically with a man's attitude to his fellow men. The breach of any of them would in one way or another disturb and disrupt the unity and fellowship of the people of God. The final commandment utters a warning against self-seeking desires which prompt wrongful acts. The word translated 'covet' has a slightly wider meaning, so that the commandment probably meant 'do not lay hands on your neighbour's property'.[17]

Exodus 31^{18}–32^{35} (J, E)—*The Golden Calf*

Exodus 31^{18} refers the reader back to Chapter 24, where we are told that Moses was on Mount Sinai for forty days and nights. In the meantime the Israelites encamped at the foot of the mountain, believing that Moses had either disappeared or had forsaken them, became restive and demanded an image to worship. The bull image and the licentious nature of the worship offered to this 'god' are reminiscent of the Canaanite fertility cults. It is possible that the writer is calling upon his knowledge of the Canaanite religious festivals for the details which he gives in this chapter, and it is also probable that there is a veiled condemnation of the images which Jeroboam set up at Dan and Bethel after the disruption of the kingdom (1 K 12^{28-9}, cf. Ex 32^{4b}).

The next paragraph (verses 7–14) may be regarded as a dramatic commentary on the second commandment. In vivid language we are made to feel the enormity of the sin of displacing God by some other object of worship. The naïve anthropomorphism which can speak of God's wrath and of His repentance, and which can appeal to His pride (verses 12–13) may seem to us to be objectionable and unworthy descriptions of God, but we do well to note what this kind of language really emphasizes—that God is Holy and that He is merciful, and that consequently there is a place for intercession, for here in this paragraph and later in the chapter we are shown Moses interceding for his people.

Though Moses intercedes for his people, yet he does not hesitate to mete out the severest punishment to the offenders. The massacre of the 3000 contrasts strangely with Moses' offer to be 'blotted out of Thy book which Thou hast written'. Yahweh declined Moses' offer, instead He commands him to lead the people onward 'to the place of which I have spoken to you'. The apostasy is not to be allowed to thwart the purpose of God.

[17] H. Cunliffe-Jones, *Deuteronomy*, p. 56.

Exodus 33^{1-23}—'*Go, lead the people*'

The journey towards Canaan is to be resumed; the golden calf has been destroyed but the sin of the people has broken the intimate communion with Yahweh. This again is expressed in anthropomorphic terms. Yahweh will give the Promised Land to Abraham's heirs, but will send His 'angel' to lead them. Israel's mourning and repentance for her sin are expressed by the throwing away of their ornaments.

Finally in a passage of great beauty Moses pleads for God's presence as the march is resumed. It is not sufficient that he alone should find favour with God; he identifies himself with Israel in the twice repeated phrase, 'I and Thy people' (verse 16). The chapter comes to rest at length on the note of mercy. The wrath of Yahweh passes, but His grace remains. 'I will be gracious to whom I will be gracious, and will show mercy on whom I will show mercy' (verse 19). For Moses there is the vision of the 'after-glow' of God.

Numbers 13–14—*A Glimpse of the Promised Land*

After leaving Sinai Moses led the Israelites northward into the wilderness of Paran. From thence he sent out spies into Canaan to spy out the land preparatory to making a general advance. Since this expedition was made in the summer ('the season of the first-ripe grapes,' Num 13^{20}, i.e. July), the spies were able to report enthusiastically on the fertility of the land, and to bring back material evidences of it (13^{23}), However, only Caleb and Joshua were confident that the land could be conquered; the 'evil report' of the majority so demoralized the Israelites that they refused to go forward in spite of the entreaty of Caleb and Joshua.

Numbers 14^{11-45} describes in a graphic manner the consequences of Israel's rebellion. The arguments which Moses used with Yahweh recall Exodus 32, but because Yahweh is 'abounding in steadfast love' (14^{18}) so Moses dared to plead yet again for Israel. But none of that generation except Caleb and Joshua would enter Canaan.

The subsequent attempt to enter Canaan, this time against Moses' advice, was a miserable failure (14^{44-5}).

Deuteronomy 34—*The Death of Moses*

It is fitting that the Pentateuch should close with this account of the death of Moses. He had led the Israelites out of Egypt, he had tolerated their complaints and ingratitude for forty years, he had made intercession with Yahweh for them, he had bound them by a solemn covenant to Yahweh. Miriam had died; Aaron had died and all that generation who had come out of Egypt. Moses had brought their descendants into the plains of Moab, to the verge of Jordan. Now he climbs to the summit of Pisgah, as once he had climbed the heights of Sinai; and Yahweh showed him in that instant of time all the land which centuries before had been promised to the seed of Abraham. G. A. Smith has described the scene. 'The whole of the Jordan valley is now open to you, from Engedi, beyond which the mists become impenetrable, to where on the north, the hills of Gilead seem to meet those of Ephraim. The Jordan flows below, Jericho is visible beyond. Over Gilead, it is said, Hermon can be seen in clear weather, but the heat hid it from us. The view is almost that described as the last on which the eyes of Moses rested, the higher hills of western Palestine shutting out all possibility of a sight of the sea.'[18]

So, alone, on the heights of Pisgah, Moses died. But now there was no demand in the camp of Israel for other gods when 'this man Moses' failed to return, for Israel knew that her leader had been taken. 'And the people of Israel wept for Moses in the plains of Moab thirty days' (Deut 34^{8}). 'The great leader is dead, but there is something more important than the great leader. The Lord's work must go on, and it is a tribute to his greatness that it does.'[19]

MOSES

When the Israelites fled from Egypt they were an ill-assorted, ill-disciplined horde of slaves daunted by the first obstacle in their way. Forty years later, when Joshua advanced across the Jordan into Canaan, he led an army which struck terror into the inhabitants of the well-fortified cities of the land. The transformation which had taken place during those forty years, in which a slave rabble had become a well-organized people, is a tribute to the work of Moses.

The Old Testament represents the Israelites as descendants of a common ancestor, Jacob, but there are suggestions in Exodus and Numbers that the descendants of Jacob were also joined by other slaves who took the opportunity to escape from bondage. Exodus 12^{38} refers to the 'mixed multitude' which formed part of the company led out by Moses. This heterogeneous collection of people had made a common cause to escape from Egypt, but once safely away what was to

[18] G. A. Smith, *Historical Geography of Holy Land*, p. 563.
[19] H. Cunliffe-Jones, *Deuteronomy*, p. 189.

prevent them splitting into rival and quarrelling factions? Some common loyalty was needed to counteract and to override the lesser loyalty of family or clan. Loyalty to Yahweh, expressed in the covenant, provided the necessary unifying factor. Moses' supreme work was the establishment of the covenant at Sinai.

Moses had returned to Egypt from Midian with the conviction that he had been called by Yahweh to bring Israel out of Egypt, and he was equally sure that the escape from Egypt was the work of Yahweh. These convictions lie at the root of the covenant which Yahweh established with Israel. It is important to remember that it is Yahweh's covenant, a fact which is emphasized in the words of the prophet Jeremiah, 'my covenant which they broke' (Jer 31^{32}). It appears that the form of the covenant relation was well known in the Ancient Near East, and it is typified by the treaties made by the Hittite kings with their vassals. It is not an agreement between equals, but rather a relationship of mutual support freely offered by the stronger party and accepted by the weaker. The vassal is under obligation, in return for the protection freely offered by his overlord, to eschew all relations with other foreign powers, not to rebel against his overlord, and to preserve peaceful relations with other vassals.

Yahweh's covenant with Israel follows this pattern. The ground of the covenant is Yahweh's action on behalf of Israel—'I am Yahweh thy God who brought you out of the land of Egypt.' The stipulations of the covenant are essentially stipulations ensuring loyalty to Yahweh alone. In return for their loyalty, Israel will be 'My own possession among all people' (Ex 19^{5}). The covenant is made with Israel as a whole, the ceremony being described in Exodus 24^{1-11}. The obligations under the covenant were inscribed on stone tablets, which were kept in the Ark to serve as a permanent reminder of Israel's duty to Yahweh. This again finds a parallel in the secular sphere, for the treaty, by which the vassal king was bound to his overlord, was deposited in the temple and read periodically at public gatherings to remind the people as a whole of their duties. This periodic public reading served also as a reminder that the whole people was bound by the covenant.

The Ten Commandments lay down basic principles of conduct demanded of Yahweh's people. In any community, however, disputes inevitably arise. According to Exodus 18^{14-16} Moses initially acted as sole arbiter in the name of Yahweh for the whole people. On the advice of Jethro, he delegated as much as possible of this task of arbitration to men specially chosen for their uprightness of character. This must have formed the basis of such administrative machinery as was necessary at this period. The mention of the 'seventy' in Exodus $24^{1, 9}$ and especially Numbers 11^{16} also indicates some form of organization which enabled Moses to share out 'the burden of the people' (Num 11^{17}).

One of the ever-recurring names given to Moses in the Bible is 'servant of Yahweh' or 'my servant' (see e.g. Ex 14^{31}, Num 12^{7}, Deut 34^{5}, Josh $1^{1, 2, 13, 15}$). Equally we are impressed, as we read the record of his life, with his twofold concern for the honour of Yahweh, and for the welfare of Israel. He knows, none better, that the Israelites are stiff-necked, rebellious, and ungrateful; but with all their failings they are God's people, through whom His purposes are to be wrought out. So Moses, combining the offices of prophet and priest, speaks to Israel for Yahweh, and speaks to Yahweh for Israel, indeed pleads for Israel when Israel would scarcely plead for herself. There is an impressive number of occasions recorded in Exodus and Numbers when Moses pleads and intercedes for Israel. The incident of the golden calf calls forth from Moses one of the greatest intercessory prayers of the Old Testament (Ex 32^{31-2}). He pleads with Yahweh not to forsake His people in the wilderness (Ex 33, cf. 34^{9}). When the rigours of the desert life were breaking the heart of the people, Moses' pleading for them becomes almost irreverent anger (Num 11^{1-15}). He prayed for Miriam even after she had spoken slightingly of him (Num 12^{13}), he prayed that Israel's refusal to enter Canaan might be pardoned (Num 14^{19}). In a passage vibrant with primitive terror we read how Moses refused to leave his plague-stricken people, but 'stood between the dead and the living: and the plague was stopped' (Num 16^{48}).

Again the primitive fear of holy things kept the people away from the tent of meeting (e.g. Num 17^{13}), which was erected outside the camp. Thither Moses must go his lonely way to consult Yahweh on behalf of the people (Ex 33^{7-11}), as he had also climbed Sinai alone to receive the Law. But Moses' closer communion with Yahweh brought its own reward and demanded its own price. Ever after the experience on Sinai something of the divine splendour shone from his face; but this very splendour became a barrier between the people and himself, and ever afterwards in their presence he must veil his face (Ex $34^{29\,ff}$, cf. 2 Cor $3^{7\,ff}$).

Through the pages of the Bible we follow him, 'servant of Yahweh', serving Yahweh's rebellious people. Blamed for their misfortunes, his authority at times questioned, still he leads them on and pleads for them, bearing 'the burden of this people'. He must bear too the secret burden of his own loneliness and suffering, until at length it seems that his cup of suffering must overflow as he learns that he cannot enter Canaan. But from Pisgah's summit he sees with one sweep of those eyes, old but still 'undimmed', the whole of the Promised Land, and he knows that his task is complete. So on Pisgah he 'died, lonely in his death as he had always been in his life'.[20]

Psalm 114—'*When Israel came out of Egypt*'

'And when they had sung a hymn they went out to the Mount of Olives' (Mk 14[26]). But of course the 'hymn' was not chosen at random. Our Lord had been eating the Passover meal with His disciples and the celebration, which commemorated the Exodus, concluded with the singing of the second part of the Passover 'Hallel' (i.e. hymn of praise) comprising psalms 114 to 118. The practice was for one member of the company, at the Last Supper probably our Lord Himself, to sing or recite the verses of the psalms whilst the rest responded with 'Hallelujah' ('Praise the LORD') after each half verse.[21] The first psalm (114) of this part of the Passover 'Hallel' is 'a triumphant hymn of praise to God for His works in the Exodus'.[22]

With great economy of expression the poet portrays the triumphal progress of Israel from Egypt to Canaan. As he surveys the accomplished fact all the rigours and hardships of the desert journey are forgotten. The crossing of the Red Sea and of the Jordan are briefly recalled in verse 3. Yahweh's part in the Exodus is not mentioned until the final verses of the psalm (verses 7–8), but this is not an afterthought. The psalmist wishes the congregation in the Temple to recall first the onward march of the People of God from Egypt to Canaan, and then to remember that 'this is the LORD's doing'. So he calls on all the earth to tremble at the presence of Yahweh, whose power was sufficient to give their fathers water from the rock.

[20] G. von Rad, *Moses*, p. 16.
[21] cf. J. Jeremias, *The Eucharistic Words of Jesus*, pp. 172 ff.
[22] G. Hebert, *When Israel came out of Egypt*, p. 15.

CHAPTER FIVE

JOSHUA TO SAMUEL

I—THE BACKGROUND TO THE CONQUEST

THE ISRAELITES, encamped in the plains of Moab across the Jordan from Jericho, could look over the river towards the land which they or their descendants were destined to possess. What sort of a land was it into which they were preparing to follow Joshua? What kind of people would they encounter?

The land was organized, and had been for many centuries, into numerous independent city States. During the periods when Egyptian authority was strong, these city States had to acknowledge the overlordship of Egypt. At other times a number of cities might form a defensive alliance against a common enemy. Joshua had to meet one such alliance, whilst Barak later led an attack against another. These States were quite small, consisting of the capital city and a few miles of territory surrounding it. Canaanite society was feudal; at the head of each small State was the king, who was supported by a small property-owning aristocracy. The bulk of the population lived in servitude to this aristocratic minority and were engaged chiefly in agricultural labour. The city itself was fortified by one or more walls with heavily guarded gates. Inside the walls the houses were crowded closely together, the miserable hovels of the serfs often adjoining the larger and better appointed dwellings of the rich. The cities were small by our standards, being typically about a quarter of a mile or less from one side to the other.

Associated with each city were its villages (cf. Josh 13[23, 28]). These were small unfortified settlements housing the agricultural labourers. They would be abandoned in times of emergency when the inhabitants would seek refuge in the cities. It is probable that many of the agricultural workers, who possessed houses in the city, lived for a part of the year in temporary shelters in the open country, especially at harvest time when they would be busy in the fields. Except when the weather was very inclement this mode of life would be preferable to the overcrowding which must have been the lot of the poorer folk.

By contrast the rich minority lived in considerable luxury. Excavation of the remains of the ancient Canaanite city of Ugarit (Ras Shamra in Syria) has provided a picture of the life and culture enjoyed by the nobility during the Late Bronze Age, i.e. the period of the Israelite conquest. The houses of the upper classes consisted of a number of rooms arranged around a small courtyard. These were two-storied buildings, the upper rooms being used as living-rooms whilst the lower ones served as store rooms or workshops. These magnificent residences were equipped with bathrooms, the baths of stone or pottery being connected to the main town-drainage system! It is not surprising to find other evidences of affluence. In the ruins of these houses were found ornaments of gold, silver, and electrum (an alloy of gold and silver), as well as bronze. Some of the objects were of local manufacture, others had been imported from Greece or Asia Minor or Egypt. Ugarit was probably the richest of the Canaanite city States, those of Palestine perhaps did not enjoy quite the high standard of living evidenced in Ugarit. Nevertheless we may take the evidence from the latter city as giving a typical picture of Canaanite culture. Commerce was an integral feature of this urban civilization, and the memory of it persists in the Old Testament where the name 'Canaanite' often means simply 'a merchant' or 'a trader'.

In addition to the wall or system of walls which protected the city, the king had at his disposal a chariot force manned by the nobles. The Israelites first encountered this formidable weapon in Canaan. Thanks to their chariots the Canaanite kings were able for many years to confine the Israelites to the hill country where the chariots could not be used.

The greatest concentration of cities was in the valleys, near to the streams which ensured a supply of water. There was an important group in the plain of Esdraelon and the valley of Jezreel, forming a chain of fortresses which for a long time penned the Israelites in the mountains of Ephraim to the south. This chain ran from Beth-shan in the Jordan valley via Taanach and Megiddo and then along to Aphek in the coastal plain. Brief notes in Joshua 17^{11-18} show that these cities remained a severe obstacle to Israelite expansion. Another similar chain of cities straddled the land in a south-westerly direction from Jerusalem to Gaza. The rulers of three of these cities, Jarmuth, Lachish, and Eglon, joined with the kings of Hebron and Jerusalem in an alliance which attempted to bar Joshua's passage into the heart of Canaan (Josh $10^{1\,ff}$). It was only when the Canaanites had discovered how to store water in cisterns dug into the rock, that a few cities were built among the hills.

Almost every feature of Canaanite life contrasted with that of the Israelite conquerors. The towns with their permanent dwellings contrasted with the tents of the nomads; the iron-clad chariots of the Canaanite patricians with the primitive weapons of the Hebrew warriors; the servitude of the lower classes with the freedom and equality of the Israelite tribesmen. But nowhere was the contrast so marked as in the sphere of religion. Inscribed clay tablets from Ugarit have provided detailed information about the beliefs and practices of the Canaanites. In common with the religion of the surrounding

Figure 4. Alphabetic cuneiform writing (from Ras Shamra).

nations the religion of Canaan was polytheistic. The supreme god was El, but being the chief god he was so remote from his people that his son Baal and the goddesses Astarte and Anat were the objects of popular worship. Baal was recognized as the storm god, and also, in association with the goddesses, as the giver of fertility. He was the personification of vegetation, and the aim of all the religious observances was to secure the fertility of the earth each year. The hot Palestinian summer which scorches all the vegetation was identified with the god Mot (Death) who had killed Baal. Anat the sister and wife of Baal seeks out her husband and restores him to life again. This 'resurrection' was marked by the onset of the autumnal rains which had defeated the drought of the summer (Mot). This myth of the gods was represented annually at the New Year Festival (the Canaanite New Year was celebrated in the autumn) by a ritual drama in which the king played the part of Baal and the high priestess the part of Anat. The climax of the ceremony was the 'sacred marriage' of the king and the priestess which was believed to ensure fertility for the ensuing year.

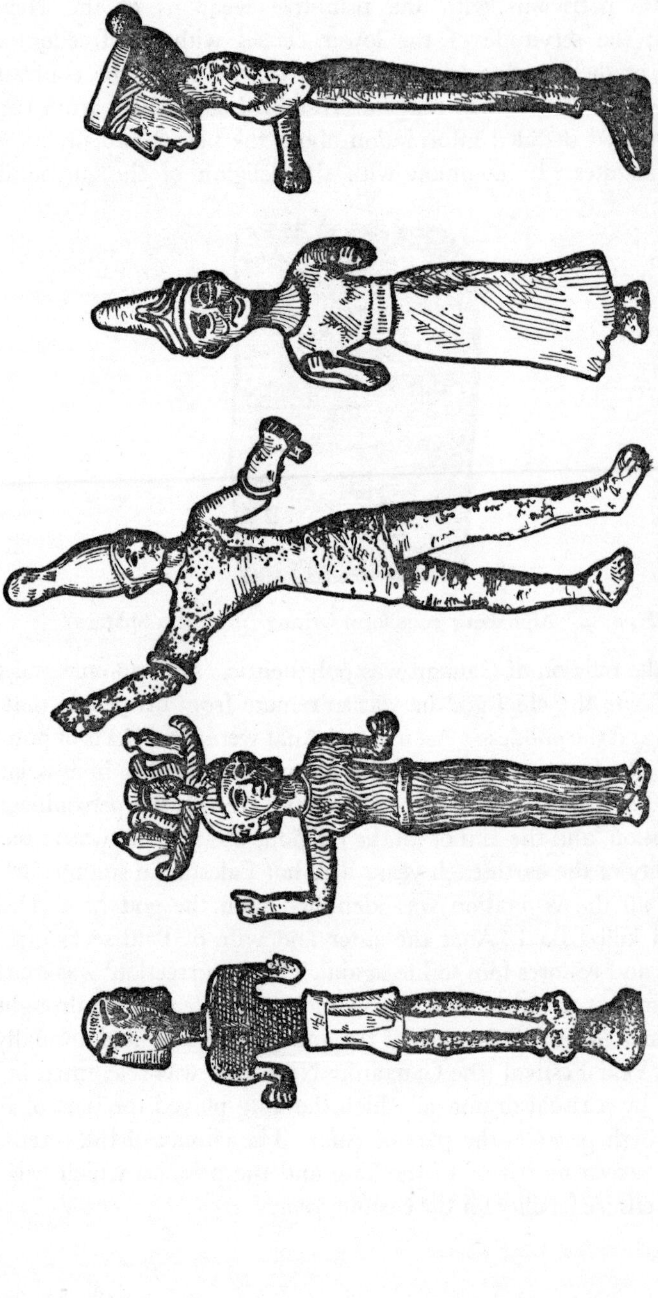

Figure 5. Phoenician deities. The first on the left is adorned with a collar and girdle of gold.

The cult of the mother goddess seems to have been very popular judging from the large number of small figures of the nude goddess which have been found in the ruins of the Canaanite cities. These figurines, which are only a few inches high, were recovered mainly from private houses. Since the primary purpose of the cult was to ensure fertility it is not surprising to find that one of the chief features of the ritual was 'sacred' prostitution—a feature which is regularly condemned by the Old Testament prophets. In addition sacrifices were offered to the gods. These were usually animal or vegetable gifts, but occasionally, in times of exceptional crisis, human sacrifices might be offered.

Such then was the civilization which the Israelites encountered when they entered Canaan; one which for the upper classes meant lives of luxury, sophistication, and sensuous pleasure, but which was supported by a mass of peasants who were little better than slaves. But it was a civilization which was doomed to succumb to invaders from East and West, for as the Israelites were penetrating from Transjordan, the Sea Peoples (Philistines) were sweeping down the Syrian coast towards Egypt.

II—THE COLLAPSE OF THE LATE BRONZE AGE CIVILIZATION

Excavations at many sites in Palestine all tell the same tale. Sometime between the middle and the end of the thirteenth century BC (1250–1200) many of the Bronze Age cities were ruthlessly destroyed by fire. The more favourably situated ones were able, by the use of their war chariots, to hold out longer against the invaders, but some of these were captured and destroyed during the next century. By the time that Saul was made king over Israel (*c.* 1000 BC), Canaanite power was broken whilst Philistine and Israelite contended for possession of the land. The period from Joshua to Saul covers about 200 years, and begins with Joshua preparing to cross the Jordan about 1210 BC.

III—PASSAGES FOR STUDY

Introduction

The biblical account of the conquest of Canaan is contained in the Books of Joshua, Judges, and 1 Samuel. This portion of the history as it now appears in our Old Testament was compiled from the stories of the great tribal heroes of the past. These stories will first have been remembered within the various tribes as part of the tribal history, and then later became part of the common stock of early Israelite history.

However, in the Hebrew Bible the collection of writings Joshua to 2 Kings is grouped together under the general heading 'The Former Prophets'. This should serve as an important reminder that there was a predominantly theological motive in presenting this account of Hebrew history. This becomes very evident in the books of Kings where, for example, we find politically important reigns dismissed in a few verses; thus the reign of Omri receives only six verses. The keynote of this historical writing is the first commandment: 'I am Yahweh your God, who brought you out of the land of Egypt: out of the house of bondage. You shall have no other gods before me' (Deut 5^{6-7}).

The history is written to emphasize the duty of obedience to Yahweh and to show the consequences of disobedience and idolatry. The outworking of this scheme necessarily involves a certain amount of idealization in the presentation of the history. Thus Joshua, the obedient successor of Moses, is represented as effecting a rapid conquest of Canaan and the extermination of its original inhabitants. This is the broad picture which the compiler presents in line with his theory of what ought to have happened. There are, however, scattered notes in the Book of Joshua which show that even at Joshua's death, and for a long time afterwards, much of the land was still firmly held by the Canaanites, whilst centuries after the conquest had been achieved the baneful influence of Canaanite religion persisted in Israel. If the extermination of the Canaanites had been as complete as some parts of Joshua suggest, then Baalism would hardly have been a problem in later years.

This theological interpretation of the history is stated at length in Judges 2^{6}–3^{6}. The people forsake Yahweh and turn to the Canaanite gods; they are punished by suffering oppression at the hands of their enemies; a 'judge' who is inspired by Yahweh and is a loyal follower of Yahweh saves Israel, whose obedience persists only as long as the judge is alive among them. Similarly in the eyes of this historian the tragedy of Saul is a direct consequence of his disobedience.

JOSHUA'S CAMPAIGN

Joshua 1^{1-9}—*Introduction*

The first nine verses of the Book of Joshua form a general introduction to the book. Under God, Moses had accomplished the task that had been laid upon him, the Promised Land is in sight, Israel must prepare to enter into her inheritance, and Joshua is commissioned to lead Israel over the Jordan into Canaan. Yahweh promises to aid Joshua (verse 5), but it is also made plain that the condition of success is obedience. Twice Joshua is solemnly warned to be 'careful to do according to all the law' (verses 7–8). Throughout he is portrayed as one whose aim is to serve and obey Yahweh. In accordance with the writer's view of history, Joshua is represented as enjoying almost unbroken success, even though the disobedience of Achan results in a temporary setback to the Israelite advance.

Joshua 1^{10}–6^{27}—*The Destruction of Jericho*

The account of the destruction of Jericho is exceptionally detailed in comparison with the description of the rest of Joshua's campaigns. It is evident that the overcoming of the first major obstacle in the way of the advancing Israelites was a memorable feat. It proved that the Canaanite cities, even though they were 'fenced up to heaven', were not impregnable. But not all the cities were taken as easily as Jericho, indeed the Jebusite fortress and city State of Jerusalem retained its independence until the time of David.

Joshua 1^{10}–5^{15}—*Preparation for the Invasion*

The invasion of Canaan could not be undertaken without adequate preparation. Joshua instructs his officers to prepare the people for the advance which was about to begin. In the meantime Joshua sent out two men to reconnoitre enemy territory and to report on the defences of Jericho. It transpired that word had already reached Jericho of the impending invasion, and the spies learnt that there was no will to resist on the part of many of the inhabitants. This is not surprising when we remember that the majority of the population of the Canaanite city States were little better than slaves, so that many like Rahab may have welcomed the invaders as liberators. If this were the case then the apparently ruthless policy of extermination of the Canaanites, which is described in Joshua, will have been directed only against the ruling aristocracy. This indeed accords with the fact mentioned both in Joshua and Judges that the inhabitants of Canaan were not driven out. It may well have been that the defection of Rahab and her family to the Israelites was typical of the behaviour of many of the inhabitants.

After receiving a favourable report from his spies Joshua struck his camp at Shittim and moved towards the Jordan. Here a temporary halt was made whilst the people prepared themselves for their entry into Canaan by 'sanctifying' themselves. The invasion was regarded as a religious act to undertake which they must be ceremonially clean.

'Sanctification' included the washing of garments and abstention from sexual intercourse. The Jordan, which was in flood, would normally have presented a considerable obstacle to the invaders, but the crossing was facilitated by some unusual occurrence which temporarily impeded the normal course of the river. Thus Yahweh, symbolized by the Ark, leads His people across the river into the Promised Land.

Once across the Jordan, Joshua established a base camp at Gilgal. To commemorate the crossing of the river twelve stones were set up, probably in the form of a circle, at any rate the name 'Gilgal' means 'a circle'. Gilgal may have been a sacred place in pre-Israelite times, and it was certainly regarded as a sacred place by the Israelites from the time of Joshua. Whilst at Gilgal the practice of circumcision was revived, and the passover was celebrated. The writer notes that thereafter the manna ceased. Israel was entering the 'goodly land, a land flowing with milk and honey' and the food of the wilderness was no longer necessary.

It is evident that the attack on Jericho was not launched immediately after crossing the Jordan. Joshua $5^{13\,ff}$ gives an account of a vision which Joshua saw in circumstances which suggest that he was making a preliminary survey in order to plan his attack. The capture must have appeared a quite formidable undertaking.

Joshua 6—*The Fall of Jericho*

The capture of Jericho is described in this chapter. The greater part of the chapter is devoted to a detailed description of the role played by the seven priests, who, preceded by the army, carried the Ark around the city to the accompaniment of loud blasts on the trumpets. We should describe this display of strength as psychological warfare, designed to weaken further the already unsteady nerves of the inhabitants. It would not be wrong to suppose that at the same time other and more directly military operations were being undertaken to force the surrender of the city. Assyrian engineers, for example, boasted that they could make the necessary preparations for storming a city in six days. Some scholars have supposed that the walls of Jericho collapsed as a result of an earthquake which occurred at the critical moment, and earlier archaeological work seemed to confirm this view. More recent investigations have, however, shown that the existing remains of the city, including the fallen city wall, belong to a much earlier city than the one captured by Joshua. Of the latter city scarcely any traces remain. This being the case it seems sufficient to attribute the fall of Jericho to the combined effect of the 'war of nerves' which intimidated the population, the successful mining-operations of the invading army which weakened the walls, and the existence of sympathizers within the city itself.

After the capture of the city it was 'devoted' (6^{17-18}), i.e. the city was destroyed by fire, its treasures were preserved as Yahweh's property, and all the inhabitants, except Rahab and her family, were put to the sword. We should remember that 'family' had a wider connotation in the ancient world than now, so that the number of those spared (Israelite sympathizers) could have been quite large.

NOTE. 'Devoted', or 'put to the ban'. If any person or thing was devoted to Yahweh it became sacred and was no longer available for profane or secular use. Persons or animals were 'devoted' by slaying them, cities by destroying them; precious objects were sometimes reserved for religious use. The alternative translation 'utterly destroy', whilst indicating what actually happened, does not bring out the religious significance of the destruction.

Joshua 7–8^{29}—*Achan's Sin: The Fall of Ai*

Joshua's plan of campaign was evidently to secure territory in the centre of Palestine between Jerusalem, which was too well defended to be taken easily, and the plain of Esdraelon, where the Canaanite chariots were as yet more than a match for the invaders. Thus Joshua singled out Ai as his next objective. A small force of Israelite warriors was deemed sufficient to take Ai, but instead of gaining the expected victory they suffered a resounding defeat. Joshua attributed this to divine disfavour, and subsequent enquiry revealed that Achan had kept some of the spoil taken at Jericho for his own use. The punishment meted out for this misappropriation of 'devoted' things would be regarded by us as both extremely severe and also unjust. The whole of Achan's family was put to death and his property destroyed. The sin of the individual brought retribution on the whole family, but this was not regarded as unjust by the ancients. The unit of society was the family group, the sin of the individual was the sin of the group; the whole group must bear responsibility and share the punishment. This doctrine was to be challenged by Jeremiah and Ezekiel who were to stress the responsibility of the individual, but we do well to reflect that the older teaching enshrines an important truth in stressing the fact that the actions of an individual often have far-reaching effects, and furthermore the family group may in some measure be responsible for the behaviour of the individual members. The place of execution was marked by a great heap of stones—' monument of disgrace'.[1]

A second attack was now launched on Ai, this time with a considerably larger force ('all the fighting men'—Josh $8^{1,3}$), and with a carefully-worked-out strategy. The main body of men who had made a night march into the vicinity of Ai, hid themselves to the west of the city. At dawn, Joshua appeared before Ai with a small company of men, the inhabitants of the city, emboldened by their former victory, went out to attack the Israelites, leaving the city undefended. Joshua feigned defeat, his men fled and were pursued by the elated men of Ai. The stratagem succeeded and Ai fell to the main body of Israelites, who at a signal from Joshua poured out of their hiding-places. The conquest of Ai opened the way into the centre of Palestine and caused consternation amongst the city States of the central regions.

Archaeological note

Joshua 8 is one of the problem chapters of this book. Archaeological evidence from the site of Ai indicates that this city was destroyed about 2000 B C and never reoccupied. This destruction cannot be the one referred to in Joshua 8; and indeed the name of the city 'Ai' means 'Ruin'—hardly a likely name for an inhabited city. The simplest solution to this puzzle is to suppose that Joshua 8 refers not to the destruction of Ai, but of Bethel, which was only about a mile away to the west and which is known to have been captured at about this time.

Joshua 9–11—*The Rest of Joshua's Campaign*

These three chapters should be read over in order to get a general picture of the rest of Joshua's campaign. The superficial impression of a swift and complete victory is corrected in the Book of Joshua itself by such observations as Joshua 10^{20} ('the remnant which remained of them had entered into the fortified cities') and especially Joshua 13^{1} ('there remains yet very much land to be possessed'). Nevertheless the wholesale destruction of many Canaanite cities late in the thirteenth century B C points to the general accuracy of these chapters. The Gibeonites, by a ruse, came to terms with Israel and this gave Israel a foothold in the central highlands. The defeat of the coalition of the five southern kings further strengthened Israel's hold on the territory already won, but seems not to have added greatly to her land.

[1] H. Wheeler Robinson, 'Joshua', *Century Bible*, p. 301.

The destruction of the great city of Hazor described in Joshua 11 has been confirmed by recent excavations on the site, though again it appears that the defeat of the northern coalition removed a serious threat to Israel's still precarious foothold in Canaan without substantially adding to her territory. In fact Canaan would not finally be won for Israel until the reign of David.

Joshua 24—*The Covenant at Shechem*

The final chapter of the Book of Joshua describes a scene at Shechem near to the end of Joshua's life. Shechem, or rather the sacred place near to Shechem, had been associated with the Patriarchs and now in the time of the conquest it was a central meeting-place for the tribes of Israel. We may wonder how the system of independent tribes maintained their unity especially when they were separated territorially by the Canaanites. This chapter suggests an answer, and also suggests why the monarchy came so late in Israel's history. The tribes were held together by their common allegiance to Yahweh, which was expressed by the covenant. This covenant was renewed at frequent intervals, possibly annually, at such a ceremony as is described in Joshua 24. An important feature of the ceremony was the public recital of the traditions of Israel, starting with the stories of the Patriarchs and reviewing above all the great central event of the Exodus. The challenge is then issued—'Choose this day whom you will serve' (Josh 24^{15}). As the tribes grew and even absorbed some of the Canaanite population, the annual renewal of the covenant ensured that these newer elements took the oath of allegiance to Yahweh (Josh 24^{16-24}) and so became part of Israel.

The words which Joshua wrote in 'the book of the law' were presumably the words of the solemn oath sworn by the people, i.e. verses 16–19, 21, 24. The preservation in the sanctuary of the treaty which defined the obligations undertaken by Israel followed the custom of the time. Copies of treaties made between heads of State were deposited in the temples of their respective capitals.

The closing verses of the chapter (29–33) recount the death of Joshua and Eleazar, the son of Aaron. Joseph's bones, which had been brought out of Egypt, were buried in Shechem as the central shrine of the confederation of Israelite tribes.

THE EXPLOITS OF THE JUDGES

Further stories from the period of the conquest and settlement are preserved in the Book of Judges. These are stories of tribal heroes who were raised up in time of crisis to deliver their own particular tribe. Occasionally they would rally a few tribes to oppose a common foe, but they never acted as national leaders. Indeed there was as yet no nation, but only a confederation of tribes held together by a common loyalty to Yahweh. Moreover, even if all the tribes had desired to act in concert on any occasion this would have been difficult, if not impossible, as the various groups were separated one from another by Canaanite-held territory. At this time the Israelites were settled in four groups. Some had remained east of the Jordan; Ephraim and Benjamin occupied the central highlands, being contained on the north by the plain of Esdraelon with its chain of strongly fortified Canaanite cities, and on the south by the Jebusite city State centred on Jerusalem. Naphtali and Zebulun had settled in the hill-country north of the plain of Esdraelon and to the west of the sea of Galilee; whilst the tribe of Judah occupied territory south of Jerusalem.

Not only did it take the Israelites a long time to overcome the Canaanites, but their occupation of Canaan was disputed by the Philistines. The latter had entered the land at about the same time as the Israelites and had seized the coastal region bordering on Egypt. From this bridgehead they were striving to conquer Palestine, a clash sooner or later between the Israelites and the Philistines was inevitable. Again even as the Israelite settlements grew and prospered they became a prey to Midianite raiders from the eastern desert. These raiders were not themselves desirous of settling in Canaan, but by their lightning raids, made shortly after harvest-time with the object of carrying off the crops, they succeeded in terrorizing the Israelite settlers.

Judges 1^{1}–2^{5}—*A Review of the Settlement in the Period of the Judges*

These verses form a general introduction to the Book of Judges. They portray the slow and painful process by which the Israelites gradually gained possession of Canaan. The tribe of Judah, and others associated with Judah, i.e. the Calebites and Kenites, won territory for themselves in the hill-country south of Jerusalem, but the valleys remained in Canaanite hands. The latter had the advantage of superior armaments —'they had chariots of iron' (Jdg 1^{19}). 'This is the first mention of iron in the Bible.'[2] The 'house of Joseph', which included the tribes of Ephraim, Manasseh, and Benjamin, settled in the central highlands but were unable to enter the plain of Esdraelon. The tribes of Zebulun, Naphtali, and Asher found land in the north near to the sea of Galilee. But above all, this introduction stresses the fact that the Canaanites were not exterminated and that many of their cities were not captured. Ultimately they were absorbed into the Israelite State, but the subjection described in verses 28 and 33 only became actual in the time of Solomon.

NOTES

(i) Adoni-Bezek (verses 5, 6, and 7)—this name should probably read Adoni-Zedek, the king of Jerusalem mentioned in Joshua 10^{1-3}.

(ii) Judges 1^{8}—This verse should be omitted as a marginal gloss (cf. Josh 15^{63} and Judges 1^{21}). Jerusalem remained a Jebusite fortress until the time of David (2 S 5^{6-9}).

(iii) Judges 1^{18}—Read with the LXX: 'Judah did *not* take Gaza etc.'

(iv) Judges 2^{1-5}—This short passage attributes the failure of the Israelites to possess Canaan quickly and completely to their failure to remain faithful to the covenant. Verse 1 probably implies that the religious centre was henceforth at Bochim. This latter place is unknown, unless the LXX, which reads 'Bethel' instead of 'Bochim', is correct. The Ark was certainly kept at Bethel during this period (cf. Jdg $20^{26\,ff}$).

Judges 2^{6}–3^{6}—*Introduction to the Theme of Judges*

This section takes up the story from the end of the Book of Joshua. So long as Joshua and the elders, who had known and worked with him, survived, so long did Israel remain faithful to Yahweh. But when the memory of Yahweh's mighty works in the Exodus had begun to fade, and the ever-present attraction of Baalism, aided doubtless by intermarriage with the surrounding peoples (Jdg 3^{6}), grew stronger, then Israel began to worship the Baalim (Jdg 2^{11}). This, in the view of the writer, was the cause of the oppressions which Israel suffered. So the pattern is worked out: Apostasy brings oppression; oppression calls forth repentance; repentance brings deliverance in the person of a 'judge'; but with the death of the judge, Israel slips back into apostasy and the cycle is complete.

[2] A. Vincent, *Le Livre des Juges*, p. 32.

Thus a 'judge' was not primarily a person who administered justice. He was a man inspired by Yahweh to deliver his people (tribe or clan) not only from the enemies who oppressed them, but also from the Baalism to which they had succumbed. 'The meaning of the word "judge" in the Book of Judges would then mostly be "judge-saviour". They were essentially men chosen by God, who re-established the rights of Yahweh in a situation compromised by the infidelity of the people. Helped by their dominant personality, they swept their tribe, and sometimes even only their clan, along to victory.'[3]

Judges 4–5—*Deborah and Barak*

The tribes of Naphtali and Zebulun, who had secured territory in the region to the west of the Sea of Galilee, were being held in a state of subjection by a powerful Canaanite confederacy in that area. The introduction to Chapter 4 (verses 1–3) represents Jabin, king of Hazor, as head of the Canaanite league. This contradicts the account of the defeat of Jabin and the destruction of Hazor given in Joshua 11. However, in spite of the earlier destruction of Hazor the Canaanite power had not been destroyed, and it appears that at the time of the great battle described in these chapters, the head of the Canaanite league and forces was Sisera, king of Harosheth.

Spurred on by Deborah, Barak raised a force of ten thousand men from the tribes of Naphtali and Zebulun and gathered them together on the slopes of Mount Tabor overlooking the valley of the river Kishon. In answer to the Israelite threat, Sisera mustered his terrible force of 900 iron-clad chariots in the valley of the Kishon. But the Israelites had chosen to give battle at the time when the river was in flood and the valley a sea of mud (5^{21}) so that the chariots were virtually useless. The Canaanite forces fell back before the fierce onslaught of the Israelites. Realizing that the situation was hopeless, Sisera fled and sought refuge in the encampment of some wandering smiths (Kenites). Here he was treacherously done to death by Jael.

This battle forms the subject matter of the great triumphal ode of Judges 5. It is thought that this poem was composed not long after the battle, and so is one of the earliest pieces of Hebrew literature which has survived. It is significant that in this poem Sisera alone is mentioned and he is evidently reckoned as the leader of the Canaanite army; there is no mention of Jabin whose name seems to have been erroneously introduced into Chapter 4.

[3] A. Vincent, *Le Livre de Juges*, p. 10.

In graphic language the poet pictures Yahweh coming to the aid of His oppressed people (verses 4–5). The misery of the Israelites forms the subject of verses 6–8. They dare not use the recognized routes (highways), but travelled along bypaths when they ventured abroad at all (verse 6); they were weak and unarmed (verse 8). At the call of Deborah and Barak the tribes bordering on the plain of Esdraelon, Ephraim, Benjamin, and Manasseh and above all Zebulun and Naphtali, rallied to the struggle and won a mighty victory over Sisera.

The poem closes with the description of the death of Sisera.

NOTE. The River Kishon: 'As a rule it is not deep or wide, and is impassable in only one or two places. In summer, parts of it are quite dry. . . . In winter, and even more in the spring, the sudden rains convert an insignificant stream into a torrent and the surrounding land into a marsh.'[4]

Judges 6–8—*Gideon and the Midianites*

These chapters give us another picture of the state of affairs during the period of the settlement rather later than the time of Deborah and Barak. Ophrah, Gideon's home town, was about five miles north-east of Jezreel. There is no mention of the Canaanite confederation which was opposed and defeated by Barak, and we may suppose that after this victory, the Israelites were able to settle in the fertile valley of Jezreel and plain of Esdraelon. But the Israelites who had settled down as farmers were not left in peace to enjoy the fruits of their labour. Raiders from the desert, using swift camels, swooped down at harvest-time carrying off or destroying the harvests. The camel had only recently (about 1100 BC) been domesticated, and its use by the Midianites turned the latter into a formidable foe, able to strike with speed at their objective and just as swiftly retire to their desert home. This situation is described in the introductory verses (1–6) of Chapter 6.

Another consequence of the settled agricultural life which the Israelites now followed was a falling away to the worship of the Baalim, the gods of the Canaanites and supposed givers of corn and oil (cf. Jdg 6^{7-10}). In this situation we meet Gideon, a loyal follower of Yahweh, threshing corn secretly lest he should be caught by marauding Midianites. He is commissioned by the angel of Yahweh to deliver Israel, but is not convinced that he has really been called to the task until his offering has been burnt, a sign that it has been accepted. Then

[4] G. W. Thatcher, 'Judges', *Century Bible*, p. 70.

he is assured that although he has seen the angel of Yahweh he will not die.

Gideon's first act is to restore the worship of Yahweh among his own kindred by destroying the local altar of Baal and building an altar for Yahweh. Gideon had destroyed the altar of Baal in the name of Yahweh, and Baal had been unable 'to plead for himself' (Jdg 6^{31}). When the Midianites appear on one of their raids, Gideon is seized by the spirit of Yahweh and rallies the Israelites to his side. He is assured by a sign that victory will be his. A numerous Israelite force gathers in the valley of Jezreel a few miles from the Midianite camp. But a small resolute band is more suited to the work in hand than a large undisciplined mob, and so Gideon sends away all who are afraid to meet the Midianites. A further test reduces the number to three hundred. The exact significance of the test by lapping water is obscure. 'The 300 may have been more alert or, in view of the night attack, knew the locality better; the banks of Ain Jalud, which is probably the spring of Harod, are still infested with leeches and no one knowing the place would put his mouth down to the water.'[5]

Gideon is further encouraged when, on making a reconnaissance of the Midianite camp, he overhears two of the enemy discussing a dream which one of them had dreamed. It was evident that news of Gideon's activity had reached the ears of the Midianites and had caused much uneasiness in the camp. The time was opportune for a surprise attack, and by a clever ruse Gideon so deployed his men and co-ordinated their actions that the Midianites were convinced that they were surrounded by a vast host of Israelites. In panic they attacked one another, and in panic they fled from their camp. This great victory secured a period of peace for the Israelites, and in later years the phrase 'as in the day of Midian' became a standard by which any mighty act of Yahweh could be judged.

NOTE. Judges 7^3 mg—'and depart from Mount Gilead'. This is the meaning of the Hebrew, but it cannot be correct. The Israelites were in or near the valley of Jezreel, whereas Gilead is east of the Jordan. A slight alteration of the Hebrew text gives the meaning, 'and Gideon tested them'. This is the reading adopted by the *RSV* and various commentators.

[5] J. N. Schofield, *Peakes Commentary* (New Edn.), p. 309.

SAMUEL THE LAST OF THE JUDGES

The events described in the first book of Samuel may be dated between 1050 and 1000 B C. Just prior to, and throughout this period, the ever-growing power of the Philistines constituted a threat to the continued existence of Israel. The Philistines had entered Palestine from the Mediterranean region about 1200 B C. This migration was part of a great movement of population in which people from the Balkans had made their way by sea to North Africa or to the coast of Palestine, whilst yet others had moved along the coast of Asia Minor and so entered Palestine. The great Hittite Empire was submerged in this migration which also threatened to overrun Egypt. The Pharaohs Merenptah (1234–1222 B C) and Rameses III (*c.* 1175–1144 B C) both waged war against these 'sea peoples', as they were called, and were able to keep them out of Egypt. Nevertheless they evidently thought it prudent to allow them to settle in the southern coastal plain of Palestine. The Philistines gained possession of the five former Canaanite city States of Gath, Ekron, Ashdod, Ashkelon, and Gaza. Although the new rulers of these five cities were independent, yet, unlike the Canaanite rulers who were often at war with each other, they formed a strong league, uniting to pursue their common objective which was the subjugation of Palestine. Each State seems to have maintained a regular army of mercenary soldiers drawn from the Canaanite and even the Israelite population. David and his followers served Achish, king of Gath, as mercenaries for a time and in payment were given the city of Ziklag.

The Philistines, who were originally confined to the coastal region south of Joppa, had moved northwards occupying the plains of Sharon and Esdraelon and the valley of Jezreel thus separating the northern Israelite tribes from the central ones. The decisive victory which the Philistines won at Aphek (1 S 4) enabled them to penetrate into the central highlands and to destroy Shiloh. For the next twenty years or more the Israelites lived in subjection to the Philistines, until the advent of Saul brought a temporary and rather precarious freedom.

1 Samuel 1–2^{11}—*The Birth of Samuel*

The scene described in 1 Samuel 1 is the great annual festival at Shiloh, which had replaced Shechem as the central shrine of the confederation of tribes. The shrine at Shiloh housed the Ark, the sacred chest, which was the visible sign of the presence of Yahweh among His chosen people. It is probable that representatives of the tribes and clans of Israel gathered annually at Shiloh for this important festival which may have been the autumnal feast of the ingathering. Here the covenant with Yahweh would be renewed, and the mighty deeds of Yahweh, particularly the story of the Exodus, would be retold (cf. Josh 24). Here the tribes would reaffirm their loyalty to one another.

The worship at the shrine was regulated by the chief priest and his sons. The office of chief priest appears to have been hereditary. When the story opens, the holder of the office is Eli who is assisted by his sons Hophni and Phineas. The character of some of the revels which accompanied this annual ceremony may be judged from the fact that Eli suspected Hannah, who was engaged in silent prayer, of being drunk. However, when he learns the reason for her earnest prayer, he blesses her and assures her that her request will be granted.

Four years later (cf. 1 S 1^{24}—children were not weaned until they were between two and three years old) Hannah attended the festival again bringing the child Samuel, who was dedicated to the service of the shrine. The section concludes with a song of praise.

NOTE. 1 Samuel 1^{24}. The Hebrew has 'three bulls' (cf. *RSV* mg). The *RSV* text follows the LXX and translates 'a three-year-old bull'. This would be 'an unusually valuable sacrifice'.[6]

1 Samuel 2^{12}–4^{1}—*The Corruption of the Priesthood*

Normally the office of chief priest would have stayed in the family of Eli. In order to prepare the reader for its transference to Samuel the writer proceeds to show that Eli's sons were unworthy of the office of priest. The crimes, of which they are accused, are the taking of more than their assigned share of the sacrifice even before the sacrifice had been offered (1 S 2^{15-17}), and immorality (2^{22}). The remonstrances of Eli were unavailing, but by contrast Samuel continued to 'grow both in stature and in favour with the LORD and with men' (1 S 2^{26}). The fate of the house of Eli, whose two sons will die on the same day and whose descendants will beg some menial task at the shrine (2^{36}), is foretold by 'a man of God' (2^{27}).

A similar judgement on Eli and his house is revealed to Samuel in a dream (1 S 3). There is no record of the passage of time in these chapters, but it is not necessary to suppose that Samuel was still very young when the vision came to him. The words 'the boy Samuel' (3^{1})

[6] H. P. Smith, 'Samuel', *ICC*, p. 10.

may be misleading as the word translated 'boy' can refer to a boy or youth of any age up to his late teens. The closing verses of this section (3^{19}–4^{1}) imply that Samuel was sufficiently mature and well known to assume the leadership of Israel in the place of Eli, so that there is no difficulty in supposing that the events of chapter 3 occurred many years after Samuel had been brought to Shiloh. (We probably tend to interpret this incident, consciously or unconsciously, in the light of Sir Joshua Reynolds's famous picture of 'The Child Samuel'. Whatever merit this picture has as a work of art, it is almost certainly a misrepresentation of the scene at Shiloh.)

1 Samuel 4^{1-22}—*'Ichabod'—The Glory is Departed*

This chapter, which is only loosely connected with the preceding one, describes one of the battles in the struggle with the Philistines. Again there is no reason to suppose that the events described here followed closely after Samuel's vision, on the contrary since Samuel presumably assumed the office of chief priest after the death of Eli and his sons, we would probably be correct in assuming a lapse of several years after the temple vision. But however long the time between the vision and the battle, the writer of 1 Samuel intends us to understand that one result of the battle was the execution of divine judgement on the house of Eli.

The LXX version of this chapter, which opens with the words, 'And it came to pass in those days that the Philistines gathered for war against Israel', makes it plain that the offensive was launched by the Philistines who were intent on bringing the central highlands of Palestine under their control. Battle was joined at Aphek and was fought out in two phases. In the first phase the Israelites suffered heavy casualties (4^{2}), the tenacity of their defence shows that they realized that their freedom was at stake. Whilst the Philistines were preparing to follow up their initial advantage, the Israelites re-formed their army and fetched the Ark of Yahweh from Shiloh to go before them into battle. This was understood by both sides as a symbol of the presence of Yahweh (verses 7–8). In spite of misgivings the Philistines, unwilling that the tables should be turned on them (verse 9), gave battle, winning a decisive victory, capturing the sacred Ark, and killing the priests Hophni and Phineas.

The tragedy on the field of battle was matched by the tragedy which overtook the house of Eli, when news of the defeat reached Shiloh. The old priest died of shock, and his daughter-in-law died in childbirth. Not even the birth of a son could lighten the dark tragedy of the hour, which was preserved in the name which one of the women standing by gave to the child: 'Ichabod'—'The glory (i.e. the Ark of Yahweh) is departed from Israel.'

Though the biblical narrative does not give any further details, archaeological evidence suggests that the Philistines followed up their victory by pressing on to the tribal centre of Shiloh, which they destroyed (cf also Jer 7^{12}, 26^{6}). After the death of Eli, Samuel must have assumed the position of 'judge', and he was able to preserve the Israelite way of life and worship in a rather restricted region. The traditions and festivals were kept alive at the ancient shrines of Bethel, Gilgal, Mizpah, and Ramah (7^{15-17}). But there was no recognized centre where the tribes could gather, and in any case the Philistines had such a stranglehold on the land that it was almost impossible to rally the tribes for any concerted action. The loosely knit tribal confederation which had been able for two centuries to resist and overcome or absorb the indigenous Canaanite population, and the raiders from the eastern desert, was no match for the highly organized, resourceful Philistines. It is true that there is an account in 1 Samuel 7^{5-14} of an engagement in which the Israelites were victorious, but such occurrences must have been isolated and the Philistines quickly recovered any ground they may have lost. They determined if possible to prevent any revival of Israelite power by forbidding the latter to manufacture weapons, even their agricultural implements were sharpened and repaired by the Philistine smiths (13^{19-20}).

CHAPTER SIX

THE UNITED MONARCHY

THE TRAGEDY OF SAUL

THE SITUATION of the Israelites was desperate, and it was obvious that, in spite of sporadic victories such as that described in 1 Samuel 7, Samuel's leadership was inadequate to meet the Philistine challenge at all effectively. Moreover, Samuel was by now an old man (1 S 8^{1}, 12^{2}), and the elders of Israel had no confidence in his dissolute sons (1 S $8^{3, 5}$), hence they ask that Samuel should give them a king to 'govern us like all the nations . . . and go out before us and fight our battles' ($8^{5, 20}$). This reasonable request, which may indeed have been opposed by those who did not wish to see the confederacy of free self-governing tribes replaced by an autocratic central government, is represented in 1 Samuel 8 as an act of rebellion against Yahweh. This appears to be a later theological interpretation influenced, perhaps, by Saul's defeat and death on Mount Gilboa. It was unthinkable that one favoured by Yahweh could come to such an ignominious end. The part played by Samuel during the reign of Saul was hardly a creditable one; unable himself to deliver Israel from the Philistine yoke, he seems to have become increasingly jealous of Saul's victories. There is more than a hint in 1 Samuel $13^{8\,ff}$ that he deliberately abused his position as judge and prophet in order to embarrass and intimidate Saul, whilst the anointing of David during Saul's lifetime can only be regarded as an act of treason.

A description of Saul's reign is contained in the last twenty-three chapters (9–31) of 1 Samuel. Unfortunately for the historian a considerable amount of space is devoted to rather unimportant anecdotes from the lives of Saul and David. The story of Saul's search for his father's asses occupies almost two chapters (9 and 10), and the slaying of Goliath, which was but one incident in the continuing struggle against the Philistines, is the subject of another long chapter (17). Nevertheless it is possible to recover from the narrative the main features of Saul's reign.

The account of the anointing of Saul by Samuel as related in chapters 8 to 10 is confused and contradictory (see below p. 112). Saul first emerges on the scene of history as the deliverer of Jabesh Gilead

(1 S 11). Philistine domination west of the Jordan evidently encouraged the neighbours of those Israelites who were settled east of the river to expand at the latter's expense. Saul, in the manner of one of the judges, rallied to the defence of the city and scored a memorable victory. As a result he was acclaimed king in Gilgal (1 S 11^{15}).

Saul's reign appears to have been quite short. 1 Samuel 13^{1b} suggests that it was only of two years' duration, this is not improbable as the Philistines would obviously make an all-out effort to crush any Israelite uprising as quickly as possible. (See the note on this difficult verse on page 113.) From the outset Saul had realized the magnitude of the task which faced him if he were to free Israel from the Philistines. He knew that the hastily summoned and ill-armed contingents from the Israelite tribes could be no match for the well-equipped and well-trained mercenaries of the Philistines. His first act, then, was to recruit a small permanent army (13^{2}) with which to harass the Philistine garrisons which had been established at Geba and Michmash. These guerrilla tactics met with some success (13^{3-4}, $14^{1\,ff}$), though not without bringing Philistine reprisals on the unhappy country ($13^{17\,ff}$). The battle described in chapter $14^{17\,ff}$ seems to have cleared the central highlands of the Philistines (14^{46}), but since only local garrisons were involved it could not be long before Saul would have to face a massive Philistine offensive. In the meantime the Israelite successes so boosted their morale, and perhaps intimidated their other foes, that Saul secured victories over Moab, Edom, Ammon, and Amalek (14^{47-8}). The campaign against Amalek is described in detail in Chapter 15, Samuel found in Saul's conduct of this campaign a pretext for withdrawing his support from the king. This was a bitter blow to the latter whose loyalty to Yahweh cannot be questioned (cf. 1 S $14^{38\,ff}$).

But the war with the Philistines continued. 1 Samuel 17 describes an engagement at Socoh, a frontier town not far from the Philistine city of Gath. This must have been typical of the continuous frontier probing and skirmishing throughout Saul's brief reign (cf. 1 S 14^{52}), but this one was remembered because of David's victory over Goliath and the subsequent rout of the Philistine forces. David soon proved himself to be very successful in guerrilla warfare, but his very success roused Saul's jealousy. The continual strain of the Philistine war, coming on top of Samuel's opposition and perhaps that of a considerable section of the population, seems to have deranged Saul's mind. So he drove from his court his ablest general. For some time David lived as an outlaw in Judah, and eventually, having gathered around him a formidable band of followers, he entered the service of Achish, king of Gath, as a mercenary.

Some sixteen months later (1 S 27^{7}) Saul fought and lost his final battle. An account of the battle is given in Chapters 28, 29, and 31 of 1 Samuel. The Philistines were clearly putting into operation a carefully prepared plan for the reconquest of Israel. The whole army of the Philistine league had gathered at Shunem in the plain of Esdraelon (28^{4}), probably in the spring of the second year of Saul's reign for 'it was the custom to embark on large-scale campaigns in the spring after the end of the winter rains (cf. 2 S 11^{1})'.[1] This vast Philistine force had advanced along the age-old military route across the plain of Sharon and into the valley of Jezreel. Before launching an attack on the Israelites who had assembled at the Spring of Harod ('the fountain which is in Jezreel', 29^{1}), the scene of Gideon's victory over the Midianites, the Philistines mustered their troops at Aphek and dismissed David and his mercenaries from their ranks.

Saul was filled with foreboding of disaster when he learnt of the Philistine preparations. Half-demented he turned for help to the shade of the dead Samuel, but he, who in life had refused to support his king, was unable to do so in his death. Cut off from possible reinforcements from the northern tribes or from those on the east of the Jordan by the Philistine army, Saul's position was hopeless. The pitifully small and ill-equipped Israelite army scattered before the Philistine onslaught. Three of Saul's sons were killed in the battle and Saul committed suicide. The bid for freedom had failed. But the men of Jabesh Gilead had reason to be grateful to Saul; at some risk to themselves they rescued the mutilated bodies of the king and his sons from the wall of Beth-shan and buried the remains in Jabesh.

PASSAGES FOR STUDY

1 Samuel 11—*The relief of Jabesh Gilead*

Taking advantage of the weakened state of Israel, the Ammonites laid siege to Jabesh Gilead, confident that the inhabitants would not receive any help from the Israelite tribes west of the Jordan. Messengers were sent out from Jabesh to seek help among the Israelite tribes for the beleaguered city. The situation seemed quite hopeless; there was sympathy for the unfortunate people of Jabesh (verse 4) but no proffers of assistance. However, when Saul heard the news he was seized by the 'spirit of Yahweh', and despatching pieces of his oxen, like some fiery

[1] M. Noth, *History of Israel*, p. 176.

cross, he speedily raised a body of resolute men and assembled them at Bezek. The latter place was 'thirteen miles north-east from Shechem on the road down to Beth-shan',[2] and a suitable place from which to launch an attack on the Ammonites. Saul divided his army into three companies and they marched by night towards Jabesh making a surprise attack on the besiegers next day.

This initial success against the Ammonites singled out Saul as the kind of leader that some of the Israelites had been hoping and waiting for. The triumphant army carried him back to the ancient shrine of Gilgal where they acclaimed him as king (1 S 11^{15}).

Notes

(i) Verse 11—'on the morrow'. Since the day according to Hebrew reckoning began at sunset (cf. Gen 1) 'on the morrow' would imply that the march started at sunset, and hence Saul was able to make a surprise attack on the Ammonites at dawn ('in the morning watch').

(ii) Verse 15—This is one of several accounts of Saul becoming king. Others are given in (*a*) 1 Samuel 8, 10^{17-27}; and (*b*) 1 Samuel 9^{1}–10^{16}. In both (*a*) and (*b*) Samuel is instrumental in making Saul king. In the first account Samuel is opposed to the monarchy but yields to popular demand. Samuel's attitude may reflect the genuine opposition of a section of the people to monarchical rule but the description of the evils of a monarchy (8^{10-18}) seems to derive from experience under later monarchs. It is hardly a description of life in Saul's kingdom. Thus the account (*a*) probably represents the reflections and opinions of the final editor of the Books of Samuel and may indeed have been composed during the exile, i.e. after 586 B C. The other account (*b*) is evidently a tale of Saul's youth, and whatever may have passed between Saul and Samuel on this occasion, Saul did not consider very seriously taking the lead in Israel until he was acclaimed king in Gilgal. It is probable that in its original form 1 Samuel 11 nowhere mentioned Samuel. The words 'and Samuel' in verses 7 and 14 are later additions connecting this chapter with the preceding ones.

1 Samuel 13—*The Revolt against the Philistines*

Saul's first act as king was to recruit a small army of three thousand men which he divided into three companies under the joint command of his son Jonathan and himself. The standard of revolt was raised when Jonathan launched an attack on the Philistine military post at

2 G. A. Smith, *Historical Geography of the Holy Land*, p. 336.

Geba (13^{3}). The Philistines reacted rapidly basing a formidable army on Michmash. In the face of this threat the majority of Saul's untrained and untried army appears to have deserted (13^{6}), leaving him with only six hundred men (13^{15b}). On their part the Philistines further intimidated the Israelites by sending out raiding-parties from their base at Michmash (13^{17}).

NOTES

(i) 1 Samuel 13^{1a}. This verse is difficult. The Hebrew text reads, 'Saul was a year old when he began to reign', which is clearly absurd. One version of the LXX has 'thirty years', but this would seem to be too young since his son Jonathan was mature enough to command the army. Probably Saul's age was unknown and the writer simply put 'Saul was —— years old', perhaps hoping to fill in the blank later. Another version of the LXX omits this verse altogether.

(ii) 1 Samuel 13^{1b}. The second part of this verse reads 'and he ruled over Israel for two years'. It is not necessary to assume with the *RSV* marginal note that 'Two is not the entire number. Something has dropped out.'

(iii) Verses 8–14 are considered along with Chapter 15.

1 Samuel 14—*Guerrilla Warfare*

The Israelites were unable to mount a full-scale offensive against their overlords. Saul had retired to his home at Gibeah, taking his six hundred retainers with him. From a vantage point outside Gibeah he kept a continuous watch on the Philistine garrison, ready to take advantage of any opportunity that might present itself. Such an opportunity arose when Jonathan and his armour-bearer made a daring raid on a Philistine outpost, killing twenty men and throwing the garrison into confusion. Saul attacked with his small band of troops and was quickly reinforced by Israelite slaves who had escaped from the Philistines and by other Israelites who had gone into hiding. The Philistines fled westward towards their own territory (14^{31}). Saul, recognizing the hand of Yahweh in this victory, forbade his men to touch food until nightfall. This injunction enshrines an ancient religious belief that the Deity would be pleased by this self-denying abstinence and would continue to fight for Israel against their foe. Even at the close of day Saul was careful to ensure that the sheep and oxen taken as spoil were slaughtered in accordance with the accepted ritual, lest the army should bring disaster upon itself by profane use of the spoil which belonged to Yahweh. 'It (the spoil) was in fact sacred, and it would be unsafe for individual Israelites to appropriate it until the first fruits had been set apart for Yahweh.'[3]

Jonathan's failure to observe Saul's command to abstain from food was discovered when Saul sought in vain to determine whether he should continue to pursue the Philistines. The penalty for not observing the prohibition was death; both Jonathan and Saul recognize this and neither pleads extenuating circumstances. In accordance with the religion of the time Jonathan heroically awaits his fate. He declares, 'here I am, I will die', whilst Saul accepts the inevitable saying, 'you shall surely die Jonathan' (14^{43-4}). The people, however, are determined to save Jonathan, the hero of the day, and so provide a ransom for him; it is probable that some member of the army died in his stead.[4] This victory over the Philistines must have liberated the central highlands, so that Saul could turn his attention to other enemies of Israel ($14^{47\,f}$).

1 Samuel 15 (13^{8-14})—*Samuel rejects Saul*

This chapter along with verses 8 to 14 of Chapter 13 belongs to that account of Saul's reign which makes him subordinate to Samuel, and so was originally unconnected with the chapters we have just studied. It was inserted at this point in the Book of Samuel because it amplifies the summary statement of 1 Samuel 14^{48} that Saul 'smote the Amalekites', but whereas in 14^{48} Saul is commended in that 'he delivered Israel out of the hands of those who plundered them', in Chapter 15 his conduct of the campaign against Amalek is given as the reason for his rejection. The quarrel between Saul and Samuel took place at Gilgal, and a comparison of 13^{8-14} with 15^{13-34} strongly suggests that we have here different descriptions of the same event. The root of the matter seems to be that Samuel equated obedience to Yahweh with obedience to himself. It is hardly justifiable to claim that Saul was usurping Samuel's privilege in offering a sacrifice (13^{12}) because Gideon, who was not a prophet, had offered a sacrifice at Ophrah (Jdg $6^{25\,ff}$).

The scene at Gilgal must have been a terrible experience for Saul. First the aged prophet, and Samuel must have been a around seventy years old, denounces the king, then with a dramatic gesture he tears his own robe and finally with a display of almost superhuman strength

3 H. P. Smith, 'Samuel', *ICC*, p. 114.

4 A. S. Herbert, *Peake's Commentary* (New Edn.), p. 325, para. 279h.

slays the unfortunate Agag, who had supposed that he was no longer in mortal danger. Thus the two, who might have co-operated to good effect, parted company.

1 Samuel 16^{14-23}—*David comes to the Court of Saul*

The quarrel with Samuel and presumably also the continuing strain of the Philistine war was beginning to have its effect on the balance of Saul's mind. 'The affliction manifested itself in sudden or unreasoning fits of terror'[5] (cf. 1 S 16^{14}). Music was a recognized means of soothing and charming away such disturbances. Thus David was introduced to Saul as one who was a skilled musician and also a tried warrior. So David took his place in Saul's modest court as one of the king's personal bodyguard. There is no hint in this account that David was the youthful shepherd lad of romantic imagination; Saul was in desperate need of seasoned warriors and it was as such that he welcomed David.

1 Samuel 17^{1}–18^{5}—*David and Goliath*

This chapter describes another incident in the Philistine war. A Philistine army had gathered near Socoh, eighteen or twenty miles west of Bethlehem. Facing them across the valley were the Israelite forces, who were being taunted to send out a man to meet their champion, the giant Goliath, in single combat. As the story now stands it raises many difficulties since it presupposes that David was unknown to Saul before this incident. Even in this story he is twice introduced to Saul (see verses 31 and 58). It may be possible to recover the original story by following the text of the LXX and omitting verses 17^{21-31} and 17^{55}–18^{5}. The story then suggests that David offered to accept Goliath's challenge and, armed with a sling, he slew the Philistine hero. It should be noted that although the text draws a contrast between Goliath's formidable weapons and David's sling, the latter was no toy, but a weapon which, in the hands of a skilled man, could be used with devastating effect (cf. Jdg 20^{14-16}). The death of Goliath caused panic among the Philistine army, and a corresponding elation among the Israelites who routed their enemies, pursuing them as far as Gath and Ekron.

1 Samuel 28–31—*The Battle of Gilboa*

Saul had been on the throne for about two years (cf. 1 S 13^{1b} and 27^{7}), and had evidently been able to ward off the Philistine attacks during

[5] H. P. Smith, 'Samuel', *ICC*, p. 148.

this period, but he had not crushed their will to reconquer the territory they had lost. Now they had mustered a formidable army in the plain of Esdraelon, and it was clear that Saul's army was no match for the combined might of the Philistine league. Saul's tragic reign was drawing to its close. He had faced great odds, his mind had given way under the strain, and in his deranged state he felt utterly deserted, forsaken by God (1 S $28^{6, 15}$). In verses dark with tragedy (28^{7-25}) we see him vainly seeking help from the shade of the now dead Samuel, but his tortured and tormented mind can only recall the fierce denunciations which Samuel had vented on him at their last meeting. Saul was already a defeated man when he left the witch of Endor.

But the men of Jabesh remembered their former deliverer, and they brought the bodies of Saul and his sons from Beth-shan to Jabesh.

2 Samuel 1^{19-27}—*The Song of the Bow*

Saul was dead, the Philistines were once again masters in Israel, but one whom he had loved, and then in his madness had driven away, paid the last tribute to the dead hero. So David lamented over Saul and Jonathan. T. H. Robinson writes: 'We know nothing of David which presents him in a better light. We can understand his references to Jonathan, who was always his friend, but the poet speaks with almost equal affection of Saul. All the mistrust, treachery, and persecution are now forgotten, and death has allowed only the king's virtues and beneficent acts to survive.'[6]

DAVID: EMPIRE BUILDER

The careers of David and Saul overlap, so that in tracing the former's amazing rise to power it is necessary to begin our account during the reign of Saul. We have already seen that David was introduced to Saul as a skilled musician and warrior. His successes against the Philistines and his increasing popularity amongst the Israelites roused Saul's jealousy and unreasoning hatred. After attempting unsuccessfully to kill David with his own hands, Saul hit on the plan of sending the popular hero on dangerous missions against the Philistines. But David seemed to bear a charmed life, and he returned unscathed from these enterprises. However, it was clear that Saul intended to destroy him, so he sought refuge among his own clan in Judah. For a time, perhaps only a few months, he used the stronghold of Adullam as his head-

[6] T. H. Robinson, *Poetry and Poets of the Old Testament*, pp. 64–5.

quarters, and quickly gathered round him a motley collection of debtors and malcontents (1 S 22^{1-4}).

David was now an outlaw, and it must have been during this period that his political ideas and ambitions began to crystallize. He set out quite deliberately to win over the Judean tribes. He gained the allegiance of some of the clans by his marriages to Abigail, the widow of a wealthy farmer from Carmel in Judah, and to Ahinoam from Jezreel in Judah. (This latter place should not be confused with the northern Jezreel.) He also went to the aid, when opportunity offered, of Judean cities which were under attack.

All the while, however, Saul was trying to seize the outlaw, and since David had no mind to engage in open and military rebellion against his king (cf. 1 S 24^{6}), he decided to quit Israelite territory altogether, and with his army of retainers, now numbering six hundred, he offered his services to the Philistine king, Achish of Gath. For his services David was given the city of Ziklag as his headquarters. This suited him admirably. He was safe from Saul and yet so far from Gath and his master Achish that he was able to keep the latter in ignorance of his plans and activities. Thus he continued to strengthen his ties with the men of Judah by making raids on their traditional enemies, at the same time assuring Achish that out of revenge he had been making raids into Judah. Fortunately for David his dubious loyalty to Achish was never put to the test. He was spared the painful decision whether he should fight against Saul at Gilboa; the 'lords of the Philistines' regarded him as a far from committed ally and dismissed him before the battle was joined.

After the disaster on Gilboa, David lost little time in returning to Judah, and, settling in Hebron, he was elected king over the 'house of Judah' (2 S 2^{4}). At the same time Abner, commander-in-chief of Saul's army, who had not been killed in the battle, made his way across the Jordan to Mahanaim and there set up Ishbosheth (Ishbaal), a surviving son of Saul, as king over Israel. By now the old confederation of twelve tribes was a thing of the past, and two new States, Israel and Judah, emerged. Abner still hoped to unify them under one crown and so began military operations against Judah. But such Israelite forces as Abner could muster were no match for David's army, the nucleus of which was the six hundred veterans who had returned with him from Ziklag, commanded by the redoubtable and unscrupulous Joab. Both Israel and Judah must have been vassals of the Philistines at this time, but so long as they were weakening and impoverishing each other by this fratricidal struggle the Philistines did not interfere.

After about two years (cf. 2 S 2^{10}, though Ishbosheth cannot have been forty years old at the time unless we suppose Saul to have been sixty or more at the battle of Gilboa), Abner realized that nothing was to be gained by continuing the struggle against David and so he made a treaty with him, whereby the latter was also elected king over Israel. Abner, however, did not live to see the enthronement of David, as he was brutally murdered by Joab to avenge his brother Asahel's death. Ishbosheth also suffered this all-too-common fate of deposed monarchs.

Now that the two kingdoms were united under David, the Philistines became alarmed and made a plundering raid into the valley of Rephaim to the south of Jerusalem. David attacked the raiders and scattered them (2 S 5^{17-21}) but the Philistines were not so easily daunted. They sent a second and presumably much larger force into the valley, but again David secured a resounding and this time decisive victory. Gilboa had been avenged, the tables were turned and the Philistine menace was over.

David continued to rule over the two kingdoms from Hebron for five years after the death of Ishbosheth. This was an inconvenient centre for administering the growing empire and it is likely that the men of Israel resented being ruled from Hebron as if Israel were subordinate to Judah. The city State of Jerusalem still remained independent; the last Canaanite stronghold in David's kingdom, it virtually cut off Israel from Judah. David therefore attacked it with his mercenaries ('his men'—2 S 5^{6}), and, in spite of its boasted impregnability, took it. He then made Jerusalem the capital of the States of Israel and Judah. One of his first acts was to bring the Ark, which seemed to have been almost forgotten, from the city of Kiriath-Jearim (or Baale Judah), where it had lain for upwards of twenty years (1 S 6^{21}, 7^{2}), to his new capital. At one stroke David gave the States an independent capital and a religious centre which all the tribes could revere. At last the old tribal centre of Shiloh had been worthily replaced, for the religious significance of Jerusalem was destined to outshine by far its political importance.

After the capture of Jerusalem, David set about to bring the various neighbouring kingdoms into his empire. Moab, whose army was treated with particular severity (2 S 8^{2}), became a vassal State. Edom in the south and Damascus and its territory in the north became provinces of the empire, administered by governors appointed by David (2 S $8^{14,\,5\,\mathrm{ff}}$, 1 K 11^{15-18}). The war with Ammon, which is described in some detail in 2 Samuel 10–12 because of the Bathsheba incident, brought yet another kingdom into David's realm. As David's overtures of peace had been slightingly brushed aside by the young Ammonite king Hanun (2 S 10^{1-5}), he took fearful revenge when victory was secured. He had himself crowned king of Ammon and then reduced the population to slavery (2 S 12^{26-31}). On the fate of Hanun the record is silent!

We do not know how long a period these various campaigns covered. The Ammonite war must have extended over two years, and Joab spent six months in 'mopping up' operations in Edom. We should not be far wrong in supposing that David spent the first ten or twelve years after the capture of Jerusalem on this programme of empire building.

During the latter half of David's reign it became apparent that all was not well within the kingdom. He had possessed himself of a large harem and this brought forth its usual harvest of court intrigue and rivalry between his various sons, resulting in one major rebellion during his reign. The story of Absalom is told very fully in 2 Samuel 13–18, from which it appears that he had been scheming to secure the throne for perhaps as long as ten years. The rape of his sister Tamar by his older half-brother Amnon provided Absalom an excuse for killing him. For three years he lived in banishment in Geshur and then for a further two years in Jerusalem before he was reconciled with David.

But besides intrigue within the court there was a growing discontent in the country. The 'men of Israel' in particular began to grumble at the delays which they suffered in getting law cases heard by the king. Absalom was not slow to fan these fires of discontent and, when he deemed that he had gained sufficient support, he caused himself to be proclaimed king in the old Judean royal city of Hebron. When David received this news, he fled from Jerusalem to Mahanaim. Fortunately the permanent army and their commander-in-chief Joab remained loyal.

Absalom moved into Jerusalem and proceeded to take control. David left two of his loyal followers, Zadok the priest and Hushai, in Jerusalem to act as secret agents. Hushai quickly became accepted as one of Absalom's advisers. Absalom was so sure that everyone of importance had deserted David that he apparently did not suspect Hushai of duplicity when the latter made his protestations of loyalty. Consequently David was kept informed of Absalom's plans and when the latter took the field with his army David was ready to meet him. Absalom's ill-trained militiamen were no match for David's regular army. The battle was fought in the 'forest of Ephraim'. Absalom's army was scattered and he himself was killed by Joab, who showed little regard for David's orders concerning his son or for his sorrow after Absalom's death. But David's troubles were by no means over after the collapse of Absalom's revolt. A quarrel broke out between the representatives of Israel and those of Judah, the former accused the latter of stealing a march on them since the elders of Judah alone were present when David was restored to his throne. Taking advantage of the tension between Israel and Judah, Sheba, a Benjaminite, stirred up the Israelites to revolt against David. By taking prompt action this rebellion was quickly suppressed, but it had revealed the continuing tension between Judah and Israel, a tension which was never resolved.

Further troubles broke out in court circles towards the end of David's life. There seem to have been two rival factions in the court, each anxious to secure power after the king's death. In fact when it became evident that David had not long to live, one of his sons Adonijah, supported by Joab and Abiathar, proclaimed himself king. The rival party headed by Nathan persuaded Bathsheba to ask David to name Solomon, her son, as his successor. On David's instructions Solomon was duly anointed king by Zadok and Nathan. After David's death Solomon endeavoured to make his own position more secure by getting rid of his political opponents. Adonijah and Joab were murdered whilst Abiathar was banished to Anathoth.

NOTE. This account should be supplemented by reading 2 Samuel 2–20 and 1 Kings 1–2.

PASSAGES FOR STUDY

2 Samuel 2–4—*David, King of Judah*

This passage is straightforward and does not call for much comment. 2^{1-11} sets the stage for the description of a battle between the servants of David and the followers of Ishbosheth. Verses 4b–7 suggest that David from the outset was planning to take over the rule of Israel if possible, so he tries to win over Jabesh-Gilead. The latter part of Chapter 2, from verse 12 onwards, describes a battle between Judean and Israelite forces. In view of 3^1 we must suppose that this was only one of many such skirmishes, but this incident is recounted in order that the reader may know how the blood feud between Joab and Abner arose.

2 Samuel 3^{2-5}. This short note names David's six sons born in Hebron to his six wives. Already David had a considerable harem. Rivalry between the different wives and their sons, each having their own following of courtiers, often led to strife in Oriental kingdoms. Such troubles were a feature of the latter part of David's reign.

2 Samuel 3^{6}–4^{12}. Abner, who was the real master in Israel, realizing that to continue the war with David could only lead to one end, came to terms with him. The transfer of sovereignty to David was accompanied by the murder of Abner and Ishbosheth. As political murders of this kind were all too common in such circumstances, David deemed it advisable to make a public protestation of his innocence.

2 Samuel 5—*The King of Judah and Israel*

2 Samuel $5^{1-3, 17-25}$. An immediate consequence of David's assumption of control of both Judah and Israel was a raid by the Philistines into his territory, but David defeated them so thoroughly that they appear to have caused little more trouble.

2 Samuel 5^{4-16}. It appears from 2 Samuel 5^{17} that the decisive encounter with the Philistines came shortly after David had been made king over Israel and so must have preceded the capture of Jerusalem described in these verses.

2 Samuel 6—*David brings the Ark to Jerusalem*

Some time after the capture of Jerusalem, David decided to bring the Ark from Baale Judah (Kiriath-Jearim) to his new capital. The removal of this sacred object required some care, and lest it be defiled it was transported on a new cart. Even so a tragedy occurred when Uzzah touched the Ark in an attempt to steady it on the cart; because he had touched the sacred object he was struck dead. Here we are moving in the realm of primitive religious ideas. Yahweh was so awesome in His majesty that only a few especially privileged persons like Abraham or Moses had been allowed to commune directly with Him. Something of His fearful majesty clung to His sacred Ark. 'Since it was the symbol of Yahweh's presence, its power was formidable. . . . Uzzah was struck dead for touching it.'[7] David was afraid to continue

[7] R. de Vaux, *Ancient Israel* (ET), p. 299.

the journey to Jerusalem, but left the Ark with Obed-Edom. Three months later the rest of the journey was safely accomplished.

2 Samuel 7^{1-17}—*God's Promise to David*

The account of the bringing of the Ark to Jerusalem leads naturally to the theme of this chapter, though in view of verse 1 we must assume a lapse of several years since that event. We know from 2 Samuel 8 that David spent several years subduing the surrounding kingdoms. During all this time the Ark had been housed in a tent, meanwhile David had built a palace for himself (2 S 5^{11}). Now he proposes to build a temple to house the Ark. The court prophet Nathan at first gave unqualified approval (7^{3}), until it was revealed to him in a dream (verses 4–17) that this was not the will of Yahweh. The major part of Nathan's message to David was Yahweh's promise that the future rulers of Israel would all be of 'David's line'. This remarkable promise begins by reviewing David's meteoric rise to power which was evidence that Yahweh was with him (verse 9). The prophetic vision then looks forward to a long line of Davidic kings; it is nevertheless thoroughly realistic as it anticipates that the kingdom will not be free from troubles: 'When he commits iniquity, I will chasten him with the rod of men' (7^{14}). Yet there is also the note of grace: 'but I will not take my steadfast love from him.' Centuries later in days of oppression and persecution promises such as this were like a beacon of hope for those who were 'looking for the consolation of Israel' (Lk 2^{25}).

2 Samuel 7^{18-29}—*David's Prayer*

The divine promise to David is matched by David's prayer which occupies the latter part of this chapter. Verse 18 seems to mean that David went into the tent and sat in front of the Ark. The prayer is almost entirely taken up with the adoration and praise of the majesty and condescension of Yahweh. David acknowledges his unworthiness and confesses that his rise to greatness has been a gift from Yahweh (verses 18–21). He then praises the power of Yahweh, which was made manifest especially in the redemption of Israel from Egypt (verses 22–4). Here once again we meet one of the great themes of the Old Testament. The prayer closes with an earnest request that Yahweh's promise to David might be confirmed, not so much that his 'house' might be great, but rather that 'Thy Name will be magnified for ever' (verse 26).

2 Samuel 8—*David's Wars*

This chapter gives a very brief account of the campaigns that David undertook against the surrounding States. These wars must have occupied a good proportion of his reign. No indication of their duration is given in this chapter, but the war against Ammon is described in greater detail in Chapters 10–12, from which we learn that this alone lasted for about two years. As a result of these campaigns David eventually controlled an empire stretching from Edom and the Sinai Desert in the south almost to the Euphrates in the north.

The chapter closes with a note giving the names of the chief officials in David's administration. Joab was commander-in-chief of the army, Benaiah had command of the foreign mercenaries (Cherethites and Pelethites) who formed the king's bodygard. At the head of civil affairs were Jehoshaphat and Seraiah, whilst Zadok and Abiathar were priests in attendance on the king.

NOTE. 2 Samuel 8^{17}—It is probable that the text should be corrected to read: 'Zadok son of Ahitub, and Abiathar son of Ahimelech', as in the Syriac version (cf. 1 S 22^{20}, 2 S 20^{25}).

2 Samuel 11^{1}–12^{25}—*David and Bathsheba*

This incident occurred during the Ammonite war. The war had already received a brief mention in the general review of David's military exploits in 2 Samuel 8. Since, however, it forms the background to the story of David and Bathsheba it is described in more detail in Chapters 10–12. The account of David's adultery with Bathsheba, of his unsuccessful attempt to conceal the consequences of his action, and finally of his callous way of getting rid of Uriah is given in 2 Samuel 11. The story is quite matter of fact, neither accusing nor excusing the king, but for this very reason the contrast between the honest and trusting Uriah and the deceitful king is all the more striking.

Shortly after the death of Uriah, David took Bathsheba to be his wife and it appeared that the whole sorry incident had been forgotten, for between the incident and its sequel (related in Chapter 12) there was an interval of many months. The first part of this chapter (12^{1-15}) describes a most dramatic interview between the court prophet, Nathan, and the king. The interview begins by Nathan ostensibly posing a legal problem. We should remember that there was a king's court in

Jerusalem over which David presided as judge (2 S 8^{15}). It is also probable that the king discussed legal cases with his leading officials, so that there would be nothing unusual in Nathan opening such a conversation. The enormity of the crime committed by the rich man in stealing the poor man's lamb is deliberately heightened by the supposition that this was a pet lamb.[8] David reacts in the manner which Nathan had fully expected.

Then the roles of king and subject are suddenly and dramatically reversed. No longer have we the courtier graciously permitted to converse with his monarch, but the prophet, who is the voice of Yahweh the Living God and King of Kings, denouncing one who is indeed king of Israel, but only by the will and grace of Yahweh. The burden of the charge against David is that he has 'despised the word of Yahweh' (2 S 12^{9}). The 'word' which has been so flagrantly set aside is the Decalogue, which is at the heart of the covenant relation between Yahweh and Israel, for David has murdered, committed adultery, and coveted his neighbour's wife (cf. Ex $20^{14, 15, 17}$). David stands convicted and condemned; he had abused his royal power, but he makes no excuses, neither does he attempt to minimize the gravity of his sin. He simply confesses: 'I have sinned against the LORD', and waits humbly to hear the word of judgement. He who had so often pronounced judgement in his royal court now waits whilst the sentence is pronounced. The sin is forgiven but its consequences cannot be blotted out. The royal example in setting aside the law will be noticed and imitated, and there will be sorrow for David in the death of Bathsheba's son. 'Then Nathan went to his house' (2 S 12^{15}).

The remainder of the passage describes the sickness and death of the child. There is a pathetic and hopeless tone in David's comment after the child had died: 'I shall go to him, but he will not return to me.' This is not a joyous expression of belief in eternal life, but a fearful anticipation of the shadowy existence in Sheol.

2 Samuel 15–19—*Absalom's Revolt*

These chapters give a detailed account of Absalom's revolt and its defeat. This has been sufficiently covered in the introduction (p. 119 f.) and needs no further comment.

[8] 'Such pet lambs are frequently seen in the houses of the poor in Syria'—H. P. Smith, 'Samuel', *ICC*, p. 322.

SOLOMON THE MAGNIFICENT

On the death of David, Solomon succeeded to a large empire stretching from Ezion-geber in the south to Riblah some seventy miles north of Damascus. His elevation to the throne was engineered by Nathan who outwitted Joab and Abiathar, supporters of Solomon's elder brother Adonijah. Shortly after his accession Solomon found pretexts for getting rid of his political rivals, endeavouring by this means to discourage would-be rebels against his authority.

Solomon's reign was untroubled by wars, and he was able to exploit the resources of his empire. He made no efforts to extend his dominions though it is likely that he received a small addition to his territory as a marriage dowry from the Pharaoh whose daughter he married. It is an indication of the strength of Israel and the weakness of Egypt that such a marriage could take place. Solomon also continued the old alliance with Tyre which David had made, to the mutual benefit of both kingdoms. Any slight territory which Solomon may have received from Egypt was more than offset by the loss of a large part of Edom and also of the city of Damascus and probably the territory to the north of the city. It is uncertain when these losses occurred, but probably quite soon after David's death. Edom had been brutally subdued by Joab, but the crown prince, Hadad, then a child, had been taken to Egypt. After David's death he had returned to Edom and managed to set up an independent kingdom at any rate in the remoter part of the land. Another rebel, Rezon, seized Damascus and set up an independent kingdom there (1 K 11$^{14-25}$). The biblical record does not suggest that Solomon took any very active measures to reconquer the lost territories, but these losses, if they occurred early in his reign, may have been in part responsible for his decision to strengthen his defences. Key cities near the frontiers were fortified and garrisoned. Hazor and Megiddo were bases for the defence of the north; Gezer, Beth-horon, and Baalah guarded the south-western frontier, whilst the base at Tamar south of the Dead Sea, served to contain Edom. Solomon also strengthened his regular army by raising a considerable force of 1400 chariots. These would be divided amongst the various garrisons. Excavations have uncovered large stables at Hazor and Megiddo believed to have been built by Solomon.

But Solomon did not confine his building activity merely to strengthening his defences. Much effort was lavished on the extension of his capital city. The old Jebusite city of Jerusalem which David had captured and made into the capital of the united kingdom was a small place. For strength it had been built on the hill-top separating the Tyropoeon valley on the west from the Kidron valley on the east. The result was a long narrow city of four to five acres extent. From north to south it may have been about 600 yards long, whilst at its widest it hardly reached 100 yards. The Jebusite population has been estimated at about 1200 people. This small city, renamed the 'city of David' became the headquarters for the administration of the rapidly growing empire. It is understandable that by the end of David's reign there must have been severe overcrowding in the city. Solomon evidently believed that his empire required a worthier capital city, and he himself desired a more imposing residence than David had left. The hill on which the ancient Jebusite city had been built extended northwards, rising even higher, and it was on this northern eminence that Solomon decided to build a temple, a royal palace, and administrative buildings. The whole formed one large complex of buildings which was as large as the city of David. Although the description of the Temple occupies pride of place in the biblical account (1 K 6), it was in fact one of the smaller buildings of the group. It was primarily a royal chapel, but since it housed the sacred Ark it also served as the central shrine of the kingdom. It did not, however, displace the local shrines.

This elaborate building work in Jerusalem and elsewhere in the kingdom (1 K 9[15]) could only be achieved by the deployment of a large labour force and also at considerable expense. A combination of heavy taxation and successful commercial enterprises provided the income for these projects; a system of forced labour provided the workers. The administration of the kingdom necessitated a vast army of officials. The names of Solomon's cabinet ministers have been preserved in 1 Kings 4[2–6]. This inner circle of highest officials included the chief priest, ministers of State (scribes), an official chronicler, the commander-in-chief of the armed forces, the chamberlain, and the minister of works. Next in rank were the twelve governors of the twelve districts into which Solomon had divided Israel. (Each district had to supply in turn one month's provisions for the court.) In addition there were three or four thousand minor officials in the government service. According to 1 Kings 9[23] there were 550 overseers in charge of the labour gangs, whilst it has been estimated that the provisions described in 1 Kings 9[23] would be enough to sustain over 30,000 people, or three to four thousand households.[9]

[9] J. Skinner, '1 and 2 Kings', *Century Bible*, p. 95.

Much of Solomon's personal wealth came from his commercial and industrial activities. With Hiram of Tyre he ran trading-expeditions from the port of Ezion-Geber (1 K 9^{26-7}) to Ophir. The latter place we now know as Somaliland, it was known to the Egyptians as Punt, a name which is sometimes used in the Old Testament. He also carried on trade with the Arabian kingdom of Sheba. One of the most spectacular discoveries of archaeology was the uncovering of a vast copper refinery at Ezion-Geber built by Solomon. Copper ore abounds in the hills southwards of the Dead Sea; this ore was mined, probably by slave labour, and then smelted and exported from Ezion-Geber. Solomon also profited from the trade in horses and chariots between Egypt and the various kingdoms north of Israel by levying a tax on all goods passing through his country. Unfortunately Solomon's expenditure exceeded even *his* vast income, and by the time he had completed his building work in Jerusalem his treasury was empty and he was on the verge of bankruptcy. To obtain ready money he was forced to sell territory, including twenty cities in Galilee, to Hiram.

The large labour force necessitated by Solomon's ambitious programme could only be raised by resorting to forced labour. About 180,000 men were impressed into this service; they were divided into three groups, each group serving for a month and then being allowed to return to their homes for two months. This measure was extremely unpopular, and, as the Judeans seem to have been exempt, it stirred up the latent antagonism of Israel to the house of David, and paved the way for the division of the kingdom after the death of Solomon.

Following ancient custom Solomon had a large harem. Many of his wives were the daughters of foreign kings, and his marriages to them would represent political alliances. Again in accordance with customary practice he allowed his wives to follow the religious observances of their own nations. Thus the cults of many heathen deities began to be observed in Jerusalem, and there was a growing danger that Yahweh too would come to be regarded as only a national god. The religious crisis which Elijah faced had its origin in the reign of Solomon.

PASSAGES FOR STUDY

1 Kings 3—*The Vision at Gibeon*

The introductory verses 1–3 acquaint the reader with Solomon's marriage to the daughter of the Pharaoh and prepare him for the account of the great celebration and sacrifice at Gibeon.

This ceremony probably took place shortly after Solomon's accession, at any rate after he had made his throne secure by getting rid of his rivals. The celebrations must have lasted for a considerable time judging by the large number of burnt offerings which were sacrificed. Solomon remained at the sanctuary doubtless hoping to receive some 'word' from Yahweh by night in a dream. He was granted a vision and requested that he might be given wisdom so that he could govern his people justly. Strangely enough we have no account of the administration of justice under Solomon, though one historian has suggested that Solomon 'may have been the first to systematize the law of Israel'.[10] The incident with which this chapter closes is given as an instance of the shrewdness displayed by the king in arriving at the truth in a difficult case.

1 Kings 6^{1-18}—*The Building of the Temple*

In the fourth year of his reign Solomon began the building of the Temple. We have seen already that this was only part of an ambitious building project by which Solomon doubled the size of his capital. However, the Temple assumed such importance in the later history of the Israelites that it came to be regarded as his greatest contribution to his people.

The main structure was rectangular, about 100 feet long, 33 feet broad and 50 feet high; this was flanked on either side by sets of small rooms for the use of the Temple officials. The entrance of the Temple faced towards the east, whilst directly opposite the entrance was the 'most holy place'. This room was cubical in shape, all its dimensions being equal to the width of the Temple. On the completion of the Temple the Ark was moved from the 'city of David' to the 'most holy place' as the symbol of Yahweh's residence in His house.

The promise contained in verses 11–13 is important in view of the belief of many in the time of Jeremiah (*c.* 600 B C) that the presence of the Temple in Jerusalem was sufficient to guarantee the safety of the city. These verses assert that Yahweh's continuing presence among His people is dependent on their faithful obedience to His laws. Yahweh may consent to dwell in the Temple, but the Temple cannot hold Him against His will.

[10] From Kittel's *History of Israel*, quoted by Montgomery in 'Kings', *ICC*, p. 107.

1 Kings 9^{26}–10^{13}—*Commerce*

Solomon had the reputation of being the richest king of his day (1 K 10^{23}). Whilst this claim may be exaggerated, he undoubtedly enjoyed a considerable income largely as a result of his commercial activities. This section gives some account of his trade with Arabia. Merchant ships sailed from Ezion-Geber, probably carrying copper from the refineries, to the distant land of Ophir from whence they brought gold and other commodities. In addition there was overland trade with the south-west Arabian State of Sheba. 1 Kings 10^{1-13} presents a rather romantic account of the visit of the Queen of Sheba to Solomon, the real purpose of which was political and economic rather than cultural. The commodities described in verse 10 were exported from south-east Arabia and the regular trade-route ran through the kingdom of Sheba. The rulers of Sheba no doubt acted as middlemen in the gold and spice trade just as Solomon did in the horse and chariot business.

1 Kings 11^{1-13}—*Solomon's Apostasy*

The practice of polygamy had baneful effects in the closing years both of David and Solomon. The intrigues aimed at securing the kingdom for first one and then another of David's sons may well have had their origin in the rivalry between his wives. In the case of Solomon the religious practices of his foreign wives diverted him from the worship of Yahweh so that he 'did not wholly follow after the LORD' (1 K 11^{6}). He built 'high places' near Jerusalem for the gods of 'all his foreign wives', and so encouraged the licentious and often barbarous practices associated with the worship of these gods. The biblical historian attributes the division of the kingdom after Solomon's death directly to his apostasy and the consequent anger of Yahweh.

We have already noted the immediate causes of the unrest in Israel —forced labour and high taxation which were necessitated by Solomon's luxurious living and his grandiose building schemes. But some of his foreign wives probably expected this kind of sumptuous provision, at any rate it pleased Solomon's vanity to provide for them in this way. Perhaps the biblical writer was near the truth when he attributed the dissolution of the kingdom to Solomon's foreign entanglements.

Psalm 132

This psalm was composed for use at the annual New Year Festival which was also the Feast of Tabernacles. This was the most important festival season of the year. Whenever 'the feast' is mentioned in the Bible without further qualification it is understood to be the Feast of Tabernacles (cf. 1 K 8², Jn 5¹). Solomon's Temple was dedicated at the New Year Festival (1 K 8²), and annually thereafter this occasion was recalled by a dramatic re-enactment of the first bringing of the Ark to the Temple. The Ark was removed from the Holy of Holies and taken to a place of assembly where the king, the priests, and great crowds of worshippers had gathered. The Ark was then brought back to the Temple in a solemn yet joyous procession, the history of its discovery by David at Kiriath-Jearim and its removal by him to Jerusalem being set forth in this dramatic psalm.

The psalm may have been composed for the dedication of the Temple, though it is more likely that it was written during the reign of one of the later kings. It was intended for liturgical use at this anniversary celebration, the various sections being used at different stages of the procession, and sung by different voices.

Verses 1–5. Before the procession moves off towards the Temple, the king (or someone acting on his behalf) sings this first section. David's piety and his concern for the Ark are recalled; he could not rest until he had 'found out a place for the LORD', i.e. a place for the Ark which represented the presence of Yahweh (3–5).

Verses 6–10. The song is taken up by the choir still recalling the story of the Ark. When David was living in Ephrathah (another name for Bethlehem) he and his companions heard that the Ark was still in existence somewhere, so they searched until they found it in the 'fields of Jaar' (i.e. Kiriath-Jearim). Now the choir exhorts the assembled worshippers to proceed to the Temple to worship Yahweh.

> 'Let us go to his dwelling place;
> let us worship at his footstool!' (verse 7).

The old battle cry is raised, 'Arise, O Yahweh', as the bearers lift the Ark and the procession moves off to the accompaniment of festal dancing (cf. 2 S 6¹⁴).

Verses 11–12. The procession reaches the Temple and the Ark is placed once again in the Holy of Holies. At this point in the ceremony sacrifices would be offered, then the next section of the psalm (verses 11–12) would be sung by one of the official prophets. This reminds both king and people of Yahweh's promise that David's descendants would continue to sit on the throne of Judah provided that they remained faithful to the covenant.

Verses 13–18. Another prophet now takes up the poem and declares that Yahweh has chosen Zion as His everlasting home. Yahweh's presence in Zion, symbolized by the Ark, will guarantee adequate provision for her people and especially for the poor and needy. Finally the prophet foresees a brilliant future for the house of David.

CHAPTER SEVEN

ISRAEL AND JUDAH

I—FROM THE DEATH OF SOLOMON TO THE FALL OF JERUSALEM

(1) *The division of the Kingdom; Rehoboam and Jeroboam*

THE GREAT empire which David had built up was already beginning to decline during the reign of Solomon. Both Edom and Damascus revolted successfully and Solomon was either unable or unwilling to bring these territories under his rule again. His failure to crush the revolt in Damascus (1 K 11$^{23-5}$) had serious consequences for Israel throughout the next two centuries, for Rezon, who had led the revolt against Solomon, founded a kingdom which became increasingly powerful under his descendants, and which dominated the Palestinian scene much as David's empire had done in its hey-day.

On the death of Solomon (*c.* 922 BC), Rehoboam, his son, succeeded to the throne (1 K 11^{43}). He seems to have been accepted as ruler over Judah without any question, but the king of Judah was not automatically recognized as king of Israel, so he went to the old tribal centre at Shechem for the ceremony of king making (1 K 12^{1}). There was, however, an influential group in Israel who were determined that the recognition of Rehoboam should be no mere formality, and in fact they took the opportunity of demanding that the intolerable burdens of taxation and forced labour imposed by Solomon be made lighter. During the next day Rehoboam consulted with his advisers. The older ones who must have realized that Solomon's oppressive measures had strained the allegiance of Israel to the house of David almost to breaking-point advised the king to conciliate the people; the younger ones, throwing caution to the winds, counselled Rehoboam to take a firm stand against the demands of Israel.

On the following day Rehoboam gave his ill-advised answer, and the empire which David had so deliberately built up fell asunder. The old war cry, sounded by Sheba when he revolted against David (2 S 20^{1}), was heard again in Israel:

'What portion have we in David?
We have no inheritance in the son of Jesse.
To your tents, O Israel!
Now see to your own house, David.' (1 K 12[16])

Still failing to realize the gravity of the situation, Rehoboam sent the most unpopular member of his government, Adoram, the minister in charge of the labour gangs, to quell the revolt. The Israelite reaction was swift and its temper unmistakable; Adoram was seized and lynched. Rehoboam fled to Jerusalem, whilst Jeroboam, who had returned from Egypt with the intention of assuming control of Israel, was made king (1 K 11[26]–12[20]). For the next two centuries Israel, which in the main was ruled by able kings in spite of the adverse judgement passed on them by the pro-Judean editor of the Books of Kings, was the more powerful and influential of the two Hebrew kingdoms.

Rehoboam's folly in handling the Israelite crisis cost him the larger part of his kingdom, but the Judeans remained loyal to him. In fact the principle of hereditary kingship had become so well established in Judah that, throughout its history as an independent kingdom, the reigning monarch was always a descendant of David save for a short period when the queen mother Athaliah, daughter of Ahab, seized power and reigned (2 K 11). No such principle became accepted in Israel so that there were fairly frequent changes in the ruling house.

Rehoboam's immediate reaction on his return to Jerusalem was to lay plans for a military invasion of Israel. This scheme was shelved on the advice of the prophet Shemaiah, but from various notes in the Book of Kings (e.g. 1 K 15[6, 8, 17]) it is evident that there was continuous border-skirmishing between Israel and Judah for almost half a century.

As soon as it had become clear that there was no danger of immediate action on the part of Rehoboam, Jeroboam set about the task of organizing his kingdom. For his capital he chose the ancient tribal centre of Shechem which he fortified. Some time later he moved the centre of government to Penuel near the river Jabbok on the east of the Jordan. It is not clear why this move, which appears to have been temporary, was made. Some scholars suggest that this military post was established to cut the great trade road which kept to the east of the Jordan and ultimately linked up with Judah. Others think that Jeroboam moved to the east of the Jordan when the Pharaoh Shishak (Sheshonq) led his great raid into Palestine.

This event occurred in the fifth year of the reign of Rehoboam

(1 K 14^{25}). Throughout the reigns of David and Solomon Egypt had not interfered in Palestine, but towards the close of Solomon's reign Shishak had seized the throne of Egypt and was determined, if possible, to restore his kingdom to its former glory. Thus when Rehoboam began to fortify his south-western frontier Shishak marched in force into Palestine. His intention appears to have been to demonstrate the might of Egypt, and his demonstration was certainly impressive. His armies destroyed the copper refineries at Ezion Geber, they overran Rehoboam's frontier forts and would have taken Jerusalem itself had not the king paid a huge tribute, robbing his palace and the Temple to do so (1 K $14^{25\,ff}$). Yet another prong of the Egyptian attack was directed into the plain of Esdraelon and this may have caused Jeroboam to move temporarily from Shechem to Penuel. After this military display the Egyptians returned home; Shishak apparently had no intention of attempting a conquest of Palestine.

As well as organizing the civil life of his new kingdom, Jeroboam thought it expedient to provide official centres of worship so that it would no longer be necessary for Israelites to go to Jerusalem. He raised Bethel and Dan, which were ancient shrines, to the status of royal sanctuaries. He instituted a new priesthood to serve at these royal chapels, which would no doubt be richly furnished in order to rival the Jerusalem Temple. The biblical historian, however, only mentions the 'golden calves' and these he roundly condemns as idolatrous objects. This appears to be a later interpretation; Jeroboam probably intended that these 'bulls' should symbolize Yahweh's throne or foot-stool, just as the Ark in Jerusalem was regarded as Yahweh's throne.

(2) *The Rise of the Aramean Kingdom of Damascus*

The friction between the two kingdoms continued throughout the reign of Jeroboam on the one hand, and the reigns of Rehoboam and his son Abijam on the other. Matters came to a crisis during the reign of Asa of Judah, Rehoboam's grandson. Baasha, who had seized the throne of Israel by murdering Jeroboam's son and successor, began to fortify the frontier town of Ramah, only five miles north of Jerusalem, with the intention of blockading the Judean capital. Asa appealed to Ben-Hadad, the ruler of the Aramean kingdom of Damascus, for help. Ben-Hadad promptly attacked Israel from the north and conquered all the northern territory bordering the sea of Galilee. Baasha withdrew to his capital Tirzah (the capital had been moved from Shechem to Tirzah during Jeroboam's reign) leaving Asa in possession of Ramah.

This incident brings on the scene the now powerful State of Damascus. Damascus had defected from the Israelite empire during Solomon's reign, and under a succession of vigorous rulers had become the most powerful State in Palestine. Israel suffered her first defeat at the hands of the Arameans of Damascus and Baasha's kingdom must have been reduced to the relatively small area bounded on the north by the Valley of Jezreel and on the south by the frontier with Judah a few miles north of Jerusalem. The Arameans were to be a thorn in Israel's side until the two kingdoms were swallowed up almost simultaneously by the Assyrians nearly two centuries later. The present defeat was but 'the first chapter in the long history of Aram's superiority over Israel'.[1]

Baasha ruled over Israel for twenty-four years and was succeeded by his son, who was murdered after a brief reign. Following a period of confusion and civil war lasting about four years Omri, an army commander, emerged as king. Although his reign is dismissed in six verses (1 K 16^{23-8}) he was 'the most capable of the north Israelite monarchs',[2] and for about forty years (*c.* 880–840 B C) Israel was ruled by Omri and his descendants.

(3) *The House of Omri*

When Omri eventually found himself in full control in Israel the plight of the country must have been desperate. The territory to the north of the Valley of Jezreel had already been lost to the Syrians (Arameans) during the reign of Baasha, and the country had been further weakened by the years of civil war. Nothing daunted, however, Omri, and later his son and successor Ahab, set about the task of building up the kingdom. In order to counter the ever-present threat from Syria, Omri made a defensive alliance with Phoenicia, an alliance which was strengthened by the marriage of Ahab with Jezebel, the daughter of the Phoenician king. This alliance, whilst politically expedient, led during the reign of Ahab to the introduction of Canaanite worship into Israel. Furthermore, Jezebel was an ardent devotee of the Canaanite Baal, and seems to have been determined if possible to replace the worship of Yahweh by the cult of Baal in Israel. We recall that Solomon permitted his

[1] Montgomery and Gehman, 'The Books of Kings', *ICC*, p. 278.
[2] Ibid., p. 284.

foreign wives to worship their own gods in Jerusalem, but this never constituted a serious challenge to the worship of Yahweh as the religion of the nation. Jezebel's 'missionary' activity did present such a challenge and provoked the implacable enmity of the prophets who found a doughty champion in Elijah.

During his reign Omri gained control of northern Moab, and exacted an annual tribute from that country which must have added greatly to the wealth of Israel (cf. 2 K 3^4). He also abandoned Tirzah as his capital, and built a new capital city on the hill of Samaria. The site was well chosen and when the fortifications were completed the city proved almost impregnable.

Ahab succeeded his father in about 869 B C. He continued Omri's policy of seeking by all means to strengthen Israel against probable Syrian attack. The long-standing quarrel with Judah was at last resolved, and Judah joined the Israelite-Phoenician alliance, this new pact being ratified by the marriage of Ahab's daughter, Athaliah, to the crown prince of Judah. At length the long-expected Syrian offensive was launched against Israel (1 K 20), ultimately Samaria was besieged and Ben-Hadad offered Ahab humiliating surrender terms. Ahab refused to accept the terms, and counter-attacking the over-bold Syrians he routed them. He again defeated a Syrian attack at Aphek in the following year, but treated the twice-defeated Ben-Hadad very leniently. There was a much more serious threat looming on the horizon; Assyria was pursuing an aggressive policy and seeking to expand westwards. The time had come for the Palestinian States to sink their differences and form a common front against the aggressor. An allied army, to which Ahab contributed two thousand chariots and ten thousand infantry, led by Ben-Hadad met the Assyrians at Karkar (853 B C). The Assyrian king, Shalmaneser III, claimed a decisive victory, but the fact remains that the Assyrian advance was halted.

With the withdrawal of the Assyrian menace the old enmity between Israel and Syria flared up again. Some two years after the battle of Karkar, Ahab attacked the Syrians in Gilead in an attempt to recover the Israelite cities which Ben-Hadad had not relinquished in spite of his treaty with Israel. Ahab's death in the battle for Ramoth Gilead brought his reign to an abrupt close.

Ahab was succeeded by his son Ahaziah who died as a result of an accident after a reign of only a few months. The throne then passed to another of Ahab's sons, so that Israel continued to be ruled by a member of the 'House of Omri' for almost another decade. Nevertheless, after the death of Ahab, Israel's fortunes began to decline. Moab revolted successfully (2 K 1[1]), and the joint forces of Israel and Judah were not able to bring her into subjection again. The war with Syria dragged on with no very decisive results for either side, although Israel seems to have recovered the ascendancy at some stage in the conflict. Within Israel there was growing opposition to the 'House of Omri' inspired by the stand which Elijah had made against the introduction of Baal worship, and the opposition was kept alive by his successor Elisha.

(4) *Jehu's Revolt*

When Elisha deemed that the time was ripe for a revolt against the ruling house he caused Jehu, an army commander who was at that time engaged against the Syrians at Ramoth Gilead, to be proclaimed king. At about the same time Elisha had also sparked off a revolt in Syria in which Ben-Hadad was murdered and his throne seized by Hazael. Immediately after being anointed, Jehu made haste to the royal residence at Jezreel where he murdered the king and the queen-mother Jezebel. The latter had persecuted the prophets of Yahweh when she was in power, and now fact-to-face with her executioner she remained defiant to the end. 'She painted her eyes, and adorned her head, and looked out of the window. And as Jehu entered the gate, she said "Is it peace, you Zimri, murderer of your master?"' (2 K 9[30-1]). The ghastly slaughter went on until all Ahab's relations and supporters and the official Baal prophets had been wiped out.

In spite of the change of ruler in Damascus, the Syrian policy towards Israel remained unchanged. After successfully withstanding an Assyrian attack on Syria, Hazael renewed the war against Israel. Jehu lost all the territory east of the Jordan, and during the reign of his son, Israel was reduced to a vassal State. Relief came when the Assyrians under their ruler Adad-nirari III once again attacked northern Syria, and in a series of campaigns from 805 to 802 B C considerably weakened the power of Syria. Adad-nirari's successors in Assyria did not continue his aggressive policy, so that both Israel and Judah were able to take advantage of the weakness of Syria and the inertia of Assyria. The next half century saw a remarkable revival both of power and prosperity in Israel and also in her sister State of Judah, but before the century was over Israel had ceased to exist.

(5) *The Age of Affluence*

Jehu's grandson, Joash (801–786 B C), made three campaigns against the Syrians and drove them out of Israelite territory, whilst Amaziah of Judah reconquered Edom. In the flush of this victory the latter provoked a quarrel with Joash who marched into Judah and met and defeated Amaziah at Beth Shemesh. The Israelite troops then swept down on Jerusalem which they raided and looted, reducing Judah to a state of helplessness. But Joash had no desire to annex Judah and so he permitted Amaziah to continue as ruler.

The period of recovery and expansion reached its zenith during the reigns of Jeroboam II of Israel (786–746 B C) and Uzziah (or Azariah) of Judah (783–742 B C). Jeroboam pushed the northern frontier of Israel beyond Damascus whilst Uzziah extended his territory as far south as Ezion Geber and westwards into Philistine country so that all the empire over which Solomon had ruled was once again in Israelite or Judean hands. The two kingdoms now commanded the main trade-routes so that their wealth increased rapidly. The prophecies of Amos and Hosea give some indication of the luxury of the upper classes in Israel and their descriptions have been amply supported by archaeological investigations.

Jeroboam added to the fortifications of Samaria, making his capital city so strong that many years later it withstood a siege of three years duration before eventually falling to the Assyrians. Finely wrought ornaments of ivory were available in abundance for those who could afford them. Things were not very different in Judah; from 2 Chronicles 26 we learn that Uzziah strengthened the fortifications of Jerusalem and also constructed forts ('towers', verse 10) to defend his frontiers.

In spite of the peace and prosperity which prevailed in Israel, all was not well with the land. Great wealth existed side-by-side with poverty. Wealthy land-owners used every misfortune of their poorer neighbours to buy up their small inheritances, consequently much land and property came into the possession of a small, but wealthy and influential minority. There was little redress in law for the poorer victims of injustice when a verdict in favour of the rich could be bought 'for the price of a shoe'. Again in spite of Jehu's purge which swept the worship of the Tyrian Baal out of the country, popular religion was still corrupted by the influence of the old Canaanite fertility cults which continued to be practised in Israel.

(6) *Assyrian Expansion and the Fall of Israel*

Jeroboam died in about 746 B C and at about the same time Tiglath Pileser usurped the throne of Assyria. These two events were to have a profound effect on Israel. Although the reign of Jeroboam had been a period of great prosperity there was nevertheless discontent with the ruling house, so that his son was murdered after a mere seven months as king. This marked the end of stable government in Israel; during the next twenty-five years the realm had six kings and most of them secured the throne by murdering their predecessor. Only Uzziah of

Figure 6. Horse in harness, engraved on the golden panel of an Egyptian fan.

Judah recognized the immediate threat to Palestine from the renascent Assyria, and he seems to have organized an anti-Assyrian coalition which was however smashed by the Assyrians. Shortly afterwards Uzziah died (*c.* 742 B C) and the Palestinian States submitted to Assyria.

The last attempt to throw off the Assyrian yoke was made about eight years later. Rezin of Damascus and Pekah of Israel had hopes of re-forming the grand alliance of the days of Ahab against their Assyrian overlords. Peaceful overtures to persuade Ahaz of Judah to join the alliance failed, so they invaded Judah in order to force her into the alliance. Ahaz, against the advice of the prophet Isaiah, appealed to Tiglath Pileser for help. The Assyrian armies moved swiftly across Palestine into Philistia, thus isolating Israel and Damascus. Parts of northern Israel were devastated by the Assyrians, some of the population being deported (2 K 15^{29}). At the same time Pekah was murdered by the pro-Assyrian Hoshea, who then ruled Israel as a vassal of Assyria. The Assyrians completed the destruction of the alliance by capturing Damascus and overrunning Syria which was then turned into an Assyrian province (732 B C). Hoshea continued to pay annual tribute to Assyria until the death of Tiglath Pileser in 727 B C. Regarding this as a favourable time to attempt to throw off the Assyrian yoke, he withheld the tribute and concluded an alliance with one of the petty kings of the Nile Delta, for Egypt seems at this time to have been split into a number of small kingdoms. Some three years later Shalmaneser V, son and successor of Tiglath Pileser, invaded Israel. Hoshea endeavoured to make peace with his overlord (2 K 17[4]), but Shalmaneser, having no faith in his protestations of loyalty, seized him and threw him into prison. The Assyrian advance continued, Samaria was besieged, and three years later it fell to Sargon, Shalmaneser's successor. This was the end of Israel. The Assyrians deported a large number of the population to other parts of their empire, and repopulated the new Assyrian province of Samaria with captives from distant parts of their empire.

(7) *Judah and Assyria; Hezekiah*

Judah escaped the fate of her northern sister; it is probable that Ahaz remained faithful to his Assyrian overlord. His loyalty was given concrete expression when he introduced elements of Assyrian worship into Judah, much to the dismay of the true followers of Yahweh. After the fall of Samaria in 721 B C Sargon had to meet troubles much nearer home. A rebellion flared up in the province of Babylon led by Merodach-Baladan and aided by the king of Elam. Sargon lost control of the province and it was about twelve years before it was again brought under Assyrian rule. In fact during the first decade of his reign Sargon had trouble in many of his provinces and so he never led a major campaign into Palestine. These troubles in Assyria coincided with the emergence, after a period of weakness, of a line of vigorous rulers in Egypt who lost no time in encouraging the Assyrian vassals in Palestine to revolt.

Ahaz died about 715 B C and was succeeded by his son Hezekiah. The new reign brought a change of policy aimed at securing the independence of Judah. Hezekiah did not embark immediately on open military revolt, but taking advantage of Sargon's preoccupation elsewhere, he began to rid Judah of the more obvious signs of Assyrian domination. The chief of these were the altar and other symbols of Assyrian worship which Ahaz had introduced into the Temple. Hezekiah also tried, though not altogether successfully, to close the local shrines which had become the scenes of a paganized form of worship. He also destroyed an ancient relic (a bronze serpent) to which some Judeans were presumably offering worship. This nationalistic and patriotic movement, which was being fostered by Hezekiah, flared up into open rebellion at the death of Sargon (705 B C). He was succeeded by his son Sennacherib who was immediately faced with a revolt in Babylon, again led by Merodach-Baladan. The latter sent an embassy to Hezekiah (2 K 20^{12-13}) to encourage a general revolt in the west. Hezekiah on his part sent envoys to Egypt to seek aid there.

Figure 7. Assyrian war chariot. 7th century.

Meanwhile he began to look to his own defences and, in anticipation of a possible siege of Jerusalem, constructed the famous Siloam tunnel to ensure a supply of water to the city.

Sennacherib eventually brought Babylon to heel and turned his attention to the western provinces, invading Palestine in 701 B C. He defeated an Egyptian army which had gone into Palestine to strengthen the rebels, and then he fell upon Judah. City after city fell to the Assyrians so that Sennacherib could claim—'But as for Hezekiah, the Jew, who did not bow in submission to my yoke, forty-six of his strong walled towns and innumerable smaller villages in their neighbourhood I besieged and conquered. . . . He himself I shut up like a caged bird within Jerusalem, his royal city'[3] (cf. 2 K 18^{13-16}). Realizing that this bid for independence had failed, Hezekiah came to terms with Sennacherib, who demanded heavy reparations which could only be met by despoiling the Temple and the king's palace of their treasures.

In 2 Kings 18^{17}–19^{36} there is a full account of another siege of

[3] D. Winton Thomas (ed.), *Documents from Old Testament Times*, p. 67.

Jerusalem and its subsequent relief. This siege was apparently contemporaneous with the presence in Palestine of an Egyptian army led by the Pharaoh Tirhakah (2 K 19⁹), who was ruling in Egypt from about 690 B C. Another uprising in Babylonia at about the same time was occupying Sennacherib's attention so that Hezekiah, probably urged on by the Egyptians, decided to make another attempt to throw off the Assyrian yoke. After crushing the Babylonian rebellion, Sennacherib invaded Palestine. Part of his army was engaged against the Egyptians and the rest besieged Jerusalem. Hezekiah was offered terms of surrender even harsher than those which he had accepted in 701 B C, but this time, encouraged by the prophet Isaiah, he refused to surrender. The siege was not pressed and for reasons which remain obscure the Assyrian forces were withdrawn.

Though Sennacherib had to call off the siege of Jerusalem which he had mounted in about 690 B C in answer to Hezekiah's rebellion, it seems probable that the latter's death shortly afterwards saved him from Assyrian reprisals. There was a complete reversal of policy with the accession of his son Manasseh, and since the latter was only a lad of twelve when he came to the throne we must suppose that the policy of submission to Assyria was dictated by his advisers. As a sign of loyalty to their Assyrian masters the rulers of Judah permitted, or perhaps even encouraged, the reintroduction of Assyrian rites and practices.

Sennacherib's reign in Assyria terminated abruptly in 681 B C when he was assassinated by two of his sons (cf. 2 K 19³⁷). He was succeeded by a third son, Esar-haddon (681–669 B C), who began to re-enforce Assyrian dominion first over Babylon and then over Egypt. The latter had used every opportunity to stir up rebellion among the various Assyrian satellite States. In 669 B C Esar-haddon was succeeded by his son Asshur-banipal (669–633 B C); this latter ruler was essentially a man of peaceful pursuits. His interest in history and literature led him to collect a vast library of cuneiform tablets in his palace at Nineveh. The recovery and decipherment of these documents has furnished much valuable information on the earlier history of Assyria. During his reign Assyrian power began to wane. Pharaoh Psammetichus (663–609 B C), who was originally permitted to rule over a small part of Egypt as an Assyrian vassal, gradually extended his boundaries until all Egypt acknowledged his sovereignty. About 655 B C he withheld tribute from Assyria and asserted his independence. The Assyrian empire was beginning to disintegrate. A few years later, in 652 B C, a rebellion led by Asshur-banipal's brother broke out in Babylon, and this, as usual, was the signal for uprisings in other outlying provinces of the empire. It is probable that Judah was involved and that the record of Manasseh's imprisonment (2 Chr 33^{11-13}) recalls his rebellion and its suppression.

Asshur-banipal was able to restore order throughout his dominions and even allowed Manasseh to return as king to Jerusalem; he probably regarded Judah as a valuable buffer State between Assyria and Egypt. For the rest of his reign there was peace throughout the empire, but after his death in 633 B.C. it rapidly fell to pieces. In 626 B C a Babylonian prince, Nabopolassar, seized power in Babylon and in the following year he drove the Assyrians from Babylon and set up an independent Babylonian kingdom.

After his abortive rebellion, Manasseh remained loyal to Assyria and reigned until his death in 641 B C. He was succeeded by his twenty-two-year-old son, Amon, who continued his father's policy. Amon, however, only enjoyed a brief reign; he was murdered by some of his courtiers in his second year as king. But the conspirators did not live to harvest the fruits of their crime for 'the people of the land [i.e. the free citizens] slew all them that had conspired against king Amon'. Then they exercised their ancient prerogative of choosing their king by putting Amon's young son Josiah on the throne.

(8) *From the Accession of Josiah to the Fall of Jerusalem*

We are not given any details of the early years of Josiah's reign when he himself was clearly too young to control policy, but we may presume that a policy of continued loyalty to Assyria was observed until the declining power of Assyria encouraged Josiah to take an independent line. This independence found expression in a religious reform aimed at stamping out all traces of Assyrian forms of worship and idolatry, and also in political and military activity designed to recover for Judah all the territory formerly ruled over by David. Thus whilst Assyria was being attacked by a formidable coalition of Babylonians and Medes from the south and east, and being ravaged by Scythian raiders from the north, Josiah was gradually incorporating into Judah the former Assyrian provinces into which Israel had been divided.

Asshur, an important city and one-time capital of Assyria, fell to the Medes and Babylonians in 614 B C. Two years later Nineveh, the capital of the Assyrian empire, was captured and destroyed, an event which caused the prophet Nahum to exult (cf. Nahum 3^9). The

Assyrians then transferred their seat of government to Haran in an endeavour to carry on the struggle, but they were driven out in 610 B C. Egypt now comes on the scene, but this time as an ally of the greatly weakened Assyria. Clearly Egypt had little to fear from Assyria now, but much from the rising power of Babylon. The Egyptian forces under Pharaoh Neco moved northward intending to join the Assyrians in an attempt to recover Haran. They were met at Megiddo (609 B C) by Josiah's forces, for Josiah regarded that part of Palestine through which the Egyptians were passing as part of his new empire. In the ensuing battle Josiah was killed and Judah once again lost her independence. In spite of Egyptian aid the Assyrians were not able to recover Haran and the Assyrian State disappeared.

Jehoahaz succeeded to the throne of Judah on the death of his father Josiah, but within three months he had been deposed by Pharaoh Neco and deported to Egypt. The Egyptians replaced him by his elder half-brother, Jehoiakim, who reigned for the next four years (609–605 B C) as an Egyptian vassal. In the year 605 B C came the almost inevitable clash between the two great powers Egypt and Babylon. The contending armies met at Carchemish, the Egyptians were defeated and lost their independence. Thus Judah became a Babylonian vassal State. The closing years of the kingdom of Judah were marked by futile rebellions against Babylon; Jeremiah seems to have been one of the few people who realized how hopeless these were. Jehoiakim rebelled against his Babylonian master, Nebuchadnezzar, some three years after the battle of Carchemish, an action which led to the invasion of Judah and ultimately to the siege and capture of Jerusalem (597 B C). However, Jehoiakim died before the capital city was taken. Jerusalem was besieged early in the reign of his son, Jehoiachin, who eventually surrendered and, along with many of the nobility of Judah, was taken captive to Babylon.

Nebuchadnezzar replaced Jehoiachin by Zedekiah, a younger son of Josiah. Intrigue with Egypt and rebellion against Babylon proved to be his undoing, and brought disaster upon Judah. The Babylonians again laid siege to Jerusalem and after about eighteen months the city fell to the invaders (586 B C). Zedekiah and his sons escaped from the city, but were captured near Jericho, and taken to Riblah where Nebuchadnezzar had his base camp. The royal princes were put to death, and the king was taken captive to Babylon.

Jerusalem was sacked and burned by the invading army, and a further deportation of the population took place. Judah now became a Babylonian province, though the Baylonians appointed a native governor, Gedeliah, to administer it. Since Jerusalem had been almost completely destroyed, the nearby Mizpah was chosen as the administrative centre of the province. Gedeliah had begun to restore some order to the battle-scarred land when he was treacherously murdered by a certain Ishmael, a member of the royal family who had not been captured by the Babylonians. The few remaining people of any consequence, fearing reprisals from Babylon, fled to Egypt taking the now aged prophet Jeremiah with them.

II—THE PROPHETS OF THE OLD TESTAMENT

A considerable portion of the Old Testament is taken up with the Books of the Prophets. Who were these men whose lives and messages are recorded in this literature? What distinguished a prophet from the rest of his fellows? In popular usage the word 'prophet' describes a person who foretells the future, and whilst it is undeniable that prediction was one element in the work of a prophet it is by no means an adequate description of prophetic activity. Basically a prophet is a person who 'tells forth', that is he preaches or proclaims a message. Furthermore, the message is one which he has received from God. The prophet therefore speaks under constraint, and hence he prefaces his message with the announcement, 'Thus saith the LORD', or some similar phrase.

Prophets were known outside Israel, and it seems likely that there were prophets associated with the shrines of pre-Israelite Canaan. From the earliest times prophets were often recognized by their strange behaviour, so much so that the Hebrew verb 'to prophesy' also meant 'to behave like a madman'. The prophet who anointed Jehu was called derisively by Jehu's fellow officers a 'mad fellow' (2 K 9^{11}). The prophets often lived together, especially at the famous religious centres, forming religious communities or schools, who would have some duties connected with the local shrine or high place. Celebrations at the high places included some form of wild ritual dancing (dervish dancing) which could so excite the onlooker that he too would be impelled to join the prophets in their frenzied exercise (cf. especially 1 S 10^{5-13}). But these outward signs of prophetic inspiration took on varied forms, as when Elijah performed the superhuman feat of running before Ahab's chariot from Carmel to Jezreel (1 K 18^{46}). At other times the prophet might go into a trance-like state in which he 'sees' visions of things to come. Thus in such a state Elisha 'sees' what havoc Hazael will wreak on Israel when he becomes king of Damascus (2 K $8^{11 ff}$; verse 11 apparently describes the fixed stare of the prophet when he fell into the trance).

The prophets often performed symbolic actions to accompany their spoken messages. Ahijah tore his new garment into twelve pieces, giving ten to Jeroboam and saying: 'Behold, I am about to tear the kingdom from the hand of Solomon, and will give you ten tribes' (1 K 11^{31}). Such actions were believed to be more than vivid illustrations of the prophetic message, rather they were regarded as a powerful means of ensuring that the predicted result would follow.

Above all it was the task of the prophet to deliver oracles. The earliest records suggest that the prophet only gave his message when someone went to him 'to inquire of Yahweh'. The inquiries could be of the most trivial kind, as when Saul consulted Samuel as to the whereabouts of his father's asses. It was also customary to pay the prophet when he 'inquired of Yahweh'. Not unnaturally the prophets sometimes gave flattering replies, especially if their client happened to be the king himself. A striking instance of the contrast between the flattering answer of the court prophets and the unwelcome answer of one who spoke the truth as he had received it, without fear or favour, is provided in the story of Ahab's preparations to attack Ramoth Gilead (1 K 22). The court prophets promised Ahab victory—the answer he wanted to hear: 'Go up, for the LORD will give it into the hand of the king.' Then after taunting the false prophets, Micaiah delivers his own unpopular oracle: 'I saw all Israel scattered upon the mountains, as sheep that have no shepherd' (1 K 22^{17}).

This incident also underlines what seems to be a distinction between the true 'men of God' and the official guilds of prophets. The former did not belong to the schools of prophets but worked alone, or perhaps with a few disciples at most. Elijah was a solitary prophet who seems to have been ignorant of the existence of any other true Yahweh prophets; Amos denied having any connection with any school of prophets; whilst Jeremiah was opposed by the court prophets of his time. These men no longer waited to be consulted but pronounced their oracles unasked, and often made themselves unpopular in consequence. They were the true champions of Yahweh protesting, on the one hand, against the paganization of the worship of Yahweh, and criticizing, on the other hand, the moral standards of their contemporaries in the light of the moral demands of Yahweh, whose character became increasingly clear through the teaching of the 'writing' prophets.

III—ELIJAH

Elijah has been described as 'the greatest religious personality that had been raised up in Israel since Moses'.[4] The narrative in 1 Kings 17–19 and 21 only covers about three years of his life, but it enables us to realize the gravity of the conflict in which he was engaged. Ever since the settlement in Canaan there had been the tendency to adapt Canaanite worship to the worship of Yahweh; and even a century after Elijah, Amos and other prophets were protesting against the licentious practices which masqueraded under the name of worship. Sacred prostitution and drunken revelry at the shrines and high places were recognized features of popular worship. Since such practices passed as Yahweh worship there seems to have been little protest until the time of Elijah. The coming of Jezebel brought a new factor into the situation. The worship of Melkart, the Tyrian Baal, which she introduced into Israel, was superficially not very different from the popular religion of Israel, but Jezebel's intention was to oust the religion of Yahweh from Israel in favour of her own form of worship and belief. She brought her own retinue of prophets who were maintained at her expense, and also seems to have persecuted some of the prophets of Yahweh (1 K 18^{3-4}). To Elijah the issue was clear. It was Yahweh or Baal; no longer was there room for compromise. Yahweh alone was God; the fertility of the land and the life-giving rain was His to give or to withhold. Baal, to whom the people turned in their time of need, was impotent to help, and so Elijah issued his dramatic announcement of the impending drought, and would later invite the prophets of Baal to an equally dramatic contest on Carmel.

PASSAGES FOR STUDY

1 Kings 17—*The Drought*

Elijah appears before Ahab with the dramatic suddenness that characterizes all his appearances. A native of Gilead, he presents himself to Ahab, makes his announcement and then disappears again to a desolate place east of the Jordan. Gradually the effects of the long drought make themselves felt. The streams and wadis dry up, there is no pasture

[4] J. Skinner, 'I and II Kings', *Century Bible*, p. 222.

for the flocks nor food for the poorer folk (1 K 18^5, $17^{9\,ff}$). Elijah is sustained at first near the brook Cherith and then later at the home of a Phoenician widow.

1 Kings 18—*Elijah on Carmel*

About three years later Elijah again confronts Ahab, who accuses him of bringing disaster on Israel. Elijah maintains that the disaster stems from the policy of Omri and Ahab who permitted the introduction of the cult of Melkart and Asherah into Israel. The prophet is now determined to bring the issue, Baal or Yahweh, to a decision. The story of the contest on Carmel is too familiar to need much comment, though we may note that the broken altar of Yahweh is an indication of the ruthless steps which Jezebel had taken to stamp out the worship of Yahweh.

Elijah's faith was vindicated, and in the enthusiasm of the moment the assembled Israelites seized the prophets of Baal, and bidden by Elijah, took them down to the river Kishon at the foot of the hill and there slew them. Elijah is now able to assure Ahab that the drought is over, and after the king had refreshed himself the prophet bade him get to Jezreel with all haste before the rain made the road impassable.

1 Kings 19—*Reaction*

Elijah was soon to learn that Jezebel was too redoubtable an opponent to be discouraged by his success on Carmel. Threatened by the queen, his elation turned to black despair, and he fled from Israel making his way southward till at length he came to Horeb. There, like his great predecessor Moses, he waited on God on the holy mountain, and received the strength and consolation which he so desperately needed. As Yahweh had appeared to Moses on Sinai to the accompaniment of thunder and lightning, so now a great storm convinces Elijah that he is in the very presence of God. He realizes moreover that the storm, terrifying though it is, only heralds His coming. When the storm has given place to the 'still small voice', Elijah goes to the entrance of the cave to commune with Yahweh, but not before he has covered his face with his mantle lest he should see God and die.

The prophet pours out his complaint that his efforts have been in vain; he sees himself as the last one to remain faithful to Yahweh and even *he* is a fugitive from Jezebel's wrath. For answer Yahweh allows Elijah a glimpse into the future. He is still in control, and judgement will yet fall on the house of Omri and on the faithless in Israel. It will be a fearful judgement involving bloody revolution when Jehu seizes the throne and exterminates the descendants of Ahab, and invasion and loss of territory when Hazael and the Syrians sweep into Israel. These were the swords of Jehu and Hazael—what the sword of Elisha was we do not know, but he too played a part in the downfall of the house of Omri.

Even so Elijah was not quite alone for there would still remain a faithful minority, seven thousand who had not bowed the knee to Baal. 'It is an anticipation of the later prophetic doctrine of the Remnant, the pious kernel, the Israel within Israel, to whom belongs the promise of the future.'[5]

1 Kings 21—*Naboth's Vineyard*

It is a characteristic of the Hebrew prophets that they did not hesitate to rebuke even the king himself if his conduct merited reproof. Elijah did not flinch from challenging the king for allowing Jezebel to introduce the cult of the Tyrian Baal into Israel, neither did he flinch from condemning the king for conniving at the murder of Naboth and confiscating his property. Elijah holds Ahab to be equally responsible with Jezebel for the murder, for whilst Ahab may have been ignorant of the details of her scheme, he must have realized that such a ruthless woman was capable of any crime to get her own way.

Naboth's stubborn refusal to sell his property appears superficially almost as unreasonable as Ahab's childish exhibition of bad temper when his request was refused. Naboth was, however, simply observing ancient custom in not letting the property pass out of his family. In fact he does not regard it as his own property, so much as a trust handed down by his fathers and which he in turn must hand on to his sons.[6]

The ease with which Jezebel was able to fix a charge of blasphemy and sedition on Naboth is striking evidence of the way in which justice could be perverted for personal gain. But beyond human injustice there is divine justice; the king is confronted with the crime (which may also have included the murder of Naboth's sons—cf. 2 K 9^{26}), which must have outraged the moral sense of all decent citizens, by Elijah who pronounces Yahweh's sentence on the house of Ahab.

5 J. Skinner, 'I and II Kings', Century Bible, p. 241.
6 For further information see R. de Vaux, *Ancient Israel,* Chapter 5, pp. 52 ff.

Psalm 51—*The Great Penitential Psalm*

This is one of the seven psalms (the others are 6, 32, 38, 102, 130, 143) which since the time of Origen (A D 185–253) have been known as the 'Penitential Psalms'. They are the psalms appointed for use on Ash Wednesday. Psalms 6, 32, and 38 are read or sung at Matins; psalms 102, 130, and 143 at Evensong, and psalm 51 is prescribed for use in the Commination Service (see the Book of Common Prayer).

By common consent Psalm 51 is the greatest of these penitential psalms. The psalmist recognizes the true nature of sin, that it is ultimately an offence against God. This leads to confession which is the prerequisite of asking for and receiving divine forgiveness. The psalm falls into five sections. It begins with the psalmist calling on God to take away his sin (verses 1, 2) and ends on a note of praise and thanksgiving (verses 15–17). The last two verses are commonly believed to have been added to the psalm after the exile in order to justify the offering of sacrifice in the restored Temple.

Verses 1–2—*'Have mercy on me, O God'*

The psalm opens with a plea for mercy. It is characteristic of this psalmist that he does not attempt to excuse himself, nor plead any previous good deeds to offset the present burden of his guilt. His sure hope lies in the character of the God to whom he appeals; his God is full of compassion (abundant mercy). The threefold description of sin (transgression, iniquity, sin) which the psalmist uses reveals a deep understanding of the nature of sin. 'Transgression' is literally rebellion against a superior, thus from this point of view sin is open defiance of God and His demands. 'Iniquity' carries the meaning of depraved actions and also the guilt resulting from such behaviour. 'Sin' means missing the mark, or wandering from the appointed pathway. Corresponding to this threefold description of sin is a threefold description of the forgiveness which the psalmist is seeking. 'Sin leaves a bad record, makes a person dirty, and contaminates morally and spiritually',[7] hence forgiveness must 'blot out' the record, 'wash' away the stains, and 'cleanse' or 'refine' out the dross.

Verses 3–5—*Confession*

The psalmist recognizes that sin is ultimately sin against God. This knowledge that he has rebelled (transgressed) against God haunts him

[7] A. B. Rhodes, 'Psalms', *LBC*, p. 86.

('my sin is ever before me'). Like St Paul he had found by bitter experience that it was much easier to do wrong than to do right, and he realizes that this is a general feature of human nature (verse 5). This verse must not be interpreted as implying that his parents were outstandingly wicked; rather 'it is the tragedy of man that he is born into a world full of sin'.[8] But even sin, though it is disobedience and rebellion against God does not put a man beyond His reach. The dark tragedy of sin serves to throw into relief the awful majesty and perfection of God. 'The consequences of his sin, and therefore in a sense its purpose, . . . is to enhance before men the justice and holiness of God, the absolutely Righteous and Pure'[9] (cf. also Rom $11^{32\,ff}$).

Verses 6–9—*The Prayer for Forgiveness*

The act of confession is a proper preparation for the prayer for forgiveness. In the parable of the Pharisee and the Publican the latter first makes humble confession to God, signified by his bowed head and the act of beating on his breast with his hands, then he prays: 'God be merciful to me a sinner' (Lk 18^{13}). Forgiveness means the taking away of sin; the psalmist uses figurative language to describe this spiritual cleansing. Hyssop was used for the ritual purification of persons who had become ceremonially unclean (cf. Lev 14^{1-9}, Num 19^{14-19}). Verse 9 introduces yet another description of forgiveness, namely that God hides His face from the sin.

Verses 10–14—*Prayer for Renewal*

The prayer for forgiveness leads quite naturally into the prayer for renewal. The psalmist realized that, because sin is an intrinsic part of man's nature (verse 5), the forgiveness and cancellation of past sin was not enough. His whole nature, which was prone to sin, must be renewed and re-created. In verses 10 and 11 we come close to the New Testament teaching of man's rebirth by the indwelling of the Holy Spirit. The new 'moral life is in the last analysis not an achievement of man, but the gracious gift of God'.[10] The characteristics of the new life lived in the continual presence of God (verse 11) are joy (verses 8, 12) and an eager readiness to bear witness to others of the new life which he now enjoys (verse 13).

[8] A. Weiser, *Psalms* (ET), p. 405.
[9] A. F. Kirkpatrick, *Psalms*, p. 290.
[10] A. Weiser, *Psalms* (ET), p. 407.

Verses 15–17—*Praise and Thanksgiving*

The psalm fittingly closes on a note of praise. A hymn of Henry Francis Lyte sums up the psalmist's sentiments:

> 'Praise my soul, the King of Heaven,
> To His feet thy tribute bring,
> Ransomed, healed, restored, forgiven,
> Who like thee His praise should sing?' (*MHB* 12).

Sincere praise from a thankful heart is the only sacrifice that God ultimately desires. Like the great prophets the psalmist dares to claim that God has no delight in animal sacrifices, rather it is the one who daily turns to Him in sincere penitence who will not be despised.

Verses 18–19—*An Appendix*

These verses are quite out of keeping with the thought of the rest of the psalm. It seems clear that a compiler of the Book of Psalms added this footnote to Psalm 51 as a protest against the disparagement of sacrifice in verse 16. Verse 19 is a very pedestrian note justifying the sacrificial rites of the post-exilic Temple.

NOTE. The heading attributes the psalm to David, and regards it as an expression of remorse and repentance following Nathan's rebuke. The historical value of this heading has been questioned by many scholars. The last two verses of the psalm are post-exilic, and even though the bulk of the psalm may be pre-exilic there is nothing in the contents to link it specifically with the Bathsheba incident. Verse 16 criticizes the sacrificial cult in a manner reminiscent of the prophets (cf. Amos 5^{21}, Hos 6^{6}, Isa $1^{11\,ff}$, Mic $6^{6\,ff}$, Jer 7^{21}), and would suggest dating the psalm long after the time of David.

TABLE II

From the Death of Solomon to the Fall of Jerusalem

Judah	*Israel*	*Prophets*	*Internal Affairs*	*External Events*
Rehoboam (922–915)	Jeroboam (922–901)		Shishak's raid into Palestine (917) Conflict between Israel and Judah for twenty years	
	Omri (876–869)		The Grand Alliance against Assyria	Assyria begins to expand westwards
	Ahab (869–850)	*Elijah*	Battle of Karkar 853	
	Jehu (842–815)			
Uzziah (783–742)	Jeroboam II (786–746)	*Amos*	Period of great prosperity in Israel and Judah	
			Syro-Ephraimite War (734)	Tiglath Pileser III (745–727)
Ahaz (735–715)		*Isaiah, Hosea*	Fall of Samaria, **End of Israel (721)**	Assyria invades Syria and Israel Shalmanezer V (727–722) Sargon II (722–705)
Hezekiah (715–688)			First siege of Jerusalem 701 Second siege of Jerusalem 689	Sennacherib (705–681)
Manasseh (688–641)				
Amon (641–639)				
Josiah (639–609)			Josiah's Reform 626 Law Book found 621	Fall of Nineveh 612
Jehoahaz (3 months)		*Jeremiah*	B. of Megiddo 609	
Jehoiakim (609–598)				
Jehoiachin (598–597)			Jerusalem captured 597	
Zedekiah (597–586)			Jerusalem destroyed 586	
EXILE				

CHAPTER EIGHT

PROPHECY AND CRISIS (I)

THE PROPHETS OF THE EIGHTH CENTURY

IT IS SIGNIFICANT that the prophets who exerted a permanent influence on the religion of the Old Testament proclaimed their messages in times of crisis. The first of the 'writing' prophets exercised their ministries during the later years of the kingdom of Israel and the quarter of a century following the fall of Samaria (from *c.* 750 to 690 B C). The rapid decline and annihilation of Israel after the splendour and luxury of the reign of Jeroboam II must have caused thoughtful people to ask questions about the ability of Yahweh to preserve His own chosen people. Beginning with Amos (*c.* 750 B C), the next three and a half centuries produced a remarkable line of men, prophets, to whom was granted a growing insight into the moral character and demands of Yahweh, and who therefore were able to interpret the crises of history in terms of the will and purpose of Yahweh. Four such prophets emerged during the latter half of the eighth century B C—Amos, Hosea, Isaiah, and Micah. Hosea alone was a native of the northern kingdom, Israel, a fact which probably accounts for the special poignancy of his oracles as he contemplates the downfall and ruin of his own native land.

AMOS

The few biographical details together with references in his prophecies to the things which he has observed and experienced (cf. especially $3^{4, 5, 12}$) enable us to form some impression of this first of the 'writing' prophets. Amos was a countryman; a shepherd who kept his flocks in the wilderness of Tekoa. The city of Tekoa was about ten miles south of Jerusalem and twelve miles west of the Dead Sea, which lay 4000 feet below. The wilderness of Tekoa was not quite barren, sufficient herbage grew on the small plains which surrounded the city to provide pasture for sheep and small cattle. The hardy sheep-farmers could supplement the income from their flocks by cultivating the sycomore (fig) trees which grew on the lower levels nearer to the Dead Sea. Amos 3 gives illuminating glimpses of the rigours of the life of a shepherd in these wild regions where seldom would another person be seen except by arrangement (verse 3), where beasts of prey would lurk in the scrub (verse 4), or where a man might snare a bird to augment his meagre food supply (verse 5).

Though living away from the larger centres of population Amos was not ignorant of the affairs of the wider world. He knew a great deal about the luxury and corruption of Israel, he knew also of the threat which the ever-growing power and ambition of Assyria presented to Israel. Neither was he illiterate. Whether he himself wrote down any of his oracles or visions is uncertain, they will in any case have been spoken before they were committed to writing, yet we may suppose that Amos brooded long over his message before the call, which sent him to prophesy against Israel at the royal chapel of Bethel or in the royal city of Samaria, came to him.

The opening verse of the book gives us a precise date for the work of Amos, namely: 'two years before the earthquake'. This must have been an earthquake of such magnitude that it was remembered for many a year as '*the* earthquake'. Unfortunately the date of an earthquake, unlike that of an eclipse, cannot be recovered by calculation, so that this piece of information does not help us in fixing the date of Amos's ministry. The remainder of the verse tells us that he prophesied in the reigns of Jeroboam of Israel (*c.* 786–746 B C) and Uzziah of Judah (*c.* 783–742 B C). The general impression gained from the book as a whole is one of a nation of which the upper classes were enjoying a life of ease and luxury indicative of great prosperity. The great mass of the people were at the mercy of this unscruplous upper class, cheated at every turn and receiving scant justice from the judges who were hand-in-glove with the well-to-do. This is the picture which Amos paints—a picture which fits very well with the closing years of the reign of Jeroboam when the threat of Assyria was veiled from all but the prophet's eyes. We may then tentatively date Amos's appearance as a prophet in Bethel at about 750 B C.

THE BOOK OF AMOS

The Book of Amos falls into three well-defined sections. First there is a series of eight oracles (1^{3}–2^{16}) pronouncing the judgement of Yahweh against the various nations of Palestine because of their crimes, some of which may have been the barbarities and atrocities associated with war. The words with which each oracle opens, 'For three transgressions of ——, and for four, I will not revoke the punishment', may have been taken by Amos from part of the liturgy of the temple. If he did use some well-known phrase in this way it must have had a telling effect on his hearers. The eighth oracle—judgement against Israel—leads naturally into the second section of the book (3^1–6^{14}). This consists of a series of oracles or addresses in which the prophet lays bare the religious and moral corruption of the Israel of his day, and pronounces Yahweh's judgement on the land. The final section of the book describes and interprets visions which Amos saw. Once again the theme is judgement on the rebellious land, which is likened to a wall found to be unsafe when tested with a plumb-line, or to a basket of over-ripe and rotting fruit.

PASSAGES FOR STUDY

Amos 7^{10-17}—*A Fragment of Biography*

Called by Yahweh, whilst following his occupation as a herdsman in Tekoa, to prophesy against Israel, Amos made his way to the royal sanctuary at Bethel. As he was mistaken by Amaziah the priest for one of the prophets attached to the temple, we may assume that Amos had joined himself to the regular temple prophets in order to get a hearing. However, his message was so unpalatable, so terrifying indeed, that Amaziah sought to drive him away from Bethel. He recognized that a professional prophet was entitled to be supported from the temple funds for his professional activities, so he bade Amos go and seek a livelihood by prophesying in Judah. Amos then disclaimed any connection with the prophetic guilds which were attached to the temples and high places. This seems to be the meaning of 7^{14}: 'I am no prophet, nor a prophet's son (i.e. a member of a prophetic guild), but I am a herdsman. . . .' Since he was not a professional prophet belonging to the royal sanctuary, Amaziah had no authority over him. Amos was speaking under divine compulsion, and his final and terrible words (verse 17) must have filled Amaziah with horror and foreboding.

Amos 3^1–6^{14}—*The Message of Amos*

The series of oracles which now forms the middle section of the book contains the core of the prophet's teaching. These words will not have been spoken on one occasion, nor perhaps all at the same place. The short fragment 4^{1-3} may well have been uttered in Samaria, whilst the incident involving Amaziah shows that Amos certainly prophesied at Bethel.

Amos 3^{1-2}—*The Charge against Israel*

These words, and especially verse 2, form the theme of Amos's message to Israel. Yahweh is the God of all nations, this is made clear in Chapters 1 and 2, but of His own free will He has chosen Israel, redeemed her from bondage, and established His covenant with her. By her debased worship, and her unjust and oppressive dealings with the weak, Israel has denied and broken the covenant. Therefore as Yahweh has 'known', i.e. had intimate and gracious dealings with Israel, so also will He 'visit' her in judgement and punishment. This theme is worked out in detail in the rest of this section.

Amos 3^{3-8}—*The Prophet's Justification*

Perhaps in reply to a demand that he should make good his right to bring so serious a charge against Israel, Amos fires out a series of questions emphasizing the relation of cause and effect. Two will not meet in the wilderness unless they have already made an appointment; the lion roars only when he has seized his prey. Prophets enjoy the confidence of Yahweh (verse 7) and when He speaks they must proclaim His word (verse 8). For those who can see beyond the immediate present the roaring of the lion of Assyria is already threatening (verse 8).

Amos 3^{9-15}—*Judgement on Samaria*

Amos now becomes more specific. He visualizes a great host drawn from Assyria and Egypt gathered on the mountains and looking down on Samaria. What a sight greets their eyes! For all the apparent peace and prosperity there is in actuality robbery, cheating, injustice, violence, and oppression: 'They do not know how to do right.'

Then Amos draws a picture of the catastrophe that will overtake the city. A pitiful remnant may escape, like the torn portions of a lamb which the shepherd rescues from the mouth of a lion. The great houses with their luxurious furnishings and finely wrought ivory ornaments will become but a heap of ruins.

Amos 4^{1-3}—*High Society in Samaria*

Amos returns time and again to the theme of the extravagance of the upper classes contrasted with the sorry plight of the poor. In this short oracle the upper-class women of Samaria are the subject of scathing comments. They are compared with the sleek, well-fed cattle which were reared in Bashan. Their lives consisted of a never-ending round of parties, resulting in continuous demands on their husbands (lords) to provide the necessarily luxurious food and drink. Much of the wealth which was squandered in this way had been gained by sharp practices in which the poor were further impoverished.

The end, as Amos sees it, is that the women will be led out like cattle through the breaches of the city wall with hooks in their noses; a prophecy which received terrible fulfilment when the Assyrians eventually conquered Samaria.

Amos 4^{4-13}—*Popular Religion*

Verses 4 and 5 are an ironical description of the popular religious practices in Israel. Amos does not condemn the formal or mechanical aspects of worship as such, but he condemns the unreality of a religion which conceives its whole duty to consist in the meticulous payment of tithes and the correct observance of the ritual of sacrifice, whilst its devotees can perpetrate the greatest injustices against their fellows.

In verses 6–13 Amos interprets the various calamities which have from time to time smitten the community as evidences of divine displeasure. Famine, drought, pestilence, and war have struck the land, 'yet you did not return to me, says the LORD'. This five-times-repeated refrain is taken up again in a rather different form in the next chapter ($5^{4, 6, 14}$, 'Seek me and live', etc.).

Amos 5^{1}–6^{14}—*'Seek Me and Live'*

This section with its repeated call to repentance also contains denunciations of those features of Israelite life which the prophet found so abhorrent. The passage is headed by a brief dirge (5^{2}) on the fate of Israel, here described as a young girl. This metaphor is also used by Hosea and other prophets. The comment in verse 3 on this dirge shows that Amos is thinking of disaster brought about by war.

He then turns to specific evils, corruption of justice and oppression of the poor (5^{10-13}), and he can only see hope for the 'remnant of Joseph' (5^{15}). For the majority the 'Day of Yahweh' will be a day of 'darkness and not light'. Once again Amos singles out a popular idea for comment and reinterpretation. He has already denounced the popular conception of religion, that attention to the mechanical details of worship was all that was required. Now he denounces the popular idea of the 'Day of Yahweh', that it would be that 'grand and glorious day, when the Lord would defeat and destroy all Israel's enemies, and give her the privilege of rule, and shower upon her all the material advantages her patriots desired'.[1] So Amos has to point out that Yahweh's enemies may actually be in Israel, and for such it will be a day of reckoning, even a day of terror. He emphasizes his point by a vivid illustration which was surely drawn from his own experience (5^{19}).

After reverting briefly to the theme that formal worship is worthless when it is unaccompanied by right living, Amos brings his message to a focus with his great declaration: 'But let justice roll down like waters, and righteousness like an ever-flowing stream' (5^{24}).

Chapter 6 adds little to the message of Amos. It is evident, however, how deeply the existence of extremes of wealth and poverty, luxury and degradation side by side had offended his moral sense, calling forth the passionate plea for justice and righteousness already quoted.

The final note of this section of the prophecy is a comment on the proud boast of the impregnability of Samaria. This boast moved him to remind its inhabitants that other mighty cities had fallen before a determined invader, and that Samaria in turn would fall.

NOTE. Amos 6^{9-10}. The precise meaning of these verses is very obscure, but it is clear that a grim situation is envisaged, perhaps during a siege when the dead outnumber the living and the latter search among the corpses for possible survivors.

HOSEA

Amos prophesied towards the close of the long reign of Jeroboam II, about 750 BC, but superficially there was little reason to suppose that the period of prosperity, which Israel was enjoying, would soon come to an end. For a brief while the impassioned words of the man from Tekoa may have stirred the consciences of some of his hearers, or struck fear into the hearts of others, but he was quickly sent back to Judah and meanwhile life went on much as before.

Amos had spoken of the disaster which must surely overtake Israel, but Hosea lived through that disaster. The introductory verse to his prophecy (Hos 1^{1}) suggests that his ministry fell during the latter half of the eighth century, but references in the prophecy itself further suggest that his active ministry was confined to the years between the death of Jeroboam and the fall of Samaria. The intrigue, regicide, and confusion of these last years of the kingdom of Israel are reflected in the following lines of Hosea:

[1] J. Myers, *Hosea to Jonah* (SCM), p. 129.

'There is swearing, lying, killing, stealing, and committing adultery;
they break all bounds and murder follows murder' (4^2).

One writer has summed up the situation in these words: 'The great Jeroboam is dead and society, so dependent in the East on the strong individual, is loosened and falling to pieces.'[2] Within a year of the death of Jeroboam, two kings had been murdered and doubtless many of their supporters had suffered the same fate, whilst the one who had climbed to the throne, Menahem, sought Assyrian help lest he should be deposed. Hosea comments:

'When Ephraim saw his sickness, and Judah his wound,
Then Ephraim went to Assyria, and sent to the great king' (5^{13}).

Hosea seems to allude to the same period of confusion in $7^{6\,ff}$, whilst verse 11 of the same chapter probably refers to the stupid policy of Hoshea, who vainly trusted in Egyptian aid to throw off the Assyrian yoke. He was deposed and carried off to Assyria;

'Ephraim is like a dove, silly and without sense,
calling to Egypt, going [i.e. as captives] to Assyria.'

Political confusion during the last quarter of a century of Israel's existence was also accompanied by the moral collapse of the nation. Popular worship, which had for so long been contaminated with elements of the Canaanite fertility cults, had become an excuse for drunken orgies and sexual excesses. Hosea marvelled, not that the nation was rushing to its inevitable doom, but that the God whom it had so completely abandoned should hold His hand so long. He found the answer in his own tragic domestic experience, for his own constant and unrequited love for his erring wife became a symbol of Yahweh's constant love for Israel.

THE BOOK OF HOSEA

The Book of Hosea falls into two sections (*a*) Chapters 1–3, (*b*) Chapters 4–14. The first section gives an account of Hosea's tragic marriage and the parallel which he drew between his own experience with Gomer, and Yahweh's experience with Israel.

The second and longer section of the prophecy is a collection of oracles uttered by Hosea at various periods of his ministry. These are mostly short poems, but the theme which runs through them all is

[2] G. A. Smith, *The Book of the Twelve Prophets*, I.273.

Israel's rejection of Yahweh—'they have broken my covenant, and transgressed my law' 8^{1b}). As a husband, or as a father, Yahweh had loved Israel, but Israel has gone after the Baalim.

PASSAGES FOR STUDY

Hosea 8^{1-3}—*The Call of Hosea*

There is no detailed description of Hosea's call to be a prophet, but this short poem may contain allusions to it.[3] The meaning seems to be that the prophet is called to sound the alarm because the judgement of Yahweh is hovering like an eagle ready to swoop on Israel. The indictment is that 'they have broken my covenant, and transgressed my law'.

Hosea 1^{2-8}, 3^{1-5}—*Domestic Tragedy*

These few pathetic verses sum up many years of Hosea's married life, years which were full of sorrow and heartache. But it was out of his bitter experience that he learnt much about the steadfast love of Yahweh for Israel. It is certainly true of Hosea that 'his knowledge of God comes to him from the realities of his own life'.[4] Hosea had married Gomer, who had proved unfaithful to him. The names given to the second and third child suggest that these may not have been Hosea's children, though apparently he did not divorce Gomer in spite of her unfaithfulness to him. This itself is remarkable in view of the ease with which a husband could obtain divorce in ancient Israel. The brief biographical sketch given in Chapter 1^{2-8} probably covers a period of at least six years following Hosea's marriage.

Gomer is not mentioned by name in Chapter 3, but it is likely that this fragment of autobiography is Hosea's description of the sequel to the events of Chapter 1. The implication is that Gomer had left him to live with 'lovers' who eventually abandoned her. She then sold herself into slavery and was later redeemed by Hosea who took her back to his house, but the former relationship of husband and wife could not be restored immediately. There must be for Gomer a time of discipline, a time for repentance before she could again be received as Hosea's wife (3^3).

The names given by Hosea to Gomer's children were also intended to convey a message from Yahweh. The dynastic struggles which followed the death of Jeroboam II reminded Hosea that Jehu had secured the throne by the massacre of all the descendants of Ahab in Jezreel

[3] J. Lindblom, *Prophecy in Ancient Israel*, p. 185.
[4] W. Eichrodt, *Old Testament Theology* (ET), I.33.

(2 K 10[11]). Now the house of Jehu was tottering and soon the kingdom would cease to exist, all this is ominously symbolized in the name 'Jezreel'. The other two names symbolize Israel's apostasy—'Lo-ammi', i.e. 'Not my people', and 'Lo-ruhamah', i.e. 'Not pitied'.

Hosea 2[2–15, 21–3]—*Yahweh and Israel*

In this long poem, Hosea, drawing on his own experience, endeavours to interpret to Israel her own history as the out-working of Yahweh's steadfast love for His people. The opening lines of the poem seem at first sight to be but a poetic description of Hosea's own tragedy, but it soon becomes clear that 'your mother' (verse 2) is not Gomer, but Israel, whose 'lovers' are the Baalim who were being worshipped at every shrine and to whom were being attributed the bounties of the harvest. As surely as Hosea had felt it necessary to punish Gomer for her faithlessness even while he still lived with her, so surely was Yahweh punishing Israel in the troubled times through which the nation was passing. The hope, which Hosea entertained that he might recall Gomer back to her former state as his wife, is paralleled by the hope which he expresses that, after the time of punishment is over, Israel will once again be 'my people' (verse 23).

SELECTIONS FROM THE POEMS OF HOSEA

Hosea 4[1–3]—'*Wickedness in high places*'

This short poem may describe the confusion following the death of Jeroboam II and the intrigue and murders which eventually placed Menahem on the throne. Lack of a strong government encourages the outbreak of violence and lawlessness (verse 2), and 'therefore the land mourns, and all who dwell in it languish' (verse 3).

Hosea 4[11–14, 17–19]—*The Spirit of Idolatry*

The worship of the Baalim involved licentious orgies which are vividly described here. The drunken revels lead to such a dulling of the intellect that the worshippers expect to be heard by wooden idols, and also issue in such sexual licence that the wives and daughters join the cult prostitutes at the shrines. Was Hosea remembering Gomer as he uttered these lines?

Hosea 5[1–7]—*Another poem on the spirit of idolatry*

In the first two verses the prophet passes judgement on the leaders who have 'ensnared' the people by their encouragement of the popular, but syncretistic, cultic practices at the high places such as Mizpah, Tabor, or Shittim. In the troubled times in which Hosea lived, Israel was attending assiduously to the formalities of religion. He had seen worshippers, presumably the wealthy land-owners ('house of Israel'), driving flocks before them to be offered as sacrifices (verse 6), but all is of no avail. This is not what Yahweh requires ('For I desire steadfast love and not sacrifice', 6^{6}), and so though the worshippers seek Him they will not find Him.

Hosea 5^{8-14}—*Alarm in Israel*

This poem was evidently evoked by some grave crisis which threatened Israel. Gibeah, Ramah, and Beth-aven (i.e. Bethel) were all near the border with Judah. The alarm in these cities suggests that this poem was uttered during the Syro-Ephraimite campaign against Judah, after Ahaz had called in Assyrian aid (see p. 139). If Syria and Israel were engaged in the attempt to hold off Assyrian attacks, Judah may well have attacked Israel's southern frontier and so earned Hosea's condemnation (verse 10).

But there was no victory either for Israel or Judah. Judah became tributary to Assyria when Ahaz appealed for help against Israel, Israel herself became subject to Assyria when Hoshea assumed the throne after murdering Pekah.

But though the Assyrian overlord will for a time ensure peace between Israel and Judah, Israel will soon succumb to the temptation to play power politics in an effort to secure Egyptian aid against Assyria, and will all too soon be carried off into captivity. Judah's turn would come later, but Hosea like the prophets who followed him saw beyond and behind the political events, 'the moral judgement of God against a recalcitrant and self-willed people'.[5]

Hosea 5^{15}–6^{6}—*'Mercy and not Sacrifice'*

The disturbances and dangers of the times seem to have called forth some superficial gestures of repentance in the nation (6^{1-2}). In this poem Yahweh's passionate longing for Israel's true repentance alternates with His judgement on His people (6^{4-5}). Hosea had learnt in his own bitter experience what it cost in suffering and sorrow to love Gomer, and something of the tension in his own heart is revealed in these verses, in which with great daring he attributes a similar kind of suffering to Yahweh, as He yearns over the wayward nation.

[5] J. Myers, *Hosea to Jonah*, p. 32.

Hosea $11^{1-9, 10-11}$—*'My son'*

This has been described as one of 'the greatest chapters in the Bible'.[6] As Hosea himself, by the constancy of his love for Gomer, has striven to win her back, so Yahweh has borne patiently with Israel. Yahweh's loving care for His people is beautifully described as a father's love for his son (verses 1–3). The infant nation had been called out of Egypt, and lovingly nurtured in its years of immaturity (verse 3 is perhaps a reference to the wilderness period under Moses). The figure of speech changes as Hosea likens Yahweh's love to the peasant's compassion for his oxen when he eases their yoke and provides their food.

The note of compassion vanishes abruptly as Hosea contemplates the apostasy of his people. Verses 5–7 reflect the political turmoil of the times in which Hosea sees the outworking, in history, of the judgement of Yahweh on Israel. The easy yoke (verse 4) which Yahweh would have His people wear gives place to the terrible yoke of captivity (verse 7) into which their life is inevitably leading them.

But the thought which he has expressed in verse 7 is too much for Hosea. Can it be that Yahweh's love is to be defeated by Israel's apostasy? that He should lose the child He has nurtured? Though Israel must be punished, and punished by captivity, yet she will not be utterly blotted out as were the cities of the Plain, Admah and Zeboim (cf. Deut 29^{22-3}). 'Justice and mercy strive together, God determines that Israel shall be both justly punished, and mercifully relieved.'[7]

But in spite of Hosea's optimism that Yahweh would not come to destroy (verse 9b), Israel did disappear as a nation. Nevertheless Israel as a holy people lived on in Judah and then survived even the catastrophe of the Babylonian exile. It is probable that a later writer added verses 10 and 11 as a sequel to Hosea's oracle. It is a fitting conclusion which fully vindicated Hosea's faith in the strength and patience of the love of Yahweh for His people. After the purifying experience of the exile the captives hear Yahweh calling them home and 'they shall come trembling like birds from Egypt, and like doves from the land of Assyria' (verse 11).

NOTE. Egypt and Assyria must be understood as poetic descriptions of the land of exile.

6 J. Myers, *Hosea to Jonah*, p. 55.
7 R. F. Horton, 'The Minor Prophets', *Century Bible*, p. 61.

ISAIAH

Isaiah's prophetic ministry extended over almost half a century. He received his call as a prophet 'in the year that King Uzziah died' (6^{1}), i.e. about 742 B C, and his latest utterances were provoked by the siege of Jerusalem by Sennacherib's army in 690 B C. The introductory verse (1^{1}) which serves as a title to the Book of Isaiah gives the additional information that his father's name was Amoz and that his prophecies concern 'Judah and Jerusalem' though in fact some of the oracles have other nations as their subject. The intimate dealings which Isaiah had with the king have led some scholars to believe that he belonged to one of the aristocratic families of Jerusalem if not to the royal family itself.

The brilliant reign of Jeroboam II in Israel had been paralleled by the equally brilliant reign of Uzziah in Judah; the material prosperity of Israel was matched by that of Judah; the social inequalities of Israel, which had provoked Amos's prophetic outburst, were echoed by a similar state of affairs in Judah, which inspired equally forthright condemnations by Isaiah (cf. Isa $3^{1\,ff}$, $5^{7-8,\,23}$). The upsurging of Assyrian power and ambition, which swept away the kingdoms of Syria and Israel and even threatened Judah with annihilation, forced the prophet to face and answer questions concerning the future of Israel, not as a nation, but as Yahweh's holy people, and concerning the role of the great heathen powers, such as Assyria, in the divine plan.

THE BOOK OF ISAIAH

We noted above that the verse (1^{1}) which stands at the head of the Book of Isaiah refers only to prophecies concerning Jerusalem and Judah. This is manifestly inadequate as a description of the whole book, but it provides a clue to the nature of the book as we now possess it. Examination of the contents shows that it is appropriate as a title to the prophecies contained in Chapters 1–12. These chapters may well have constituted the first edition of the prophecies of Isaiah. The process by which the book attained its present form seems to have been both complex and lengthy. It is sufficient to state that the majority of Old Testament scholars recognize that it is largely compiled from the prophecies of three prophets. The oracles of Isaiah, son of Amoz (sometimes called Isaiah of Jerusalem, or First Isaiah), are contained in Chapters 1–39 of the Book of Isaiah, though even some of these chapters come from a time long after the death of Isaiah. The remainder of the book belongs to the exilic or post-exilic period and will be dealt with later.

NOTE. For an account of the composition and growth of Isaiah see e.g. 'Isaiah' by O. C. Whitehouse in the *Century Bible* series, or *Prophecy in Ancient Israel* (pp. 285 ff), by J. Lindblom.

PASSAGES FOR STUDY

Two major national crises occurred during Isaiah's long ministry, and many of his oracles are set against the background of, and offer a comment on, these crises, in both of which the kingdom of Judah, and in particular the capital city of Jerusalem, was being attacked by foreign powers. In 735/4 BC Rezin of Damascus and Pekah of Israel sent a joint force against Judah in an attempt to force Ahaz into an anti-Assyrian alliance. In 701 and 690 BC Assyrian forces under Sennacherib overran Palestine and laid siege to Jerusalem. The first two groups of passages selected for study relate to these two crises. The third group illustrates Isaiah's teaching on the holiness of Yahweh and the doctrine of the remnant.

Isaiah 6^1–9^7—*Isaiah and the Syro-Ephraimite War*

Isaiah 6—*The Call of Isaiah*

In this and the following chapters we have some autobiographical fragments, headed by a detailed account of Isaiah's call to the prophetic office. This striking experience is quite precisely dated—'in the year that king Uzziah died'—and as G. A. Smith has pointed out[8] there may well be a contrast here between the passing away of the glory of Uzziah, struck down by leprosy in his later years, and the everlasting glory of Yahweh, a glimpse of which Isaiah was allowed to see in this vision in the Temple. The description of the vision suggests that the prophet 'saw' Yahweh under the form of an Assyrian monarch wearing his robes of State, seated on his throne and accompanied by his attendants. The Assyrian kings were accustomed to style themselves 'King of Kings'; in his vision Isaiah meets the true King of Kings, and is so overpowered by His majesty, and so overwhelmed by the sense of His holiness, that he can only confess his own sinfulness and that of his compatriots whilst he waits, trembling and fearful, for the fate which must, he believed, overtake one who has seen Yahweh—'I am lost' (6^5).

[8] *The Book of Isaiah*, I.59–60.

But the vision was granted to Isaiah as a preparation for the commission he was about to receive. His spontaneous confession of sin, evoked by the vision of Yahweh in all His Majesty, calls forth, not divine wrath, but divine forgiveness symbolized by the purification of the prophets lips by the burning coal. God's messenger has been prepared and now he willingly responds to the call 'go for Us'. Only then does he learn what will be the cost, in frustration, of his mission, and what its outcome will be. He is warned that his message will only serve to harden still further the heart of the apostate people, and that the inevitable outcome must be the destruction of the nation. The latter, likened to a flourishing tree, will be reduced to an apparently lifeless stump, but hidden within this stump is the 'holy seed', a righteous remnant which is the hope for the future.

Isaiah 7^{1-17}—*Isaiah and the Syro-Ephraimite Invasion*

The Syrian and Israelite forces had invaded Judah in an attempt to force Ahaz to join an alliance against Assyria, and now Jerusalem itself was being threatened. Isaiah found Ahaz, obviously disturbed by the situation, inspecting his defences and particularly the water supply in preparation for the anticipated siege. The prophet endeavours to reassure the king that this threat will come to nothing; he brings the word of Yahweh, 'It shall not stand, and it shall not come to pass' (verse 7). But lack of faith in this promise and entanglement in foreign alliances, for presumably Ahaz was already contemplating calling in Assyrian aid, will ultimately lose for Judah the independence which Ahaz is trying to preserve. 'If you will not believe, surely you shall not be established' (verse 9).

A little later, perhaps a few days, Isaiah once again attempts to dissuade Ahaz from his policy of making an alliance which can only mean subservience to Assyria. This interview may have taken place in the palace. Isaiah's offer to convince the king with a sign from Yahweh is hypocritically refused, and, furious at the king's obstinacy, the prophet then proceeds to give Ahaz the sign of 'Immanuel'.

This sign seems to contain both a threat and a promise.[9] The king's fear for the future of his throne and kingdom must have raised in his mind the question of the continuance of the Davidic dynasty. The sign of Immanuel contains a promise that the Davidic line would continue. The young woman about whom the prophet spoke was probably one

[9] For a different interpretation of the sign see S. H. Hooke, *The Siege Perilous*, pp. 222 ff.

of the king's wives: the promised son would then be a royal child. Some scholars have indeed identified 'Immanuel' with Hezekiah. But the circumstances under which the child would be reared contain a threat of the disaster which will overtake the land when the Assyrians overrun it. It appears that Isaiah envisaged not only disaster in Israel (verse 17), but that in some measure Judah would also suffer either as a result of Assyrian intervention, or possibly the allusion is to the devastation that the land would suffer at the hands of Syria and Israel before their defeat by Assyria (cf. 2 Chr 28).

Notes

Verse 3. 'Shear-jashub'. The name means 'A remnant shall return'. The lad was old enough to accompany Isaiah when he went to meet Ahaz, so that he was probably four or five years old at any rate. If he was born shortly after Isaiah's call, the prophet may well have given his son this symbolic name as a permanent reminder of the outcome of his prophetic ministry. Again this sign may be interpreted both as a threat and a promise—'Only a remnant shall return' but 'a remnant shall turn'. 'Turn', i.e. repent rather than return.

Verse 14. 'young woman'. This verse has given rise to much debate. It is now generally agreed that the old translation 'virgin' (see margin) does not convey the force of the Hebrew *'almah'*. The better translation is 'young woman' and the implication is a 'young woman of marriageable age, but who has not yet borne a child'. Neither the word nor this verse have any connection with a doctrine of virgin birth.

Verse 15. 'Butter [or curds] and honey'. This was 'the plain fare of a nomad, betokening the desolations of war which have left the land bare of everything but the simple products of the desert'.[10] This state of desolation is graphically described in the four short oracles with which Chapter 7 closes (verses 18–23).

Isaiah 8^1–9^7—*Isaiah's reaction to the policy of Ahaz*

The appeal to the king and court having failed, Isaiah now endeavoured to convince the ordinary citizens of the folly of becoming embroiled with Assyria. To this end he prepared a large placard bearing the cryptic phrase *'Maher Shalal Hash Baz'*, i.e. 'The Spoil Hastens, The Plunder Comes Quickly'. Isaiah explained the meaning of this slogan (cf. verse 4) to the two witnesses who watched his symbolic action. Isaiah's conviction of the imminent downfall of Israel and

[10] O. C. Whitehouse, 'Isaiah', *Century Bible*, I.135.

Syria was emphasized by the name which he gave to the son who was born to him later.

His efforts were in vain, the people would not heed any more than the rulers; they were all rushing headlong into the arms of Assyria. Isaiah seems to have retired from public life for a time. He had proclaimed the message which Yahweh had given to him, but lest the word of Yahweh be lost, he charged his disciples to preserve his oracles (verse 16). Meanwhile the prophet and his children, with their symbolic names, must serve as silent preachers to a hardened generation.

The closing verses of Chapter 8 ($^{19\,ff}$) probably describe the scene in Israel as the Assyrians rampaged through the land. In their distress the people try to penetrate the future by appealing to mediums and wizards who purport to consult the shades of the departed. Famine stalks through the land and the despairing people curse both God and king. Yet this scene of darkness and gloom inspired Isaiah to one of his noblest utterances (9^{2-7}). With his unruffled confidence in the sovereignty of Yahweh, first expressed in the sign of Immanuel, he now confidently asserts that the time will come when the anguish and distress will give place to great rejoicing. Ahaz and his like will not reign for ever, but in those days to which Isaiah looks forward, the ruler will be a worthy successor of the mighty David. His reign will bring peace, and his rule will be just and righteous.

Isaiah 29–31—*Isaiah and Sennacherib's Invasions*

There are numerous allusions in Isaiah to the diplomatic exchanges between Hezekiah and the Egyptians. Hezekiah wished to be free from the Assyrian yoke to which Ahaz had committed Judah, whilst the Egyptians were anxious to keep the Assyrians as far from their frontiers as possible. The oracles in which Isaiah denounces the alliance with Egypt were probably delivered during the years 705–690 B C. Isaiah has no confidence in the Egyptian ally, which was indeed described scornfully by an Assyrian officer as a 'broken reed of a staff' (2 K 18^{21}), but equally he is confident that the Assyrians will not destroy Jerusalem. The following passages illustrate this twin theme of mistrust of Egypt, and unwavering trust in Yahweh as the only deliverer of Jerusalem.

Isaiah 29^{1-14}—*'Ariel'—The Beleagured City*

In this magnificent poem Isaiah describes Jerusalem under siege and expresses his confidence in her ultimate survival. The name which the prophet applies to the city—'Ari-el'—is something of an enigma to the modern reader at any rate. The Hebrew word, used here as a name for Jerusalem, means 'the mountain of God' and refers to the great altar of the Temple. The word also means a 'shade' or 'ghost' and this is the meaning required in verse 2b (cf. 29^{4b}). The city which David had captured will once again experience the horrors of siege, so that instead of the sounds of rejoicing at the annual festivals, there will be lamentation as from a city of dying and dead. Yahweh will deliver His 'Ariel', and the time of distress will pass as a nightmare with the break of dawn.

In the final stanza of the poem (verses 9–14) the prophet remarks on the spiritual blindness of the people who seem incapable of realizing the danger which threatens (because of their intrigues with Egypt?) or of trusting in Yahweh who is their real hope.

Isaiah 30^{1-7}, 31^{1-9}—*Poems Criticizing the Alliance with Egypt*

In these two poems Isaiah expresses his antagonism to the alliance with Egypt. He is convinced that in time of real trouble Egyptian help will be valueless. Isaiah's advice has been consistent throughout: that Judah should avoid entangling herself with the great powers, whether Egypt or Assyria. In Yahweh alone is her hope; this present wooing of Egypt is the act of 'rebellious children, who carry out a plan, but not mine; and who make a league, but not of my spirit' (30^{1}).

The second poem elaborates the prophet's teaching that Yahweh will deliver Jerusalem. He will watch over the city like a young lion watches its prey and the Assyrians will be as helpless as shepherds who are called out against the beast but cannot intimidate him.

THE REMNANT

Like his contemporaries Amos and Hosea, Isaiah was profoundly disturbed by the moral decay of his people. His concern turned to dismay when he was confronted by Yahweh, the Holy One of Israel, in the Temple vision. He who was righteous Himself surely demanded righteousness from His chosen people. 'He looked for justice, but behold bloodshed; for righteousness, but behold a cry.' Isaiah could see no future for his people but destruction (e.g. $5^{8\,ff}$); yet this was Yahweh's chosen people, and even if the nation were sooner or later to be utterly destroyed this was surely not the last word. So in Isaiah's teaching we find a new idea. If the nation because of its unrighteousness must be destroyed, there would survive a remnant who would turn to Yahweh 'they would be a holy people, in them the election would be fulfilled'.[11] This idea of the remnant, which the prophet received at his call (6^{13}), crops up in numerous passages and usually in a context of denunciation and threatened destruction. This is the hope that Isaiah brings, symbolized by the name of his eldest child 'Shear-Yashub'—'A remnant shall turn'.

Isaiah 1^{2-31}—*A Rebellious People*

This long poem in which Yahweh stands both as accuser and judge of the people recalls the judgement of Amos and Hosea on Israel. There is the same accusation of injustice and the same story of meticulous, but meaningless ritual observance (verses 12 ff); but disaster (in the form of the Assyrian invasion of 701 BC) has already fallen on the nation (verses 7 ff). Even amidst this tale of woe the prophet holds out a hope, like a faint light in the encircling gloom, a beacon in a storm. In verse 9 there is a hint of a few survivors, and in verse 19 the condition for their survival is stated.

Isaiah 5^{1-7}—*'The Song of the Vineyard'*

In this poem Isaiah makes use of the familiar figure of the vine and the vineyard as a symbol of the chosen people (cf. Hos 10^{1}, Jer 2^{21}, Ps $80^{8\,ff}$). In a picture obviously drawn from life Isaiah shows us the owner of the vineyard making every preparation calculated to secure a bumper harvest, nothing is neglected, no expense spared, only the best vines are planted, but all to no purpose. The plants prove to be worthless, and the whole project is abandoned. In this parable Isaiah holds out no hope at all. Israel and Judah are both doomed to destruction.

Isaiah 6^{11-13}, 10^{20-7}, 14^{32}, $28^{5,\,16}$, 37^{32}—*The Remnant*

Isaiah's teaching on the remnant runs like a scarlet thread throughout his prophecies of disaster. The various passages cited above enable us to build up a picture of this remnant. When Isaiah received his call he was left in no doubt about the effect of his message; it would fall on deaf and incredulous ears, and only the stump of the nation would survive the disasters that must overtake the rebellious, unrighteous people. At first then he sees a stump, but it is a living stump and a sign of hope (6^{13}).

In that day towards which Isaiah looks, the remnant which then remains will have learned to lean in faith on Yahweh, no longer depending on those who oppress them. So the prophet can exhort this

11 J. Lindblom, *Prophecy in Ancient Israel* (ET), p. 367.

faithful remnant ('my people', who are presumably not all the inhabitants of Zion, but Isaiah's disciples—cf. 8^{16-18}) to stand fast whilst the storm of Assyrian invasion blows itself out. Who constituted the remnant? There is a possible hint in 14^{32}; they are the 'afflicted of Yahweh's people' who will find refuge in Zion. (In the psalms in particular the truly pious followers of Yahweh are often called 'the humble' or the 'afflicted ones'; cf. also Zeph 3^{12}). But though 'afflicted' and 'humble', people of no account in the eyes of the hardened nation, when their day comes this despised remnant will have its glory. As the king ought to be the glory of the nation, so Yahweh Himself will be their glory (28^{5}).

Finally in contrast to the scoffers who rule in Jerusalem (28^{14}), but who are destined for destruction, Isaiah speaks of the Godly remnant which is the true foundation of Zion (28^{16}). The remnant is described here as a 'stone', a well-tested stone, tested by the scales of justice and the plumb-line of righteousness (verse 17) and hence fitted to be the foundation of a renewed Israel (37^{32}).

CHAPTER NINE

PROPHECY AND CRISIS (2)

I—DEUTERONOMY AND JOSIAH'S REFORM

HEZEKIAH'S bid for independence failed, and it is probable that only the death of the king and the adoption of a policy of submission to Assyria saved Judah from further invasion. But submission also involved the reintroduction of Assyrian cults into the land, so that Hezekiah's religious reform seemed to have had no permanent value, and as a gesture of defiance against Assyria it was futile. It would be wrong, however, to see this reform merely as one facet of the bid for independence. Hezekiah had made an attempt to stamp out the old Canaanite cults, which had been practised side by side with the worship of Yahweh from the times of the Judges (2 K 18^{4}). In this work the king must have had the support of those who had been influenced by the teaching of the prophets of the ninth and eighth centuries.

During the reign of Manasseh the uncompromising advocates of Yahweh must have gone underground, and it is not unlikely that they devoted themselves to collecting and editing the traditions which had been preserved in Israel, and had been brought to Judah after the fall of the northern kingdom. One book which appears to have been compiled during this period was Deuteronomy. The traditions and laws which the book preserves were of great antiquity, and had almost certainly been known in Israel, whence they were brought to Judah after the fall of Samaria. (One pointer to the Israelite origin of the traditions preserved in Deuteronomy is the use of the name 'Horeb' for Sinai; cf. 1 K 19^{8}, where 'Horeb' is used in the Israelite story of Elijah.) The book was stored in the Temple and forgotten; it came to light again when the Temple was being restored during Josiah's reign (2 K 22$^{8\,ff}$).

We have already seen (p. 143) that the failing power of Assyria during the early years of Josiah's reign encouraged the latter to attempt to regain independence for his kingdom. (Indeed by the time of the fateful battle of Megiddo, when Josiah lost his life, he had succeeded in extending his kingdom to include much of the former kingdom of Israel.) A religious reform aimed, as usual, at stamping out the cults of the foreign deities, for whom altars had been erected in the Temple, was undertaken. As this involved carrying out repairs in the Temple so the 'Book of the Law' was found.

The stress which Deuteronomy lays on the duty of worshipping and serving Yahweh alone, found a ready response in the mind of the king, who redoubled his efforts to rid his kingdom, not only of foreign cults, but of the ancient Canaanite practices which were still observed at the high places of the land. Although sacrifice at the high places was forbidden, it appears that it was not possible to carry out the more radical step of bringing all the priests to the one central sanctuary at Jerusalem (cf. 2 K 23^{9}).

According to the account in the Book of Chronicles, Josiah's reforming activities were begun in the twelfth year of his reign, which was also, significantly, the year in which the Assyrian monarch died. A highlight of the reform was a great celebration of the Passover in the Temple in the eighteenth year of Josiah's reign (2 K $23^{21\,ff}$). Although the first steps towards the removal of alien worship from Judah were probably taken, as Chronicles suggests, some years before the discovery of Deuteronomy it seems clear that the teaching of this book exercised a considerable influence in the later stages of the reformation. A comparison of the details of the reform given in 2 Kings 23 with various passages from Deuteronomy will indicate how closely the measures carried out followed the prescriptions of the newly found Law Book.

(*a*) The Centralization of Worship: 2 K $23^{5,\,8,\,12\,ff,\,16,\,19}$; cf. Deut 12^{1-7}.

(*b*) The Passover to be celebrated at the Temple, not at home: 2 K 23^{21-3}; cf. Deut 16^{1-8}.

(*c*) The suppression of various pagan practices:
2 K $23^{4,\,5,\,11}$; cf. Deut 17^{3}.
2 K $23^{4,\,6,\,7,\,14}$; cf. Deut 16^{21-2}, 12^{3}.
2 K 23^{10}; cf. Deut 18^{10}.
2 K 23^{7}; cf. Deut 23^{18}.
2 K 23^{24}; cf. Deut 18^{11}.

INTRODUCTION TO DEUTERONOMY

Deuteronomy is cast into the form of three speeches delivered by Moses to the Israelites who are gathered on the plains of Moab just prior to their entry into Canaan. The opening verse of the book shows that in fact it was composed *after* the settlement in Canaan, when the writer would naturally refer to the region east of the Jordan as 'beyond

Jordan'. If, as we have already suggested, the book was compiled, in the main, during the reign of Manasseh by a member of the reforming party[1] then we must regard it as a reinterpretation of the ancient laws and traditions in the light of the teaching particularly of the eighth-century prophets. From this it follows that the Israel which is being addressed in Deuteronomy is not in fact the Israel which stood at the foot of Horeb with Moses, or waited for the signal to cross over the Jordan into the Promised Land; rather it is the 'Israel' of the seventh century which is being exhorted. The ancient covenant which bound Yahweh and Israel together is still valid, for Israel is still the same Israel called by Yahweh out of Egypt. 'Six centuries wasted in sin and constant apostasy are cancelled out, and Israel is set once more at Horeb to hear Yahweh's word of salvation, which has not lost its power.'[2]

Superficially Deuteronomy appears to be a heterogeneous mixture of history, legislation, and exhortation. It is, in fact, primarily an exposition of the covenant. The historical introduction (Ch 1–4), which many scholars believe to have been added during the exile, illustrates Yahweh's gracious dealings with His people. The twin emphases of the book are (*a*) Yahweh's election of Israel, which was most emphatically not due to any merit on Israel's part; and (*b*) Israel's duty of loyalty and obedience to Yahweh alone. This loyalty is shown when Israel observes and performs the 'Laws, ordinances and statutes', but here too the apparently legalistic attitude of Deuteronomy is offset by its requirement that what is most important is to act from a right motive. Deuteronomy understands that it is more important to carry out the spirit of the law rather than merely to observe its letter. This is well illustrated in the case of the 'law of release' (Deut 15^{1-11}). The law is stated in verse 1, and this may well have been the extent of the original statement of the law. The remainder of the passage is commentary on the law, and the spirit in which Deuteronomy interpreted this law is finely shown in verses 9 and 10. This, as G. von Rad has remarked, 'is law preached'.[3]

Deuteronomy falls into four sections as follows: (*a*) historical introduction (Ch 1–4), followed by an exposition of the first commandment (Ch 5–11); (*b*) the detailed demands of the covenant (Ch 12–26); (*c*)

[1] It may be possible to identify the reformers as belonging to the 'people of the land' who put Josiah on the throne, 2 K 21^{24}; and cf. G. von Rad, *Studies in Deuteronomy*, p. 63.

[2] G. von Rad, ibid., p. 78. [3] Ibid., p. 16.

the blessings of obedience and the curse of disobedience (Ch 27–30); (*d*) an appendix concluding with an account of the death of Moses.[4]

PASSAGES FOR STUDY

Deuteronomy 6–11—*A Sermon on the First Commandment*

The whole section comprising Chapters 6–11 should first be read straight through to catch something of the spirit of Deuteronomy. In passionate language the writer pleads with his readers to 'remember' Yahweh, the mighty God, who had brought their ancestors out of Egypt; Yahweh, the gracious God, who had chosen the unworthy people of Israel to be His people; Yahweh, the jealous God, who demands undivided loyalty from His chosen people. Notice how often in these chapters the reader is exhorted to 'remember'.

Deuteronomy 6—'*Hear O Israel*'

Verses 4–9 form part of the Jewish confession of faith which is recited morning and evening by orthodox Jews to this day. It is known from its opening word in Hebrew as the 'Shema' ('*shema*'='hear'). Verses 4 and 5 were quoted by our Lord as the first commandment. This kind of 'commandment' is far removed from mere legalism. God cannot be loved to order, and hence the writer a little later (verse 12) exhorts his readers to remember Yahweh 'who brought you out of the land of Egypt'. For it is only as the people 'forget not all his benefits' (Ps 103^1) that there will rise up in their hearts love of Yahweh, and reverence (fear) for Him. In the pagan atmosphere of Canaan, it was all too easy to forget Yahweh and to 'go after other gods', so there is the oft-repeated exhortation to remember: 'We were Pharaoh's slaves in Egypt' (verses 21–2).

NOTE. Deuteronomy 6^4. The translation of this verse presents some difficulties. Three possible alternative translations are given in the margin. The third rendering, 'The LORD is our God, the Lord alone', suggested by the medieval Jewish Rabbi, Ibn Ezra, perhaps gives the best sense and is in line with the sentiments of the passage as a whole.

Deuteronomy 7—'*A Chosen People*'

To anyone like the writer of Deuteronomy, who took the first commandment seriously, the cults of Canaan were a problem. We cannot, however, condone his ruthless proposal to deal with the problem by

[4] H. Cunliffe-Jones, *Deuteronomy*, pp. 5 ff.

exterminating the Canaanite population, but we must remember that when Deuteronomy was written there was no separate Canaanite population, so that the proposal represents an 'ideal' which 'ought' to have been carried out at the conquest of the land. Verse 5 is more realistic; the destruction of the high places and the associated objects of worship was undertaken during the Josianic reform.

Starting from the first commandment Deuteronomy first stresses that Yahweh, and Yahweh alone, is Israel's God. In this chapter (verses 6 ff) the writer goes on to state the complementary truth that Israel is Yahweh's people, and this by Yahweh's choice. But there is more to be said about this choice. Deuteronomy knows it as a fact of history that Israel has never merited this divine favour. They were an insignificant people (7^{7}), even a stubborn people ($9^{6\,ff}$), but unaccountably Yahweh loved them and so He chose them 'out of all the peoples that are on the face of the earth' (7^{6}; cf. 10^{14-15}). This is the principle of justification by faith, that God accepts people *as they are*. 'The basis of election never lies in the one who is chosen, but exclusively in the One who chooses. Election means precisely this : that Israel knows itself to be wholly dependent upon the grace of the One who has chosen her, and that she ought to live in this attitude of continual dependence.'[5]

But Deuteronomy does not understand this election in any sentimental manner, for though election cannot be merited, yet the fact of being chosen brings its own obligations of loyalty and love towards Yahweh. Furthermore it is possible to reject Yahweh, and the consequences are destruction ($7^{9\,ff}$). The reward of loyalty to Yahweh is material prosperity ($7^{12\,ff}$). This is the characteristic teaching of the Old Testament, and it is not true to experience; the lesson had yet to be learned that 'a man's life does not consist in the abundance of his possessions' (Lk 12^{15}). A repeated warning to destroy all traces of Canaanite worship concludes the chapter.

Deuteronomy 8—'*Take heed lest you forget*'

In the next three chapters the writer illustrates the two points which he has already made, that Yahweh alone is Israel's God, and that Israel is God's chosen people, by recalling some events of the Exodus. The wilderness experience showed Israel's utter dependence on Yahweh, but the lessons of the past were too easily forgotten so that this chapter is punctuated with phrases such as, 'You shall remember', or 'Take heed lest you forget'.

[5] E. Brunner, *Christian Doctrine of God* (ET), p. 310.

Deuteronomy 9–10[11]—*'You are a stubborn people'*

The writer has already stated that Israel's election is due to divine grace alone ($7^{6\,ff}$). This theme is hinted at in the opening verses (1–7) of Chapter 9, but here the emphasis is on the fact that the gift of the Promised Land was in no way merited by Israel. The description of Israel as 'a stubborn people' (verse 6) reminds the writer of the apostasy of Israel even at Horeb itself, so he recounts in some detail the episode of the Golden Calf.

Deuteronomy 10[12]–11[32]—*The Application of the Sermon*

Deuteronomy 10[12–22]—*'What does the* LORD *require of you'*

The writer has dealt at length with God's gracious dealings with Israel, but both Yahweh and Israel are parties to the covenant. Yahweh has said, 'I will be your God', and one of the implications is His choice of Israel. What then is required of Israel? In this passage three requirements are asked for. The first, which recalls the words of the Shema, is that Israel must fear and love God 'with all your heart and all your soul'. In this context fear is not to be contrasted with love; fear is the proper attitude of reverence which man must always adopt in the presence of his Creator, the One to whom belongs 'the heaven and the heaven of heavens, the earth with all that is in it' (verse 14). Secondly Israel must imitate God (verses 16–19). The influence of the eighth-century prophets, with their concern for the fatherless, the widows, and the alien, is very evident in these verses. The alien (sojourner) is particularly recommended as the object of the faithful Israelite's love (verse 19). At all times resident aliens (i.e. members of other tribes or nations) seem to have constituted a part of the population. Whilst not slaves, they neverthless did not enjoy all the rights of the Israelite citizen. It may be that the number of such aliens had been greatly increased in Judah at the time when Deuteronomy was being written by an influx of refugees from the former northern kingdom.[6] If there was a 'refugee problem' in Judah at the beginning of the seventh century then it would give added point to this verse. Finally, Israel must be thankful. This passage ends as it began with the injunction to fear, to serve, and to cleave to Yahweh. With a nice economy of words (verse 22) the writer recalls the mighty act of Yahweh in redeeming Israel from Egypt and therefore can say: 'He (and He alone) is your praise.'

[6] R. de Vaux, *Ancient Israel*, p. 75.

Deuteronomy 11 (cf. Deut 30^{15-20})—*The Two Ways*

In this final chapter of exhortation the writer takes up again the theme mentioned briefly in $7^{9\,ff}$. The way of obedience is the way of blessing and life; the way of disobedience is the way of destruction and death. The destruction of Pharaoh and the fate of those who rebelled against Moses in the wilderness (Num 16) is used as an illustration and a warning. Of course such an interpretation of history is an over-simplification. Misfortune is not always a consequence of sin and disobedience, but Deuteronomy is right in insisting that the basis of life is obedience to a moral demand. The assumption that there is a difference between right and wrong is the corner stone of every legal code. The limitation of Deuteronomy is that it interprets the 'blessing' to mean material prosperity alone; the experience of saints down the ages has proved that obedience brings a blessing which is quite independent of material goods, in fact these same saints were often poor in material wealth.

Deuteronomy 12^{1-28}—*The Law of One Sanctuary*

The demands of the covenant are worked out in detail in the second section of Deuteronomy (Ch 12–26). We shall study only the opening chapter of this section. Loyalty to Yahweh as Israel's God required that all other worship be eschewed. After the conquest, the ancient Canaanite shrines (high places) continued to be used for the worship of Yahweh, and many of the features of the earlier worship were adopted by the Israelites. This impure worship was roundly condemned by the eighth-century prophets, and it became evident to the Deuteronomic reformers that a drastic solution of the problem was called for. Their proposal was to destroy all the local high places, and bring the officiating priests to one central shrine, the only place authorized for worship and sacrifice. The location of the one sanctuary is not named in Deuteronomy, but when the ideas of the reformers received practical expression in the reign of Josiah it was clear that the Temple at Jerusalem must be the one legitimate sanctuary.

The manner of worship at the Temple is described in 12^{5-7}, from which it is evident that the central feature of the worship was a sacramental meal and that the keynote of the worship was thanksgiving. It was clearly intended to be a joyous festival.

The destruction of the local shrines raised one practical difficulty (verses 15 ff). Previously certain animals could only be slaughtered at the sanctuary, some of the flesh would then be offered on the altar and the rest eaten by the worshipper. It was clearly impracticable to carry out this procedure when all the local shrines had been destroyed; hence the new legislation included provision for the slaughtering of animals at home. The meat could then be used for food, provided that care was taken to pour away the blood.

II—THE PROPHETS OF THE SEVENTH CENTURY

After the death of Isaiah it was about sixty years before the voice of prophecy was heard again in Judah. Throughout the long reign of Manasseh, Judah was held firmly in the iron grip of Assyria, and prophetic utterances condemning the foreign, and particularly the Assyrian, cults which were being practised in Judah at that time would have been regarded as seditious, and perhaps punishable by death (cf. the fate of Uriah in the reign of Jehoiakim—Jer 26^{20-3}). The prophetic and reforming party will have gone underground during this period, devoting themselves to collecting and preserving the traditions and laws of their nation.

The decline of Assyrian power, which was already becoming evident by the end of Manasseh's reign, led to a radical change of policy during Josiah's reign. Prophets were able to proclaim their messages openly again. But although the time of Assyrian domination had come to an end, an even more critical period faced Judah. The whole of the Middle East was in ferment. The Scythian hordes sweeping down from the steppes of Russia had, by their attacks, weakened Assyria, and were now threatening Palestine and even Egypt. Judah was just off the line of the Scythian advance and escaped without molestation, but other troubles loomed ahead as Egypt and Babylon, which had now replaced Assyria as the dominant Mesopotamian power, struggled for the mastery of the Near East. In this struggle the kingdom of Judah came to an end just as a little over a century earlier her sister kingdom, Israel, had also ceased to exist.

These events form the background to the pronouncements of the four prophets Zephaniah, Nahum, Habakkuk, and Jeremiah, though it is possible that only Jeremiah witnessed the death-struggles of his nation. Zephaniah was probably rather older than Jeremiah, at any rate his description of the religious observances in Judah suggest that he prophesied before Josiah set his reform in motion. His work may be dated between 635 and 630 B C.

The ruin of the Assyrian empire and the imminent fall of the capital city of Nineveh were the occasion of Nahum's oracles which must have been composed shortly before that city fell to the Babylonians in 612 B C. But the collapse of the Assyrian empire only meant the rise of the Babylonian which equally threatened the existence of Judah. This Babylonian menace was the occasion of Habakkuk's prophecy. 'He saw in the Chaldeans (i.e. the Babylonians) a nation appointed to chastise his own people; but he prays for his people, hoping that through faithful adherence to Yahweh they will save their life (2^{4}).'[7] Habakkuk's prophecy may be dated somewhere between 612 and 605 B C.

But completely overshadowing these minor prophets of the seventh century stands Jeremiah. His prophetic ministry spanned upwards of forty years from his call in 626 B C as a young man, perhaps in his early twenties, to his death in Egypt.

JEREMIAH

Jeremiah was a native of Anathoth, a village three to four miles north of Jerusalem. Thither Abiathar, the priest, had been banished by Solomon for the part he had played in the attempt to make Adonijah king in succession to David (1 K 1^{18-25}, 2^{26-7}). Jeremiah was 'of the priests that were in Anathoth' and presumably a descendant of Abiathar. Whilst we have no exact details giving the date of his birth, since he is described as a young man at the time of his call (626 B C) we may presume that his birth fell somewhere between 650 and 645 B C. He left Anathoth about 621 when his life was threatened, and went to live in Jerusalem. Apart from a preaching-tour through the cities of Judah as an advocate of Josiah's reform, and a time spent in hiding when he had incurred Jehoiakim's wrath, he continued to dwell in Jerusalem until the city was destroyed by the Babylonians in 586 B C. He then threw in his lot with the pitiful remnant who were left in Judah, eventually being taken by force by them to Egypt. His last days were spent in a vain attempt to keep the small colony of refugees in Egypt loyal to Yahweh (Jer 44). There is no record in the Bible of his death, though an early Christian tradition asserts that he was murdered by his compatriots. In view of his constant opposition to their idolatrous practices this may well be true.

[7] J. Lindblom, *Prophecy in Ancient Israel*, p. 255.

THE BOOK OF JEREMIAH

In the case of the majority of the prophets we do not know what steps, if any, they took to ensure the preservation of their oracles. A passage in Isaiah ($8^{16\,ff}$) suggests that that prophet had gathered round himself a band of disciples who would be concerned to preserve the words of their master. The Book of Jeremiah gives us some precise information concerning its origin. The nucleus of the book was formed from a collection of oracles which the prophet had delivered during the first twenty-two years of his ministry. Under the rule of Jehoiakim the reforming policy of his father Josiah had been set aside, and it seemed to Jeremiah that both the efforts of the former king and his own warnings had been unavailing. He therefore engaged a professional writer, Baruch, to take down at his dictation the prophecies which he had uttered since his call (Jer 36). This scroll, which was read by Baruch in the Temple on a day of fasting some months later, eventually came into the hands of Jehoiakim who destroyed it. Jeremiah and Baruch then prepared a second edition incorporating some extra material.

To this early edition of Jeremiah's prophecies there was added at some later period an account of Jeremiah's activities up to the fall of Jerusalem and of his departure into Egypt with those who were fleeing from the Babylonians.

Unfortunately the compilers of the book had no interest in presenting their material in chronological order and consequently it is not always easy to date the individual prophecies, whilst in the narrative-portions of the work incidents belonging to the reigns of Jehoiakim and Zedekiah are jumbled together in a bewildering manner.

PASSAGES FOR STUDY

The following passages, which have been selected for special study, have been arranged as far as possible in their probable chronological order.

Jeremiah 1^{4-10}—*The Call of Jeremiah*

Verses 1 and 2 of this chapter show that Jeremiah received his call in 'the thirteenth year of Josiah', i.e. 626 BC. Verse 3—a later addition to the text—indicates that the period of Jeremiah's activity lasted until the fall of Jerusalem.

The prophet's call is described in the next seven verses of the chapter. Isaiah became conscious of his call as a result of the vision in the Temple, when he was overwhelmed by the glory and majesty of Yahweh. The circumstances of Jeremiah's call were different and if verse 11 describes another feature of the same experience, then we may conclude that it was winter and that the young man was alone, staring rather abstractedly at an almond tree. In this meditative frame of mind he hears Yahweh speaking to him, and learns that Yahweh had destined him for the office of a prophet. The sense of working under divine compulsion, which was so strong in Jeremiah (cf. Jer 20^7), and from which he shrank, is evident in the manner of his call. He was born to be a prophet. But Jeremiah shrinks from this task, which perhaps even at this stage he suspected would involve a life of loneliness, persecution, and hardship.

His plea of immaturity is brushed aside, but there is the promise that Yahweh Himself will put His word in the prophet's mouth. This promise is accompanied by another psychic experience in which it seemed that the hand of Yahweh touched his mouth in the act of imparting His word to Jeremiah.

He learns that his office will be no sinecure. He will find that his work throws him into the seething cauldron of imperial rivalries, and of national calamity and disaster.

Jeremiah 1^{11-19}—*Two Visions*

The Almond Tree

How can a prophet know that his preaching will be effective? Jeremiah had been called to pronounce judgement and doom on his people, 'to pluck up and to break down', but what certainty had he that his words would be fulfilled? As he ponders these questions his gaze becomes fixed on the twig of an almond tree. Immediately the thought seized Jeremiah: Yahweh Himself will vindicate His own word. The association of an almond tree with the idea of Yahweh 'watching over my word' is not obvious without reference to the Hebrew. As indicated by the marginal note to these verses (11–12) the Hebrew for 'almond tree' (*shaked*) and for 'watching' (*shoked*) are very similar and are in fact derived from the same Hebrew word—*shakad*—meaning 'to watch'. But there is rather more than a mere play on words here. The almond tree was named 'shaked', i.e. 'the wakeful tree' precisely because it was the first to break into life after the rigours of the winter, and it annually proclaimed the promise of approaching spring. So from seeing the almond tree the idea that Yahweh is ever watchful is born in the prophet's mind.

The Boiling Cauldron

The second vision concerns the judgement which was shortly to fall on Judah. How would this judgement come? While pondering this problem Jeremiah noticed a cauldron placed on a flaming fire. To appreciate what the prophet was looking at we must imagine 'that the cauldron was sunk down in an open-air hearth of stones or bricks forming a circle round it, but open towards the north, from where the wind blew on the fuel consisting of wood or dry thorns'.[8] The wind blowing from the north and fanning the fire gave the prophet the answer he was seeking. 'Out of the north evil shall break forth upon all the inhabitants of the land.'

Trouble was in fact already brewing in the north, the Scythians were attacking Assyria and would soon be sweeping into Palestine. Whether Jeremiah ever regarded the Scythians as instruments of divine punishment we do not know, but the foe from the north which eventually brought ruin to Judah was Babylon.

It is only at verse 16 that we have a statement of the charge against Judah: that they have forsaken Yahweh and worshipped other gods.

Jeremiah is warned that his ministry will be far from easy. He will make many enemies in every stratum of society, but his ultimate assurance is Yahweh's promise: 'I am with you to deliver you' (verse 19).

Jeremiah 2—*'They have forsaken me'*

In this chapter we have a collection of poems in which the prophet contrasts the ideal religion of utter devotion to Yahweh (verses 2b–3) with the degenerate and sensuous worship of the high places which passed for the worship of Yahweh, but was in fact scarcely to be distinguished from the old Canaanite fertility cult.

Verses 2b–3—*Pure religion*

In this beautiful little poem Jeremiah recalls the time when Israel was utterly devoted to Yahweh. Jeremiah, like Hosea before him, looked back to the wilderness period as a time when Israel's loyalty to Yahweh was undivided. Using Hosea's metaphor of marriage, he likens this early period to a honeymoon. The terrors of the wilderness (cf. verse 6) inspired no fear in the 'bride' Israel for 'her husband' Yahweh was there

[8] J. Lindblom, *Prophecy in Ancient Israel*, p. 140.

providing food (manna) and drink (water from the rock) and giving her protection.

NOTE. Both Hosea and Jeremiah regarded the period of wandering in the wilderness as a time when Israel was completely loyal to Yahweh; the tradition preserved in Exodus and Numbers is rather different, even in the wilderness Israel was stubborn and rebellious.

Verses 5–8—'*They went from Me*'

Deuteronomy exhorts Israel to remember how Yahweh had led her out of Egypt and through the wilderness. In this poem Jeremiah recalls these same mighty acts of Yahweh; but because Israel has failed to remember that 'it was the LORD's doing and marvellous in our eyes' (cf. verses 6–7), so she has been lured away, running after the Baalim.

Verses 9–13, 18–19—'*Broken cisterns*'

These two passages probably make up a single poem. Many scholars believe that verses 14–17, which interrupt the sequence, were added later. With bitter irony Jeremiah exposes the folly of Israel (verse 11). The heathen at least are loyal to their own gods, worthless though these be, but Israel has forsaken Yahweh, her glory, for the Baalim. Such folly can only be likened to the behaviour of a man who chooses to depend on a cistern, hewn with great trouble out of rock, which at best will supply flat and stagnant water, and which is liable to crack and so lose even this poor supply; all the time there is a perennial spring of fresh water at hand.

In verse 18 there is probably a slight movement of thought. The prophet is reproaching Judah for depending on these powers (Assyria and Egypt) for aid.

Verses 20–8—'*No restraints*'

In vivid language the prophet describes the wilful disobedience of Israel. The restraints of the covenant had been cast aside with the defiant 'I will not serve'. Yet the freedom thus snatched has only put the people in bondage to their lust and passion. Though the worshippers may try to deceive themselves that their ritual prostitution is a necessary part of the worship of Yahweh (verse 23), in reality they are troubled in conscience (verses 26–8). But they are so much at the mercy of their passions that they despair of any change. 'It is hopeless, for I have loved strangers and after them will I go' (verse 25).

Verses 29–37—*'I am innocent'*

When misfortune overtakes the people they complain about Yahweh (cf. 'Why does God let this happen to me?'), but the root of the trouble is that they have turned away from Yahweh and forgotten Him (verses 31–2). Their protestations of innocence (verse 35) are belied by their conduct which is such 'that even the experts in immorality are her pupils'.[9] But shameless conduct will in due time bring shame on them (verse 37). (There is an allusion to some historical situation in verse 36 in which Judah was disappointed by Assyria, but the details are now unknown.)

Jeremiah 11^{1-8}, 11^{18}–12^{6}—*Jeremiah and the Reform*

The reform inaugurated by Josiah, at about the same time that Jeremiah received his call, was further stimulated by the discovery of the Law Book in the Temple. The insistence on absolute loyalty to Yahweh and the stern prohibition of the idolatrous practices inherited from the Canaanites struck a sympathetic chord in Jeremiah. It appears from Jeremiah 11^{1-8} that the prophet took an active part in the reform by preaching in support of the covenant throughout Judah (verses 6 ff).

He evidently hoped that his advocacy of the reform would render acceptable to the people Josiah's policy of destroying the high places and of centralizing the worship in Jerusalem. Josiah's measures were, however, unpopular and the men of Anathoth, at any rate, sought to take vengeance on Jeremiah for the loss of their local sanctuary. The centralization of worship in Jerusalem enhanced the position of the Zadokite priesthood, whilst the descendants of Abiathar in Anathoth were to become of even less account. Jeremiah, the innocent enthusiast of the reform, had not calculated on the persistence of this family feud, and when he realized what plots were being made against his life he felt 'like a gentle lamb led to the slaughter' (verse 19).

Those who had sought to kill him prospered and appeared to get off scot-free. Thus Jeremiah raises one of the most acute problems of the Old Testament: 'Why do the wicked prosper?' (12^{1}). But there is at the moment neither answer for his problem nor consolation for his plight. His cup of suffering is not yet full.

[9] A. S. Peake, 'Jeremiah', *Century Bible*, I.100.

'And if in a safe land you fall down,
how will you do in the jungle of the Jordan?' (12^5).

Jeremiah 26, 7 $^{1-15}$—'*The Temple of the* LORD'

Josiah had been killed in battle at Megiddo, and the victor, Pharaoh Neco, had put Josiah's son, Jehoiakim, on the throne. The latter was of a very different stamp from his father, he had no sympathy with the reform movement, but was chiefly interested in carrying out grandiose building schemes at a time when the country was already being oppressively taxed to pay tribute to Egypt. Jeremiah compares him very unfavourably with his father Josiah, of whom he had a very high opinion (Jer 22^{13-19}).

Nothing of the spirit of the reform which Josiah had launched remained, only the formal ceremonies of the Temple were left. To the prophet it seemed that the people had only changed their trust in the gods of the high places for a trust in the Temple, rather than in the God who had chosen to be worshipped there. So he is moved to address the worshippers as they made their way to the Temple. Graphic details are given in Jeremiah 26 and there is a rather fuller account of his actual address in 7^{1-15}. This so incensed his hearers that the prophet would have been lynched on the spot had not some of the royal household appeared at the crucial moment to rescue him from the enraged mob. We can form some picture of the scene. As Jeremiah proceeded to accuse the people of injustice, immorality, and idolatry, so they countered all his arguments with the refrain: 'This is the Temple of the LORD.' But this was lip-service which was belied by their lives, and the fate of Shiloh, which had been destroyed by the Philistines, could be the fate even of the Temple in Jerusalem.

Jeremiah 36—*The Writing of the Roll*

Four years have elapsed since Jeremiah addressed the crowds outside the Temple. Though he was rescued from the mob on that occasion he was debarred from going into the Temple (36^6). The prophet, however, decided to make another attempt to turn the people from their 'evil way' (verse 7). Since he could no longer make his appeal in person he employed a professional scribe, Baruch, to write down on a roll all the prophecies which he had uttered over the previous twenty-two years. At an appropriate fast-day, when there would be many worshippers at the Temple, Baruch read the roll to those who had gathered in 'the chamber of Gemariah', one of the rooms of the Temple.

Jeremiah 29^{1-15}—*Advice to the Exiles*

Jehoiakim's attempt to free Judah from the Babylonian yoke had the reverse effect and brought a terrible punishment on the country. The land was devastated, Jerusalem besieged, and the flower of the population, including the young king Jehoiachin, were carried off into exile in Babylonia. There were those, both in Jerusalem and in Babylon, who believed that the exile would be of short duration (cf. $28^{2\,ff}$), but Jeremiah could hold out no such hope. The exile was part of the doom which he had so long predicted, but he does not regard the present disasters as spelling the utter destruction of the people of God. There will be a return, but in the meantime the exiles must be prepared for a long stay in exile and so make plans to settle in Babylonia.

Jeremiah 37–39^{14}—*The Last Days of Jerusalem*

These chapters, which are quite straightforward, give an account of Jeremiah's activities during the second siege of Jerusalem. Unlike Jehoiakim, Zedekiah had considerable regard for the prophet, but though he sought his advice he did not act upon it, as he was unwilling to oppose those who favoured resistance to Babylon. The siege dragged on to its inevitable conclusion and Jeremiah was taken prisoner when the city fell, but he was released as one who had steadily opposed the anti-Babylonian faction in Jerusalem.

NOTES

(1) Jeremiah $37^{11\,ff}$. This proposed visit to the 'land of Benjamin' was regarded by the officer on duty as an excuse for Jeremiah to escape from the capital. Jeremiah had bought some land in Anathoth (32^{6-15}) and evidently had other business to transact in connection with his estate.

(2) Rab-saris, Rab-mag. These are the titles of Babylonian officers.

Jeremiah 42^{1}–43^{7}—*Jeremiah in Egypt*

After Ishmael had murdered Gedaliah, the governor of the Babylonian province of Judah, fear of reprisals caused the leaders of the pitiful remnant still left in Judah to seek Jeremiah's advice on the best course of action to take. After ten days he was able to give them the 'word of the LORD' concerning the matter. He assured the leaders that the people had nothing to fear if they remained in Judah, but that disaster would overtake them if they fled to Egypt. In spite of this warning they nevertheless fled to Egypt compelling Jeremiah and Baruch to go with them.

The last glimpse we are given of Jeremiah shows him protesting against the pagan worship of the Queen of Heaven which was being practised by the refugees in Egypt (Ch 44).

Jeremiah 31^{27-34}—*The New Covenant*

Although Jeremiah had been convinced from the outset that Judah would suffer punishment at the hands of a foe from the north, yet he never lost hope that the people of God would continue to exist and ultimately be restored to their own land. He expressed this conviction in a quite practical manner when he purchased an estate at Anathoth although the land was then being overrun by the Babylonians.

Once again after the fall of Jerusalem he expresses the same hope (verse 27) in a passage which recalls the charge he had received at his call (cf. 1^{10}, and 31^{28}). Yahweh has declared that the time of plucking up and breaking down is over and there is to be a time of building and planting. When that time comes there will be a new spirit among the people. The old order with its excuses, 'The fathers have eaten sour grapes and the children's teeth are set on edge', and its reliance on the outward paraphernalia of religion, 'The Temple of the LORD, The Temple of the LORD', had passed away. In the new order which Jeremiah foresees, each individual will recognize his own responsibility for his own sins. Some scholars have seen in this proverb a popular statement of the idea of corporate responsibility as exemplified in Achan's sin and the consequent punishment of the whole of his family (Josh 7^{24-5}). But it seems to the present writer that this is reading too much into a homely proverb. It is more likely that the ones who were quoting it were merely using it as a convenient excuse to shift responsibility from themselves. In any case Jeremiah is saying that in the new order people will not try to shift the responsibility for their sins, but each one will recognize and accept his own.

With the passing of the old order there was also the abrogation of the covenant. The only lasting effect of Josiah's reform seems to have been to increase the veneration with which the Temple was regarded, until many people came to look upon it as a sort of talisman which would ensure their personal safety and that of Jerusalem. This was far from the spirit which Deuteronomy had sought to foster, a spirit of loyalty to Yahweh and obedience to His commandments based on love of Yahweh. (See the notes on Deuteronomy 6.)

Thus Jeremiah teaches that Yahweh will make a new covenant with the restored Israel. It is important to realize in what sense this will be new. 'The New Covenant is new not in the sense that it introduces a new moral and religious code, but that it confers a new and inward power of fulfilling the code already given.'[10] Jeremiah is thus concerned entirely with the way in which Israel will enter into the covenant. The foundations of the covenant remains unaltered: 'I will be their God, and they shall be my people', but in former times, whether at Sinai or at a ceremony in the Temple, the formal acceptance of the covenant on behalf of the nation had not ensured that the nation would honour its requirements. Not only was the foundation of the new the same as that of the old, but its content was still in essence contained in the Ten Commandments, which were concerned with loyalty to Yahweh and right dealings between men. This too had been the burden of the teaching of all the prophets; this was the law (Heb. *Torah*= 'teaching') which Yahweh would write on the hearts of 'the house of Israel' (verse 33). The engraving on stone or the writing of a code of law in a book later to be committed to memory was not enough, only when the spirit which the code embodied was joyfully accepted as expressing a valid rule of life could the covenant be said to be established. But this implies a heart attuned to the will of God. The old Israel was constantly described as rebellious, and because it was rebellious at best only a grudging acceptance of the law could be expected. Early in his ministry Jeremiah had pleaded with his people to 'circumcise yourselves to the LORD, and take away the foreskin of your hearts' (4^4) and towards the close he had given them Yahweh's promise: 'I will give them [i.e. the exiles] a heart to know that I am the LORD' (24^7). The foundation of the new covenant is the right relationship with God into which men can enter if they turn to Him. Circumcision of the heart means the opening of the heart to God; the turning of oneself to Him. No longer will the law be obeyed as an irksome duty, but of the new Israel it will be said: 'his delight is in the law of the LORD, and on his law he meditates day and night' (Ps 1^2). 'It is from that total behaviour of a man who fully responds to the will of God, that the delight in the law of God springs in all its fullness, for that behaviour imparts to man's life the meaning and value which is ordained for it by God.'[11]

In verse 34 Jeremiah continues to describe the intimate relation

[10] A. S. Peake, 'Jeremiah', *Century Bible*, II.103.
[11] A. Weiser, *The Psalms* (ET), p. 105.

which will exist between Yahweh and His people. Already the thought of a covenant between God and a whole people has faded into the background. The relationship of which the prophet writes can only be a relationship between God and each willing individual. This is further described as 'knowing the LORD'. Jeremiah has elsewhere stated what this knowledge means; it is an insight into Yahweh's character such as had in times past been given to the prophets but which would henceforth be available to all who turn to Yahweh. '. . . let him who glories glory in this, that he understands and knows me, that I am the LORD who practise steadfast love, justice, and righteousness in the earth; for in these things I delight, says the LORD' (Jer 9^{24}).

But the intimate relationship which the new covenant implies will still be imperfect so long as the sin of man stands between himself and God, so the enunciation of the New Covenant carries with it the gracious promise: 'I will forgive their iniquity and I will remember their sin no more.'

'What then are the positive features of the religious relationship established by the New Covenant? There are three: (1) *Inwardness*—"I will put my law in their inward part"; (2) *Individualism*—"all shall know me"; (3) *Forgiveness of sins*—"their sins will I remember no more".' [12]

Psalm 130—'*Out of the Depths*'

This is the sixth of the seven penitential psalms of the early Church. It was one of Luther's favourite psalms and the source of inspiration for his hymn 'Out of the depths I cry to Thee'. An English translation by Catherine Winkworth is included in the *Methodist Hymn-book* (No. 359); this should be read alongside the psalm.

The psalm may best be understood as a personal testimony made by the psalmist in the course of public worship in the Temple, for in verses 7 and 8 he addresses words of encouragement to 'Israel', i.e. to fellow Israelites gathered with him for worship. Verses 1–6 are a recital of his past experience both of the despair engendered by sin and of the unmerited grace of God.

Like the author of Psalm 51 this psalmist also recognizes the awful quality of sin which separates man from God. The agony of separation he describes metaphorically as being in the 'depths' or deep waters (cf. Ps $69^{2, 14}$), and out of these depths he cried (past tense as in the RV not 'cry' as in the *RSV*) to God. His heartfelt prayer (verses 2–4) begins on

[12] J. Skinner, *Prophecy and Religion*, p. 329.

a pleading note in which there is also an undertone of despair (verse 2). The hopelessness of his (and not his only, but everyman's) situation is expressed in the rhetorical question which follows (verse 3). Like St Paul, the psalmist recognized that 'all have sinned and fall short of the glory of God' (Rom 3^{23}). But the conclusion is not that he is condemned, but that he may be forgiven (verse 4). Again the psalmist anticipates St Paul when he insists that God's forgiveness is to be received humbly, even with fear (reverence) and trembling. Romans 2^4 is perhaps the most illuminating commentary on this verse of the psalm: 'Or do you presume upon the riches of his kindness and forbearance and patience? Do you not know that God's kindness is meant to lead you to repentance?'

The anguish of soul which the psalmist endured before he was sure of God's gracious forgiveness is suggested by the little fragment of autobiography in verses 5 and 6. Here too all the verbs should be in the past tense:

'I waited for the LORD, my soul waited, and in his word I hoped, my soul waited for the LORD....'

The watchmen wait eagerly for the break of dawn which marks the end of their vigil, but even more eagerly the psalmist had waited upon and hoped in Yahweh.

But his anguished waiting and fervent hoping have not been in vain. God is a gracious God who has forgiven him, and now he can with confidence call on his fellow worshippers to 'hope in the LORD' with the assurance that 'He will redeem Israel from all his iniquities'.

TABLE III

From the Fall of Jerusalem to the Maccabean Revolt

Judah			*External Events*	
Fall of Jerusalem	586	*Ezekiel*		
Exile				
			Cyrus gains control of Persia	550
Some Jews return under Shesh-Bazzar	538	*Deut.–Isaiah*	Cyrus takes Babylon	539
			Death of Cyrus	530
			Cambyses	530–522
The Temple is rebuilt	520–516	*Haggai* *Zechariah*	Darius I	522–486
			Xerxes I	486–464
			Artaxerxes I	464–424
Nehemiah's first period as governor	444–432			
Nehemiah's second period as governor	429?–424?			
			Xerxes II	424–423
			Darius II	423–404
Ezra's Mission to Judah	397		Artaxerxes II	404–358
			Alexander the Great conquers Persia	333
			Death of Alexander and division of his empire	323
Judea part of Ptolemaic kingdom	323–200			
Judea part of Seleucid kingdom	200–167			
Outbreak of Maccabean revolt	167	*Book of Daniel*	Antiochus IV (Epiphanes)	175–163
Temple Rededicated	Dec. 164			

CHAPTER TEN

ISRAEL IN EXILE

I—HISTORICAL BACKGROUND—586–515 BC

THE VACILLATING policy of Zedekiah and the intrigues of his pro-Egyptian counsellors brought the Babylonian armies into Judah in about 587 BC. The country was devastated, its cities sacked and finally Jerusalem itself was taken after a siege lasting eleven months. The city was ravaged and the Temple reduced to a ruin, after the conquerors had removed everything of value from it. A further deportation of population to Babylonia, and the flight of others to Egypt (after the murder of Gedaliah) left the country, already devastated by war, almost depopulated. A pitiful remnant, eking out some sort of living, continued to bring offerings to the ruined Temple (cf. Jer 41[5]), but there must have seemed little prospect that Israel could survive this overwhelming calamity. The belief that the Temple could never be destroyed had been rudely shattered. For many the ground of their faith had been cut away.

The future, however, as Jeremiah had already realized (Jer 29), lay with the exiles, but they must be prepared for a prolonged stay in Babylonia. If there had been thoughts of a speedy return and also an attempted rebellion as Jeremiah 29[7–9, 21–3] seems to suggest, it was quickly suppressed, whilst the catastrophe of 586 BC was a clear indication of Nebuchadnezzar's grip on his empire.

Unlike the Assyrians, the Babylonians did not disperse their captives far and wide throughout their dominions but settled them in Mesopotamia, south of Babylon. The conditions of their captivity do not seem to have been very oppressive. They were able to build houses and engage in agriculture. They enjoyed a normal community life, the affairs of the community being regulated by their own elders, whilst prophets such as Ezekiel were free to minister to them.

But if the conditions of the exile were tolerable, the fact of the exile posed a theological problem. Was Yahweh powerless against the gods of Babylon that He had been forced to surrender His nation, His city, and His Temple? Or was He merely capricious and so had treated His people unfairly? (cf. Ezk 18[25]). The prophets, and particularly Jeremiah and Ezekiel, who lived through the final crisis, had already answered the very questions that the exiles were asking. The tragedy which had overtaken the nation was Yahweh's judgement, but beyond the tragedy there was hope of restoration, and on this hope the exiles could rebuild their faith.

In this situation Judaism was born. The Temple with its ritual was a thing of the past, but there were other ways in which the exiles might express their devotion to Yahweh. The prophets had accused the people of not keeping the covenant, so now there was increased attention to the law, and as outward signs of their rejection of paganism the exiles were more meticulous in the observance of the Sabbath. Circumcision, which was not practised among the Babylonians, also became a distinctive mark of the loyal Jew. During this period the records of the past would become increasingly precious and were carefully preserved. These told of the mighty deeds of Yahweh in bringing His people out of Egypt and establishing them in Canaan, and so gave the exiles ground for the hope of a similar redemption and restoration in the future.

Throughout the long reign of Nebuchadnezzar (604–562 B C) there could be little chance of change, but the Babylonian empire was his creation and on his death the decline set in rapidly. He was succeeded by his son Evil-Merodach who reigned for only two years before being assassinated. This king receives mention in 2 Kings because he released Jehoiachin from the long imprisonment he had endured under Nebuchadnezzar (2 K 25^{27-30}).

The Babylonian throne ultimately passed to Nabonidus (556–539). This monarch was a devotee of the moon god Sin and so earned the enmity of the powerful priesthood of Marduk. It seems clear that during his reign the empire was split into rival factions, and so was an easy prey for any determined conqueror. Such a conqueror was already at the frontier. Cyrus the Persian, who had been a vassal king of the Median empire, had revolted successfully in 550 B C against his Median overlord and had seized control of a vast empire which stretched from Iran in the east to Asia Minor in the west and almost encircled Babylonia. For a number of years Cyrus left Babylon in peace whilst he extended his kingdom farther eastwards into Parthia (now Afghanistan). Eventually he turned on Babylon which fell with hardly a struggle. It seems likely that many Babylonians were glad to be rid of Nabonidus and welcomed Cyrus as the liberator he claimed to be.

The Persian treatment of subject peoples presents a striking contrast to that meted out either by the Assyrians or the Babylonians. The policy of deportation, pursued by the two latter powers, was reversed and the subject peoples were permitted to return to their homelands. The decree which Cyrus made, authorizing the rebuilding of the Temple in Jerusalem (Ezra 6^{2-5}), is but one illustration of the outworking of the liberal policy of this enlightened ruler, who has been described as 'generous and benevolent', one who 'had no thought of forcing conquered countries into a single mould, but had the wisdom to leave unchanged the institutions of each kingdom he attached to his crown'.[1] It is noteworthy that State aid was made available for this work of reconstruction! Cyrus also appointed native princes as provincial governors, who would be responsible for the day-to-day administration of their own people; though as would be expected the highest posts in the imperial government were held by Persians or Medes.

Some Jews took advantage of the permission granted to them to return to Judah, and Cyrus appointed Shesh-bazzar as their governor (Ezra $1^{8, 11}$, 6^{14}). This Shesh-bazzar must have been a son of Jehoiachin (=Jeconiah) if he is the person whose name is written in 1 Chronicles 3^{18} as Shen-azzar.[2] Work was begun as soon as possible on the Temple but progress was so slow that the returned exiles soon became discouraged. The older people who could just remember the magnificence of Solomon's Temple were evidently disappointed at the very inferior building which seemed to be all that was contemplated (Ezra 3^{12}). Meanwhile Shesh-bazzar, who was probably quite old when he came from Babylon, was succeeded as governor by his nephew Zerubbabel. The foundations of the new building were completed and then all work came to a standstill. A dispute arose between the returned exiles and the people still resident in the land. The latter wished to be associated with the rebuilding of the Temple, but Zerubbabel refused the aid which they offered (Ezra 4^{1-3}). In retaliation the 'people of the land' (Samaritans) began to hinder the work of reconstruction. Life must have been anything but easy for the returned exiles. They had to make their homes as best they could in a ruined city, and then a succession of bad harvests (Hag $2^{16\,ff}$) reduced their morale to its lowest ebb. There is little wonder that the sustained opposition of the Samaritans finally brought the work to a halt.

For the next sixteen years (536–520) no further progress was made on the Temple. Meanwhile Cyrus, who died in 530 BC, had been

[1] R. Ghirshman, *Iran*, p. 133.
[2] His name also appears as 'Sanabassarus' in 1 Esdras 6^{18}.

succeeded by his son Cambyses (530–522). Cambyses had no son to succeed him, and on his death Darius, one of his officers, who was also a member of the ruling house, was chosen as king by the army. Revolts broke out in every part of the vast Persian empire so that Darius was fully occupied in restoring order during the first two years of his reign. The confusion of the times was interpreted by the prophets Haggai and Zechariah as a sign that a new era was dawning, ushering in the rule of Yahweh. Haggai certainly, and Zechariah probably, regarded Zerubbabel as the Messianic king destined to rule when the Persian empire had collapsed (cf. Hag 2^{20-3}). Haggai interpreted the misfortunes of the previous sixteen years as a sign of Yahweh's displeasure that the Temple had not been restored. In view of the re-establishment of the Davidic kingdom, which Haggai was now promising, it was more than ever necessary that the Temple be rebuilt. Urged on by the two prophets, the people again set to work on the Temple. Cyrus's decree permitting the restoration of the Temple was confirmed by Darius so the work proceeded and the Temple was completed about four years later (516 BC). Haggai's predicition of the re-establishment of the kingdom under Zerubbabel was not fulfilled. Instead Darius gained complete control over the empire and Zerubbabel fades from the picture. Whether *he* had ever entertained any hopes of ruling over a re-established Israel we do not know. It is not unlikely that some rumours of the seditious (from the Persian point of view) teaching of Haggai and Zechariah came to the notice of the Persian authorities who may then have relieved Zerubbabel of his governorship. Certainly he was not replaced by another from the line of David, and any hope that a Davidic prince would rule again in Israel died.

II—THE PROPHETS OF THE EXILE

EZEKIEL

Ezekiel received his call to the office of prophet in the year 593 BC (in the fifth year of the exile of king Jehoiachin, Ezk 1^2), when he was already an exile in Babylonia. If the 'thirtieth year' mentioned in Ezekiel 1^1 refers to the prophet's age, then he would have been born in 623 and would thus be about twenty years younger than Jeremiah. There are other possible interpretations of this verse, however, but we are probably correct in assuming that Ezekiel was twenty to thirty years younger than Jeremiah. Like his older contemporary he also witnessed the overthrow of his nation, but since he had already been deported with the first group of exiles he was spared the horrors of the final siege and destruction of Jerusalem in 586 B C. This event was the watershed of his ministry. Before 586 the burden of his proclamations was the judgement and punishment of Judah and Jerusalem; after 586 his concern was with the ones who were exiled with him. For these folk he has a message of hope and a promise of the restoration of the nation.

Ezekiel was a priest (1^3) as well as a prophet, his priestly sensibilities are revealed in his horror of becoming ceremonially defiled (4^{14}) and his acute distress at the heathen cults which were being practised in the Temple (Ch. 8). He also stands in the line of the classical prophets receiving revelations direct from Yahweh in the course of abnormal psychic states of ecstasy or trance. It was in such an abnormal state that Ezekiel received his call and in such states that he was transported in spirit to Jerusalem. Like his predecessors, Amos (cf. Amos 3^8, 7^{15}) or Jeremiah (cf. Jer 1^5), he was conscious, perhaps even more vividly than they, of a divine compulsion driving him relentlessly to proclaim, by word and symbolic action, judgement and destruction against Judah and Jerusalem. He was above all sensitive to the awe-ful majesty of Yahweh, and over against this terrible and majestic God he saw the careless and rebellious nation of Judah. As Ezekiel surveys this scene and pronounces doom on his nation all human emotions are suppressed. When the final débâcle comes, and the armies of Babylon are hammering on the gates of Jerusalem, the knowledge of the suffering which the people have brought on themselves overwhelms him. All private sorrows and calamities pale into insignificance before this national disaster. It is a measure of his sensitive nature, and of the extent of his self-identification with the sufferings of his wayward nation, that he behaves in his personal bereavement as they will be compelled to behave in their national disaster. On the day that the siege of Jerusalem was announced, Ezekiel's wife ('the delight of your eyes') died; acting under divine restraint the prophet refrained from performing the customary mourning rites, indicating that when Jerusalem ('the delight of their eyes and their heart's desire') is destroyed there will be no opportunity for mourning.

The fall of the city marks the end of the first phase of Ezekiel's ministry. For seven years he had consistently prophesied the doom of Judah; now the catastrophe had happened, but for the remnant of the nation in exile there is a message of hope. 'Ezekiel's sorrowful task as a prophet of doom is complete . . . the prophet of doom becomes predominantly a harbinger of hope and restoration.'[3] Ezekiel, the prophet of doom, appears as a harsh and forbidding person; indeed he felt that he had been specially hardened by God in order to proclaim the harsh words of judgement. 'Behold I have made your face hard against their faces, and your forehead hard against their foreheads' (Ezk 3^{8-9}). Another side of his character is revealed in his later ministry as a prophet of hope. He who had hurled his denunciations against Jerusalem and Judah now speaks words of tenderness and compassion to the bewildered exiles. They were sheep without a shepherd, because those who should have been shepherds to them (their rulers and their priests) had proved worthless, therefore God Himself would be their Shepherd, gathering the scattered remnant together and leading them back to their homeland (Ezk 34^{11-16}). But the restoration of the shattered and scattered people of God involved more than a return to their homeland. Like Jeremiah, Ezekiel realized that renewal begins with the individual. So Ezekiel echoes Jeremiah's teaching on the covenant when he promises that the exiles will receive a new heart and a new spirit (Ezk 36^{26-7}). Though the exile seems to be the grave of all Israel's hope, like the dry bones of the prophet's vision (37^{1-14}), Israel will rise and live again.

But Ezekiel was priest as well as prophet, and he realized that a restored community would need a restored Temple as a centre for worship. As an expression of his hope for the future the exiled priest drew up plans for the Temple which would rise on the scarred ruins in Jerusalem, and left detailed regulations for the Temple services.

(NOTE—The above paragraphs on Ezekiel have assumed that throughout the whole of his ministry he lived in Babylonia. Some scholars, arguing from Ezekiel's detailed knowledge of affairs in Jerusalem, think that he did not go to Babylon until after the fall of Jerusalem. These scholars reconstruct his life as follows. First he lived in Jerusalem where he uttered his earliest prophecies of doom. Some time before the final Babylonian onslaught he had removed to some town or village not far from the capital and so quickly received news of the siege and its outcome. Then he went, or was taken captive, to Babylon where he ministered to the exiles.[4] The majority of scholars, however, incline to the opinion that this reconstruction creates more difficulties than it solves.)

3 C. G. Howie, *Ezekiel and Daniel*, p. 57.

4 For further details see H. Wheeler Robinson, *Two Hebrew Prophets.*

OUTLINE OF THE BOOK OF EZEKIEL

Ch. 1–24 Prophecies of doom against Judah and Jerusalem.
Ch. 25–32 Prophecies against foreign nations.
Ch. 33–39 Messages of hope.
Ch. 40–48 The Temple of the future.

PASSAGES FOR STUDY

Ezekiel 1—*The Vision of God's Glory*

In this chapter Ezekiel endeavours to describe the overwhelming experience which was the prelude to his call to be a prophet. This vision of the glory of Yahweh was clearly so unique as to be almost indescribable, so that the reader can at best only get an impression of the transcendent scene which the prophet 'saw' in his ecstatic state. Whereas Isaiah was content to describe his rather similar experience by the bald statement that he saw 'the LORD sitting upon a throne high and lifted up' (6^2) and surrounded by the seraphim, Ezekiel attempts to describe the throne which, in his vision, was mounted on a chariot. The physical background to the vision may well have been a sudden storm 'of great violence' such as 'are apt to arise in the Euphrates valley during the cold season'.[5] In his ecstatic state the prophet saw such a storm-cloud, irradiated with flashes of lightning, but as it approached, it resolved itself into a chariot bearing the throne of Yahweh. The fact that Yahweh's throne was movable was the key feature of the vision. The destruction of the Temple (where Isaiah had 'seen' Yahweh) did not mean the defeat of Yahweh. He could go where He willed, it was His Spirit which directed the course of the chariot, and so He could visit His people in exile and call Ezekiel to be His prophet even 'in the land of the Chaldeans, by the river Chebar'.

Ezekiel 2^1–3^{14}—*The Call of Ezekiel*

The prophet falls prostrate before the awe-inspiring spectacle, then he hears a voice addressing him, 'Son of man, stand upon your feet' (2^1), so he receives his commission. Like Isaiah he is warned that his message will fall on deaf ears (3^7). The vision changes, the prophet has received his commission aurally, now it is confirmed symbolically as he eats the scroll containing the words of Yahweh. It is evident that the chariot vision, the voice and the scroll vision are all part of the same ecstatic or trance experience, for, as in a dream, scenes change rapidly in this

[5] G. A. Cooke, *Ezekiel*, pp. 9–10.

type of ecstatic experience. The details of the message which Ezekiel is to give to 'the house of Israel' are not given, but the prophet already knew how dreadful was the word which he had to speak (2^{10}).

The awe-inspiring experience of the glory of Yahweh, and the terrible nature of his message struck Ezekiel dumb. 'And I sat there overwhelmed among them seven days' (3^{15}).

Ezekiel 4^{1-17}—*Prophecy of the Siege of Jerusalem*

The prophets often accompanied their spoken messages with actions which illustrated their words (cf. 1 K $11^{30\,ff}$, 22^{11}). Ezekiel performed a number of such acts, some of which, portraying the siege of Jerusalem, are described in this chapter.

Verses 1–3, 7–8. Using a plan scratched on a clay tablet to represent the city, Ezekiel mimics the various military operations involved in the siege and capture of a city.

Verses 4–6. By this symbolism Ezekiel indicates the duration of the exile. The northern kingdom which was depopulated by the Assyrians in 721 is already in exile, Judah's exile is still in the future. Since Ezekiel can hardly have lain on his left side for 390 days we must suppose that he perhaps repeated this action each day for more than a year. The numbers are not easy to interpret and the equation of the number of days with an equal number of years of exile should not be taken too literally. The symbol, whatever the detailed interpretation of the figures, indicates a lengthy period of exile for Judah.

Verses 9–17. This is a straightforward piece of symbolism enacting the privations which the besieged population of Jerusalem will suffer.

Ezekiel 8—*Idolatry in Jerusalem*

This chapter describes another visionary experience of the prophet. After the death of Josiah in 609, idolatrous practices sprang up again in Judah. Some of these are vividly described in Ezekiel's vision. There was a pagan idol at the entrance to the Temple, but worse was to follow. In an inner chamber the prophet saw seventy elders engaged in the secret worship of various pagan deities, some of which were worshipped under the guise of animals or reptiles. In another part of the Temple precincts there were women 'weeping for Tammuz'. The latter was the god of vegetation who 'died' each summer when the vegetation withered. In this ceremony the women are mourning his 'death'. Some men were worshipping the sun (verse 16), whilst some particularly offensive ritual is clearly intended by the closing words of verse 17, though we are quite ignorant of the nature of this cult.

Ezekiel 18—*A Popular Proverb*

Ezekiel takes up a moral problem which was becoming ever more insistent as Judah tottered to her ruin. The disasters which attended the close of Zedekiah's reign were being attributed to the sins of previous generations. The popular proverb, which Jeremiah had also denounced, was the current excuse and explanation of the present distresses, and God's justice was also being called in question.

Jeremiah had said that the proverb would cease to be uttered in the ideal kingdom of the future ('in those days' Jer 31^{29}), but Ezekiel realizes that it is the present generation who must be taught that God is just and treats each individual according to his own actions. In his attempt to combat the despairing fatalism of the day Ezekiel goes to the opposite extreme in suggesting that as a man lives so he will reap a reward of good or ill; he makes no allowance for the fact that the society in which a man lives does affect him. An individual may enjoy undeserved good fortune or suffer unmerited misfortune, but this does not absolve him from responsibility for his own actions; and Ezekiel is at pains to stress this latter point in his illustration of the behaviour of grandfather, father, and son.

The chapter ends on a pleading note: 'Repent and turn away from all your transgressions. . . . For I have no pleasure in the death of anyone, says the LORD God; so turn, and live' (Ezk 18^{30-2}).

Ezekiel 34—*God the Good Shepherd*

Jerusalem had fallen; the doom which Ezekiel had so often prophesied had at last overtaken the city and the nation. Was there any hope for the remnant which had been carried off to Babylon? In an earlier vision (Ch. 11) Ezekiel had 'seen' Yahweh's chariot leave Jerusalem, he had also 'seen' the chariot in Babylonia (Ch. 1). This signified to the prophet that, although Yahweh had for the time abandoned the unworthy city, He had not forsaken His people. Chapters 34, 36, and 37 contain Ezekiel's message of hope to the exiles. Yahweh Himself will gather the scattered exiles as a shepherd gathers his flock. The kings (shepherds) had been annointed by Yahweh to shepherd His people, instead they had cared only for themselves and their own comforts and ambitions. In two passages of great tenderness and beauty Ezekiel describes God's shepherding of His people (Ezk $34^{11-16, 25-31}$).

The emphasis in verse 15 should be noted. In contrast to the careless shepherds, 'Yahweh Himself will act as the Shepherd of His people—a profound and moving thought.'[6] The personal pronouns in this verse are emphatic in the original: 'I *myself* will be the shepherd of my sheep, and *I* will make them lie down.' The description 'shepherd' was commonly used of kings and rulers in ancient times (cf. Isa 63^{11}, Ps 78^{71-2}). Then as Yahweh is the Ruler of His people so He is 'Shepherd' *par excellence* (cf. Isa 40^{11}, Jer 31^{10}, Pss 23^{1}, 80^{1}; and New Testament usage, John 10^{11}, Heb 13^{20}, 1 Pet 2^{25}, 5^{4}, Rev 7^{17}).

Ezekiel 37^{1-14}—*The Valley of Dry Bones*

The nation had been scattered; like a dismembered corpse it was dead. Was it possible that it could live again? The vision of the valley of Dry Bones came as the answer to the question. It is possible that Ezekiel had actually witnessed such a scene as he describes in verse 2 on some old battle-ground, where the desiccated bones of the slain still lay scattered about. In the vision these bones are reassembled, clothed with flesh and skin, and finally brought to life as 'breath' comes into the bodies. So it will be with the 'house of Israel', and then the pessimistic saying—'Our bones are dried up, and our hope is lost; and we are clean cut off'—will be forgotten.

DEUTERO-ISAIAH

The group of prophecies which are contained in Isaiah 40–55 are thought by the majority of Old Testament scholars to be a record of the oracles spoken by a prophet whose name is now unknown, but who, for convenience, is called 'Deutero-Isaiah' (i.e. Second Isaiah). The two main themes of these chapters are (*a*) the triumphal return of the exiles to their homeland after wreaking vengeance on their captors, (*b*) an exposition of the mission of the renewed Israel, which was to proclaim the salvation of Yahweh to the Gentiles. These chapters relate to the years shortly prior to, and immediately following, the fall of Babylon to the Persians in 539 B C.

We have seen that in the case of Ezekiel the fall of Jerusalem in 586 marked a turning-point in his prophetic career. Prior to 586 his message was one of judgement and doom on the sinful nation and city, after that date he speaks words of hope to the exiles. There is similarly a critical date in the ministry of Deutero-Isaiah, the capture of Babylon by Cyrus in 539. Prior to that date the prophet had

6 G. A. Cooke, *Ezekiel*, p. 375.

confidently declared that Cyrus would destroy Babylon and that in consequence the exiles would return in glorious triumph to Jerusalem. Cyrus indeed captured Babylon, but he did not destroy the city, which seems to have welcomed him as the one who had delivered the Babylonian empire from the unpopular and ineffective government of Nabonidus. On his part Cyrus gave thanks to the Babylonian deities, Bel and Marduk, for his victory. He also gave the exiles permission to return to their homeland, but quite clearly there was to be no triumphal procession across the desert to Jerusalem; nor was there any question of exulting over the discomfiture of their former captors. In this situation the prophet came to realize that it was not Yahweh's purpose that Israel should gloat in triumph over the Gentiles, but rather that to them also should His Law be given. When the covenant is re-established the Gentiles will be included in its scope (Isa 55^{5}). This part of Deutero-Isaiah's message culminates in four poems which are usually called 'The Servant Songs'; they are Isa 42^{1-4}, 49^{1-6}, 50^{4-9}, 52^{13}–53^{12}.

It is probable that Deutero-Isaiah recited his message in the form of short poems. It has been suggested that he addressed gatherings of the exiles on days of public lamentation, possibly in the synagogues.[7] Whether the prophet himself subsequently wrote down his oracles, or whether this was done by his disciples we do not know. They were eventually collected together and published in their present form by a disciple. The oracles are not arranged chronologically; poems promising vengeance on the Babylonians and the triumphant return to Judah stand side-by-side with the later ones which portray Israel as Yahweh's preacher of the Law to the Gentiles. This intermingling of the earlier, narrowly nationalistic poems with the later ones which show a concern for the Gentiles was probably deliberate. The later poems correct the teaching of the earlier ones. Thus by placing the first Servant Song (42^{1-4}) immediately after a poem describing the victorious progress of Cyrus ($41^{25\,\mathrm{ff}}$), the compiler intended to draw a contrast between the true Servant of Yahweh and Cyrus, who had at one time been called the servant of Yahweh. Unlike Cyrus, who had in any case not fulfilled the prophet's hopes, and who had imposed his rule upon a vast empire by military conquest, the Servant would bring the rule of Yahweh to the same distant regions ('the coastlands'—i.e. the kingdom of Lydia in Asia Minor) by peaceful persuasion. (Contrast Isa 41^{25} with 42^{2-4}.)

[7] J. Lindblom, *Prophecy in Ancient Israel*, p. 270.

Both the earlier and the later teaching of the prophet sprang from the same basic conviction that Yahweh had a plan for His people and that He was able to carry it through. The fact that Yahweh's people were in exile must have tempted many of them to believe that the Babylonian deities were all-powerful, in spite of the teaching of the earlier prophets that the exile was Yahweh's judgement on the nation (cf. Isa 42^{24-5}). Yahweh was only the God of a small nation and small country; could He be a match for the powerful gods of the great empire which had overwhelmed them? Against this background of scepticism and despair Deutero-Isaiah drew his 'portrait' of Yahweh, the Sovereign Lord not only of Babylon, but of all the nations and all nature.

The prophet used at least twelve names to describe the character and work of Yahweh. Foremost was the one which his eighth-century predecessor Isaiah had already used to express the awe-inspiring sovereignty of God: 'The Holy One of Israel', in whose presence Isaiah had become aware of his own sinfulness. Deutero-Isaiah constantly reminded the exiles that Yahweh was this same supreme and exalted God before whom the Babylonian gods appeared in their true light as 'vanity' (empty). Another favourite name is 'Redeemer'. In ancient society the duty of 'redeemer' devolved on the nearest kinsman of anyone in distress. If a person had been enslaved, say for debt, his 'redeemer' must pay for his release, or if he suffered injury or death the 'redeemer' must avenge him. Other titles which the prophet used to emphasize the contrast between Yahweh and the pagan gods were: 'The Everlasting God', 'the First and the Last', and the curious phrase 'I am He' (41^{4}, $43^{10, 13, 25}$, 48^{12}). This latter phrase seems to express 'the thought that Yahweh' is 'the only, living and active God'.[8] Closely allied with the name 'Redeemer' is the name 'Saviour' which Deutero-Isaiah used occasionally.

As evidence of the superiority and power of Yahweh, the prophet referred to His past activity in creation and history. Yahweh was Lord of nature and of history. The heavens were stretched out by Him (40^{22}), and the stars called forth night by night (40^{26}); the earth and all its inhabitants owed their origin to Him (42^{5}, $45^{7, 12}$, $51^{13, 16}$), Yahweh's deliverance of His people from Egypt was for the prophet a sufficient guarantee of His ability to lead them back from Babylon (43^{16-21}, 51^{10-11}). Thus in addition to the names already mentioned Deutero-Isaiah also describes Yahweh as 'Creator' (40^{28}, 43^{15}), 'King

[8] Ibid., p. 380.

of Jacob' or Israel (41^{21}, 43^{15}, 44^{6}), 'Lord of Hosts' (44^{6}, 45^{13}, 47^{4}, 48^{2}, 54^{5}), 'the Rock' (44^{8}), and the 'Mighty One of Jacob' (49^{26}).

In contrast to this magnificent portrayal of Yahweh, the Omnipotent Redeemer, the prophet drew a scathing caricature of the idols worshipped by the heathen (40^{19-20}, 44^{9-20}, $46^{1-2, 5-7}$). In 46^{1-2} the prophet may have had in mind the Babylonian New Year festival when the idols were carried in procession through the streets of the city on beasts of burden; or there may be an allusion to the occasion when Nabonidus sought to protect the gods from the advancing Persians by removing them from the suburbs to places of safety within Babylon!

PASSAGES FOR STUDY

(a) *Passages promising the homecoming of the Exiles in triumph*

Isaiah 40^{1-11}—*'Good Tidings of Great Joy'*

This passage is made up of four short poems by which the prophet introduces his message of comfort and hope.

Verses 1–2. In this poem the prophet receives his commission to announce to the exiles that their period of captivity is drawing to an end. In verse 2, Jerusalem should probably be understood to represent the exiled citizens of Jerusalem who will shortly be returning to rebuild the ruined city. Instead of 'warfare' the alternative rendering 'time of service' is to be preferred; the exiles were not conscripts for military service, but presumably they had to perform some form of labour for the Babylonians. It is this time of forced labour which is coming to an end.

Verses 3–5. The prophet pictures a great triumphal procession of the exiles marching back to Jerusalem, a procession which would contrast vividly with the weary column of captives who had been brought across the desert by the Babylonians a generation earlier. There is perhaps also some memory of the hardships of that former journey in these verses, for a smooth and easy road is to be prepared for the return of the exiles. It is not clear who is being urged to prepare the way, but as the prophet subsequently names Cyrus as the one appointed by Yahweh to effect the restoration of Israel to her homeland, perhaps here too Cyrus is the one to whom the voice is crying.

Verses 6–8. This poem is a message of encouragement to those who doubted if the exile would ever come to an end. The transience and fallibility of mankind is contrasted with the omnipotence and eternity of Yahweh. His purpose will not be frustrated either by the might of Babylon or by the hesitation and scepticism of the exiles.

Verses 9–11. With the eye of faith the prophet already sees the triumphant procession heading for the homeland. In a remarkable figure of speech he bids Jerusalem, like a royal herald, announce to the other cities that the procession is approaching. A generation earlier Ezekiel had described his vision in which he saw Yahweh forsaking the rebellious city and nation; now the same city is bidden to raise the cry: 'Behold, your God.'

Though the scene is one of triumph, there is solicitude for those who have suffered the burden of captivity, for this same Yahweh, who is depicted as going in triumph at the head of His people, is also the Good Shepherd who is concerned for the welfare of them all, great or small, strong or weak (verse 11).

Isaiah 40^{12-31}—*'The Lord Omnipotent Reigneth'*

The prophet now turns aside to justify his own confidence in Yahweh. His power has been made manifest in creation and in history. In his description of Yahweh the Creator, the prophet surveys the whole of the then-known universe. The heavens and the earth are the theatre of His activity, nations rise and fall at His behest (verses 22–4), beside Him idols are objects of derision (verses 18–20).

Isaiah 42^{18}—43^{13}—*'I have redeemed you'*

In this poem the prophet contrasts the punishment which Israel has received with the glorious restoration which is shortly to take place. Israel is bidden to look and listen and interpret the signs of the times, but being blind and deaf she was unable to understand the meaning of the exile (cf. Isa 6^{10}). Though Babylon was a spoiler and robber (42^{24}), it was by Yahweh's permission, and now the time is ripe for Him to restore His people. This restoration is to be effected by the triumphs of Cyrus; by his conquests Yahweh's people will be returned from the regions whither they had been scattered (43^{5-6}), whilst Cyrus will receive territories as a ransom for Israel (43^{3}). But in all these troubles Israel will be unscathed (43^{2}). The poem closes with another affirmation of the omnipotence of Yahweh (43^{10-13}).

Isaiah 44^{9-20}—*What is an idol?*

This passage is very straightforward. The temptation to worship the apparently all-powerful gods of Babylonia must at times have been very strong. On the positive side the prophet stresses the omnipotence of Yahweh, and negatively he pours scorn on idol worship. In these verses 'the prophet lashes idolatry with satire in which there is a subtle mixture of ridicule and argument'.[9]

Isaiah 44^{23-8}, 45^{1-8}—*Cyrus*

In these two poems the prophet names Cyrus as Yahweh's instrument in the restoration of Israel, though the conqueror himself is unaware of the part he is playing (45^4). The prophet clearly hoped much from Cyrus, but again in these poems we are aware that the ultimate ground of his hope is his trust in Yahweh, whose love for Israel ($44^{23, 26}$, 45^4) is matched by His omnipotence. This trust in Yahweh will enable the prophet to proclaim a yet deeper message to the exiles when his hope in Cyrus has proved to be displaced.

(*b*) *The Servant of the* LORD

We have already suggested that the failure of Cyrus to send the Jews back to Palestine in triumph, and his acknowledgement of the gods of Babylon presented a serious problem to the prophet. He found the solution in a deeper concept of Yahweh's purpose. It was not enough, perhaps not even necessary, that Israel should return in triumph, gloating over the downfall of her one-time masters; on the contrary the Gentiles are waiting for Yahweh's law (*torah*=teaching). But who was to 'establish Yahweh's justice in the earth' and proclaim His law to the waiting 'coastlands' (42^4)?

There are a few passages in the prophecy (e.g. 42^{5-9} esp. verse 6) which suggest that the prophet may have entertained the hope that Israel would undertake this missionary task. But it must soon have become evident that his vision of a mission to the Gentiles was shared neither by the Jews who had taken advantage of the decree of Cyrus to return to their homeland, nor by those who remained in Babylon. On the one hand life in Babylon under the enlightened monarch Cyrus was probably quite comfortable; on the other hand the magnitude of the task of reconstruction facing the ones who had returned to Jerusalem soon filled them with despair. The prophet's earlier promises of a triumphal and glorious return to Jerusalem had proved to be exaggerated if not false; it is not surprising if his later teaching went unheeded. Any hope which the prophet may have entertained, that Israel would serve Yahweh by teaching His law to the Gentiles,

9 O. C. Whitehouse, 'Isaiah', *Century Bible*, II.108.

must soon have faded away, but his conviction remained unshaken that it was Yahweh's will that they should be taught.

By whom then was this mission to be undertaken? The prophet gives his answer in the poems which describe the character, work, and passion of the 'Servant of Yahweh'. Who was this Servant? Various attempts have been made to identify him, the following are a few of the suggestions which have been put forward: Israel, Moses, Jeremiah, Deutero-Isaiah, and even Zerubbabel. If the prophet were writing of Israel in these poems then it could hardly be the Israel he knew. The Israel of his experience had already refused to accept Yahweh's mission, so we must suppose that he was thinking either of a remnant within Israel, faithful to Yahweh and zealous to do His work, or else an ideal Israel of the future. Of the individuals who have been identified with the Servant, it is sufficient to note that although certain features in the prophet's description seem to fit them, there are others which do not. Furthermore, individuals such as Moses or Jeremiah, who were already dead when these poems were composed, could hardly be intended by Deutero-Isaiah, since he was describing, in the first poem, someone whose work lay in the future.

It seems probable that the prophet was describing an ideal Servant of Yahweh, be he an individual or a renewed Israel, who had yet to appear on the plane of history. That some features of his description recall the lives and work of the great prophets of the past need not surprise us. For as Deutero-Isaiah pondered the lives and even the apparent failure of the mission and ministry of his predecessors; as he brooded on the meaning of their sufferings and persecution, so there formed in his mind the picture of a 'Servant', who, like the earlier prophets, was destined to a life of failure and suffering, and the cost of whose mission would be death; but this final disaster would be the prelude to ultimate victory. It is likely that Deutero-Isaiah himself may have suffered persecution at the hands of his fellow countrymen when they realized that the promise of a glorious return to Jerusalem was to remain unfulfilled. This experience too will have helped to fill out the picture which he was drawing. Also the idea of vicarious suffering was not unknown in the Ancient Near East. During the annual New Year Festival the Babylonian king was publicly humiliated in front of the god and struck by the high priest. This symbolic suffering was understood to be endured for the welfare of the nation. His own experience, his knowledge of the life and sufferings of his predecessors, even his acquaintance with a pagan ritual were the ore which was fed into the crucible of the poet's mind. Under divine inspiration these experiences and ideas were fused and refined so that there emerged this portrait of the unique Servant of Yahweh.

Isaiah 42^{1-4}—'*Behold My Servant*'

The Servant is introduced in this first poem, and his character and mission are briefly sketched in. The speaker is Yahweh; He presents His Servant to the prophet,[10] as one who is specially endowed for the mission which he is to undertake. 'I will put my Spirit upon him' (verse 1). When the Spirit of Yahweh came upon a man he was enabled to perform extraordinary feats; the meaning here is that the Servant will receive all the equipment (physical, mental, and spiritual) necessary for the carrying out of his task of bringing justice and the knowledge of Yahweh to the Gentiles. Though the Servant has full power to carry out his mission, this power is not to be exercised in an oppressive or tyrannical manner. 'The normal way by which a new religion was propagated was by conquest; the gods of the conqueror became those of the vanquished.'[11] But the way of military conquest, with shouting and tumult (verse 2) and oppression of the helpless (verse 3) is not the way of the Servant. Though he eschews the way of military conquest, the Servant will persevere, undismayed by the magnitude of his task, until in the end Yahweh's purpose is accomplished (verse 4).

Isaiah 49^{1-6}—*The Servant's Preparation*

In this poem the Servant himself is the speaker. Verse 1 reminds us of Jeremiah's claim that he had been called to his prophetic task even before he was born (Jer 1^5). There is a period of preparation and then the Servant is ready for his work, like a sharp sword grasped by the hand that will wield it, or a polished arrow still hidden in the quiver but ready for instant service (verse 2). Yahweh Himself will be glorified through the work which the Servant will accomplish. In the past the prophets have ministered to Israel, and they seem to have laboured in vain. Verse 4 suggests that this also will be the experience of the Servant, but this failure is to open the way to a larger success, for Yahweh is calling him to enlarge the area of his mission. 'I will give you as a

10 Cf. J. Lindblom, *The Servant Songs.* Other scholars suggest that the scene of this first poem is Yahweh's heavenly court and that He is presenting His Servant to the court; cf. C. R. North, *The Suffering Servant*, p. 142.

11 E. J. Kissane, *The Book of Isaiah*, II.36.

light to the nations, that my salvation may reach to the end of the earth' (verse 6).

The occurrence of the name 'Israel' in verse 3 presents some difficulty. This verse appears to identify the Servant with Israel, whereas verses 5 and 6 speak of the restoration of Israel as a part of the work of the Servant, who in this case can hardly be the people of Israel. C. R. North translates the verse:

> 'And he said to me, my Servant art thou,
> Thou Israel by whom I will get myself glory.'

and he comments: 'The writer seems to say that here in the Servant is the true Israel found.' [12]

Isaiah 50^{4-9}—'*Despised*'

In this poem we are permitted to overhear the Servant as he reflects on the course of his mission. He is conscious that he has been equipped by Yahweh for his task, and that he receives instructions from Him daily as he waits upon Him. Nevertheless his efforts appear to be doomed to failure; he has encountered hostility and persecution, and has been the victim of physical violence (verse 6). He is utterly alone, with no one to befriend or help him, but in this extremity he is sure of One who will vindicate him. Buoyed up with this confidence in 'the Lord God' who 'helps' him (verses 7–9) he steels himself to continue his mission, 'Therefore I have set my face like flint' (verse 7).

Isaiah 52^{13}–53^{12}—'*Man of Sorrows*'

The cycle of Servant poems reaches its climax in this final poem. In the first one Yahweh introduces His Servant, in the second and third poems the Servant speaks for himself, but here we are invited to look upon a spectacle of terrible suffering, punishment and death, and to reflect upon its meaning and purpose. The sensitive reader cannot fail but be impressed by the mysterious and almost eerie quality of these verses. 'Most wonderful and mysterious of all is the spectral fashion in which the prophecy presents its Hero. He is named only in the first line and once again; elsewhere He is spoken of as He. We never hear or see Himself. But all the more solemnly He is there: a shadow upon countless faces, a grievous memory in the hearts of the speakers. He so haunts all we see and all we hear, that we feel it is not Art but Conscience, that speaks of Him.' [13]

[12] *The Suffering Servant*, pp. 118, 145.

[13] G. A. Smith, *Isaiah*, II.341.

Throughout the poem the Servant remains silent; the speakers are Yahweh, whose solemn declarations (52^{13-15}, 53^{11-12}) open and close the poem, and the Gentiles who have at length come to understand the true meaning of the Servant's sufferings (53^{1-10}).

The Servant has already been put to death (verses 8–9), and in the opening words Yahweh alludes to his coming exaltation. Those who had been appalled ('astonished', 52^{14}) and repelled by his loathsome appearance will be amazed by this unexpected turn of events. Thus the Gentiles are led to reflect on the mystery of the exaltation of the one-time despised sufferer. Their amazement is evident in the rhetorical questions which stand at the head of the central section of the poem (53^{1}); it seemed impossible that the sufferer in their midst, who had been the object of their contempt (verses 2–3), should be the recipient of Yahweh's special care and protection. 'And the arm of Yahweh—over whom hath it been revealed?' (53^{1}).[14]

But now the meaning of the suffering becomes clear. The Servant has borne it all, not as a punishment for his own transgressions and iniquities, but on behalf of those who had despised and shamefully used him. This they recognize in their solemn confession:

> 'Surely *he* has borne our griefs
> and carried our sorrows.
> Yet *we* esteemed him stricken
> smitten by God and afflicted.'

The pronouns 'he' and 'we' are emphatic in the original. His imprisonment, judgement, and execution are now seen to be part of this same pattern of vicarious suffering, in which 'he was stricken for the transgression of my people' (53^{8}). This is Yahweh's grand strategem ensuring the ultimate victory of His will, which is to make many righteous (verse 11).

This interpretation which the Gentiles now place on the suffering of the Servant is confirmed in the closing verses (53^{11-12}) by Yahweh Himself. The ultimate triumph of the Servant is also promised; the despised one 'shall divide the spoil with the strong' (53^{12}), i.e. 'The Servant is to be given the status of a king'.[15] But the Servant's triumph is not the last thought which the poet wishes to leave with us; so he returns at the end to his main theme of the mystery of vicarious suffering:

[14] C. R. North, *The Suffering Servant*, p. 121.
[15] E. J. Kissane, *The Book of Isaiah*, II.191.

'He bore the sin of many,
and made intercession for the transgressors.'

Psalm 22—*'Why hast Thou forsaken me?'*

This is the first and greatest of six psalms (22, 35, 41, 55, 69, 109) which have been called the Passion Psalms, and which must always recall to us the Passion of our Lord. According to Mark's account of the crucifixion the opening words of the psalm were the last words to be uttered by Jesus before His death (Mk 15^{33-7}), and it is probable that He had meditated deeply on the whole psalm during the hours of His agony.

The psalm falls into two clearly defined sections. The first part (verses 1–21) consists of lamentations and supplications. In the second part the psalmist praises God and gives thanks to Him for his deliverance.

(*a*) Verses 1–21—*The Lament*

The psalmist has suffered greatly though we are only given oblique hints of the cause of the suffering. He has been mocked and despised by his fellow men (verses 6–7), but worst of all he feels to be forsaken by God. His suffering has brought him 'to the brink of the grave and reduced him to utter despair'.[16] The tension between despair and faith is very marked in this lament. The psalmist's intense suffering induces a mood of such hopelessness that he fears that, not only is he deserted by men, but also by God Himself (verses 1–2). Then as he remembers God's dealings with Israel, and as he recalls that 'our fathers trusted and were saved' (verses 4–5), so his own faith begins to revive.

Further contemplation of his own unhappy situation, however, arouses his doubts and fears again (verses 6–8). But these begin to be allayed as he reflects now on God's care of himself since his birth, and so he prays for God's continuing succour in his present distress (verses 9–11).

The mood of hopelessness and despair returns yet again; his enemies are too strong for him. They are likened to 'strong bulls', 'ravening lions', or 'dogs' whose presence invokes in him 'the helpless fear which overcomes him at the sight of them and makes him tremble'.[17] The physical accompaniment of these strong emotions are vividly described in verses 14–15. This section of the psalm closes with a despairing plea

16 A. Weiser, *The Psalms*, p. 219. 17 Ibid., p. 223.

to Yahweh to save his life; he had already lost everything else (verses 17–18). This psalm is noteworthy in that the sufferer does not seek vengeance on his enemies (contrast Ps $69^{22\,ff}$, 109^{6-20}, 35).

(*b*) Verses 22–31—*Praise and Thanksgiving*

Verses 22 and 25 suggest that the psalm, which closes with a paean of praise to Yahweh, was composed for use in public worship. In the lament (verses 1–21) the psalmist recalls his sufferings, and the despair and doubt which they had engendered. In spite of his buffetings he had clung desperately to Yahweh, and now he knows that his trust had not been misplaced. He cannot sufficiently praise the God who has heard the afflicted when he cried to him (verse 24).

The psalmist calls first on those who fear Yahweh to praise Him, then he summons 'all you sons of Jacob' ('his adversaries, too, are probably included in 'all you children of Israel') [18] to add their praise. Still the volume of praise is not enough; not only the psalmist; not only his friends; not only all Israel; but 'all the ends of the earth shall remember and turn to the LORD' (verse 27). Even this chorus of praise is too small! As Yahweh's dominion embraces all nations (verse 28) and all generations, so generations past (verse 29) and future (verses 30–1) as well as present will do homage to Him.

Thus this psalm, which opens on a note of acutest despair and Godforsakenness, ends with a shout of triumph. The stark horror of Good Friday ends in the triumph of Easter Day. 'Guided by this psalm, he (Jesus) entered upon the way which led him through his most bitter Passion, but ended in the triumph of faith and in the victory of the kingdom of God.' [19]

[18] A. Weiser, *The Psalms*, p. 225. [19] Ibid., p. 226.

TABLE IV

Nehemiah and the Samaritans

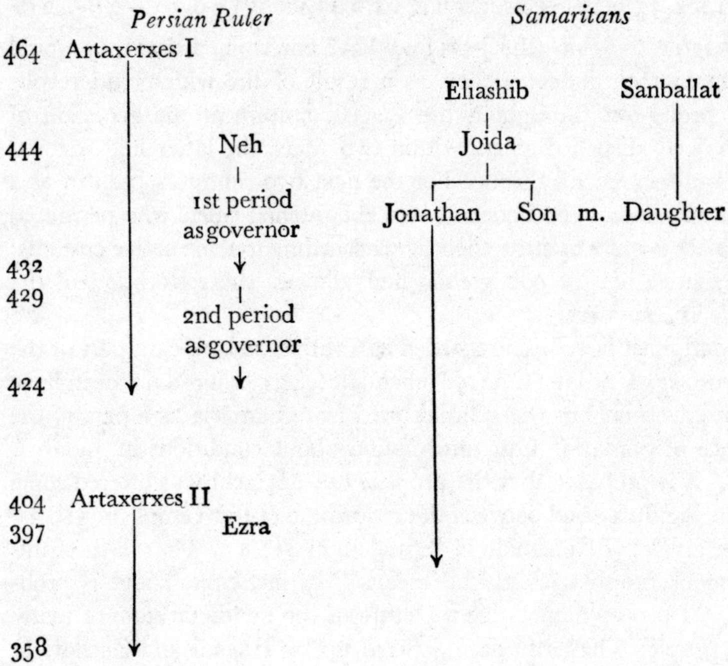

CHAPTER ELEVEN

FROM THE REBUILDING OF THE TEMPLE TO THE MACCABEAN REVOLT

I—THE JEWS UNDER THE PERSIANS 520 BC–385 BC

ANY HOPES which the Jews may have entertained that they would regain their independence, as a result of the widespread revolts which broke out throughout the Persian empire at the accession of Darius, were dispelled when, within two years, the latter had restored order and secured his throne. For the next two centuries Judah was a Persian province. The Persians were enlightened rulers who permitted the subject peoples to order their lives according to their native customs; in pursuance of this policy they had allowed the restoration of the Temple in Jerusalem.

Judah must have been regarded as a rather insignificant part of the great empire. Until the time of Nehemiah (444 BC) it did not even have its own governor, but was administered from Samaria as a part of the Province of Samaria. Our information about conditions in Judah is scanty. It is probable that the prophecy of Malachi was uttered some time during the period between the restoration of the Temple in 516 BC and the arrival of Nehemiah in Jerusalem in 444 BC. The words of this anonymous prophet ('Malachi' means 'My messenger', and is probably not a proper name) give a picture of the apathetic state of many of the people. The enthusiasm, stirred up by Haggai and Zechariah, which had encouraged the people to finish the work of restoring the Temple, had evaporated. A new generation had grown up and were living either in the still partly ruined city of Jerusalem, or elsewhere in the small and impoverished land, which was all that was left of the former kingdom of Judah.

Whilst the Persian rule was free from the harshness and cruelty so characteristic of the Assyrian, nevertheless the subject people were heavily taxed so that a state of hopeless despair seems to have settled on the small community. No longer were they buoyed up by the thought that they were God's people, rather they were in grave danger of losing their identity and of being assimilated to the surrounding people. With the disappearance of Zerubbabel, authority and leadership passed to Joshua the high priest, but the priests of this later generation, who should have inspired and led the people, were perfunctory in the performance of their duties. The spiritual bankruptcy of the time is reflected in the attitude of the priests who accepted, contrary to the prescriptions of the Law, imperfect and maimed animals for the sacrifices; the second best was good enough for God! It is also reflected in their failure to instruct the people in the way of the LORD (Mal 2^{7-9}), and finally in the frivolous manner in which they were divorcing their Jewish wives in order to marry women of foreign extraction.

The Books of Ezra and Nehemiah, which are a continuation of 1 and 2 Chronicles, give some information of the happenings in Jerusalem in the fifth century B C. Not all the Jews merited Malachi's strictures; there were some who, in spite of great discouragement, endeavoured to carry on with the work of rebuilding the city. In this they were hindered at every turn by 'the people of the land' (Ezra 4^{4}). In this verse these 'people' are mentioned in connection with the restoration of the Temple, but succeeding verses make it clear that hindrance from this quarter persisted for many decades. Who were these 'people of the land'? Ezra 4^{2} shows that they were people of mixed blood, descendants of the folk brought into Samaria by the Assyrians after the fall of the northern kingdom and the deportation of the Israelites in 721 B C. These people claimed to be worshippers of Yahweh, but were not recognized as such by the returned exiles. The descendants of these 'people of the land' were the Samaritans, who subsquently built a rival temple on Mount Gerizim (cf. Jn 4^{20}, where 'this mountain' is Mount Gerizim). The enmity between Jew and Samaritan dates from the time of the return of the exiles to Jerusalem.

Darius I had permitted the restoration of the Temple, and this was completed in 516 B C, and since this ruler was favourably disposed towards the Jews it is probable that some progress was made in the rebuilding of the ruined city. The accession of Xerxes I in 485 B C gave the Samaritans an opportunity to hinder the work; a suggestion that the Jews were rebuilding and refortifying the city could be interpreted as implying that they were preparing to rebel against the Persians. Whatever the precise charge the Samaritans brought against the Jews (Ezra 4^{6}), it seems to have been effective in getting the work stopped, as no further mention of rebuilding is made until the reign of Artaxerxes I (464–424 B C). At some time during the first twenty years of the latter's reign the Jews recommenced the building operations which had been halted by Xerxes. Once again the Samaritans intervened by suggesting in a despatch to Artaxerxes that the Jews intended rebellion

(Ezra 4[11–16]). Artaxerxes in reply gave the Samaritans authority to stop all further building work. In fact they so far exceeded their mandate that they also destroyed some of the work that had been completed, so that when, in due course, word was brought to Nehemiah of affairs in Jerusalem he learnt that 'the wall of Jerusalem is broken down, and its gates are destroyed by fire' (Neh. 1[3]). This verse can hardly refer to Nebuchadnezzar's destruction of the city in 586 B C—that event was history, not news! It must refer to the recent rebuilding and subsequent destruction of the walls and gates.

NEHEMIAH

Artaxerxes had already been on the throne for twenty years when news of the plight of Jerusalem and its inhabitants came to the ears of one who might be able to help. Nehemiah, the Jew, served as cup-bearer (butler) to the king, and so occasionally had access to him. He seems not to have been chief butler or he would hardly have had to wait three months before meeting the king in the course of his duties. Hanani, Nehemiah's brother, brought the visitors from Jerusalem to meet Nehemiah in the month Chislev (November–December; Neh 1[2]), but the latter did not see the king until sometime in the month of Nisan (March–April). Nehemiah must have stood high in the favour of the king, for when he recounted to him the news he had received, and had expressed his own concern at the plight of Jerusalem and its inhabitants, he was granted leave of absence to visit the city, and was appointed governor of the province of Judah with authority to restore Jerusalem.

Nehemiah's appointment as governor of Judah soon brought him into conflict with Sanballat, governor of Samaria. The existence of a governor in Jerusalem with the oversight of Judah meant a diminution in Sanballat's authority, since he had now lost control over Judah. It is not improbable that it had been a deliberate part of Samaritan policy to prevent the re-establishment of Jerusalem as a centre of Jewish culture and religious life. Certainly Nehemiah expected opposition, for he made his initial survey of the city by night. Then, having discovered the extent of the damage, he encouraged the citizens to repair the wall as speedily as possible. Sanballat and his supporters, Tobiah and Geshem, tried to stop the work by intimidation, and by the threat of an armed attack on the city, but such was Nehemiah's confidence and resourcefulness (Neh 4) that the wall was completely restored in fifty-two days (Neh 6[15]).

Though Nehemiah had successfully foiled Sanballat's attempt to prevent the rebuilding of the wall, he had made a dangerous enemy who would stop at nothing to get rid of him. Even while the work was in progress he had tried to lure Nehemiah to a meeting 'in the plain of Ono' (Neh 6^2), about twelve miles north of Jerusalem, presumably under the pretext of coming to some amicable arrangement, but actually to get rid of him. When this plot failed, Sanballat sent a message to Nehemiah saying that it was being rumoured that he intended to make himself king over Judah. On the face of it this message was a friendly warning that Nehemiah should take care lest such rumours reached the ear of Artaxerxes. In fact it was a scarcely veiled threat that Sanballat himself would make sure that the rumours, of which he was undoubtedly the author, did reach Artaxerxes and so discredit Nehemiah with the Persian government. But Nehemiah refused to be intimidated. Having thus failed either to capture or intimidate him, his enemies tried to discredit Nehemiah with his own people.

They paid a certain Shemaiah to warn Nehemiah that there was a plot to assassinate him on a certain night. Shemaiah then suggested that Nehemiah should hide himself in the Holy of Holies, but he contemptuously repudiated this advice that he should skulk away like a coward. Unfortunately Nehemiah also had enemies among the nobility of Judah, some of whom were bound by ties of marriage to Tobiah and who regularly reported to him any details of Nehemiah's plans which they managed to discover.

When the rebuilding of the walls was completed Nehemiah was able to turn his mind to other problems. The walls and gates would provide no real defence unless they were properly manned, so Nehemiah entrusted the defence of the city to his brother Hanani and to one of his officers Hananiah. These two recruited citizens to do regular sentry duty on the walls and at the gates, the latter being closed at night (Neh 7^{1-3}).

The derelict state of the city posed another problem. Many of the houses were still in ruins and consequently the population of the city was small, too small for the city to serve worthily as the religious and administrative centre of the province of Judah. The few who lived in the city belonged to the upper classes (11^1), and had presumably been able to build comfortable residences for themselves. But as some of these were in league with Tobiah and so of more than doubtful loyalty to Nehemiah, the latter was anxious to repopulate the city. To do this he adopted the drastic plan of choosing by lot one-tenth of the rest of the people to take up residence in Jerusalem. In addition some others volunteered to move into the city (Neh 11^{2}).

The failure of the Jewish community to organize themselves effectively before Nehemiah became governor is reflected in their failure to provide adequately for the maintenance of the Temple and its staff. This was rectified when Nehemiah appointed officials to ensure that the sacrificial offerings were supplied, and to gather in the prescribed dues for the priests and Levites (Neh 12^{44}).

A time of famine, possibly towards the end of Nehemiah's first period as governor (Neh 5^{14}), caused a crisis in the province and also brought to light serious social abuses. The poorer peasants were unable to provide enough food for their families, and the taxes demanded by the Persians were proving grievous to be borne. In desperation they were driven to selling or mortgaging their land, or to borrowing from their wealthier neighbours, or even to selling their children into slavery. The age-old evil of the wealthy taking advantage of the distresses of the needy (so roundly condemned by Amos and Isaiah) had reared its ugly head again. The desperate situation called for vigorous action, and Nehemiah proved himself equal to the needs of the hour. Since he himself, in order to help his countrymen, had not exacted the dues to which he was entitled as governor, but rather had redeemed, out of his own pocket, some who were enslaved, and had provided regularly for 150 poor Judeans, his anger against the unscrupulous wealthy was all the more severe. Although his suggestion to them (Neh 5^{11}) to restore the property which they had acquired seems to be but a polite request, it was in reality an order which he intended to enforce (cf. Neh 5^{12}).

Nehemiah's first period as governor of Judah ended in 432 B C (the thirty-second year of Artaxerxes I), and he returned to the Persian court. He had been granted leave of absence for 'a time' (Neh 2^{6}), and that time had presumably expired. Now various happenings, which would not have been tolerated while Nehemiah was in control, were permitted. The high priest Eliashib, who was evidently one of those who had maintained a friendly relationship with Nehemiah's enemy Tobiah, was emboldened to prepare a special room in the Temple court for Tobiah's use. The Levites no longer received their dues and were forced to leave Jerusalem to seek agricultural work in the country. Trade and secular employment were openly followed on the Sabbath; intermarriage with the surrounding population had increased enormously. The period, over which this decline from the strict code of behaviour enforced by Nehemiah took place, must have been a few years, time enough for the children of mixed marriages to have learnt how to talk (Neh 13[23–4]). Eventually news of the state of affairs in Judah reached Nehemiah and he sought, and was granted, permission to return to Jerusalem. On arriving in the city he set a reform on foot. Tobiah was turned out of the Temple, tithes were exacted for the Levites, all work on the Sabbath was strictly prohibited and measures taken to keep all traders out of the city on that day. Mixed marriages were proscribed, and a grandson of Eliashib who had married a daughter of Sanballat was expelled from the city.

No other details are given of Nehemiah's second period as governor, nor do we know how long it lasted though it may well have been terminated on the death of his patron Artaxerxes.

EZRA

We know nothing of the events in Judah during the last quarter of the fifth century BC. Papyri discovered at Elephantine, an island on the Nile opposite Assuan, which had been a Jewish colony long before the Persian conquest, and was a Persian military outpost after the conquest of Egypt, name a certain Bagoas as governor of Judah. One of these papyrus documents, a copy of a letter to Bagoas, bears the date 407 BC (according to our reckoning) and its contents show that Bagoas had already been governor for some years.

In 397 BC, i.e. the seventh year of Artaxerxes II, a Jewish priest, Ezra, who was resident in Babylon, received a commission from the king to go to Judah to regulate the religion of the province in accordance with 'the law of your God' (Ezra 7[26]). The text of the letter of authority which Ezra received is reproduced in Ezra 7[12–25]. In accordance with the general Persian policy of encouraging the different peoples to follow their own religious practices and customs, Ezra was granted State funds for the use of the Temple and its services (Ezra 7[20]).

On arrival in Jerusalem he was informed that both the lay people and the priests were still contracting marriages with the surrounding people. It seems that either Nehemiah's legislation against mixed marriages had never been strictly enforced, or more probably it had fallen into disregard when his governorship came to an end. Ezra's obvious distress on receiving this news communicated itself to the crowd of people who had assembled with him at the Temple. As a result Ezra and the leaders agreed on the drastic policy of divorcing all alien wives. A proclamation was issued calling all the men of Judah and Benjamin to an assembly in Jerusalem within three days, the penalty for disobedience being confiscation of property and excommunication (Ezra 10^{7-9}). The stern measure called for by Ezra and the reforming party was adopted, but its enforcement was left to officials in each city. This harsh measure was intended to preserve the identity of the Jewish people and to protect its religion from corruption by heathen practices. It is interesting to notice that both Nehemiah's and Ezra's reforms were initiated by persons who had recently returned from the land of exile. The Jewish communities in Babylon, whence Ezra came, had preserved their identity and religion by keeping themselves separate from the Babylonians amongst whom they lived. For Ezra, preservation meant separation and vice versa.

One other event which occurred whilst Ezra was active in Judah is recorded in Nehemiah 8. The people had assembled in Jerusalem for the autumn New Year Festival (the first day of the seventh month—Neh 8^{2}), and Ezra was called to give a public reading of the Law. We do not know exactly what portion of the Law of Moses he read, but it may have been part of the Priestly Code which he had brought from Babylon. In accordance with the provisions of the Law, the Feast of Booths was celebrated during the seventh month. The public reading of the Law continued daily throughout the Feast.

THE BOOKS OF EZRA AND NEHEMIAH

These two books are a continuation of the Books of Chronicles, in fact 2 Chronicles $36^{22\,ff}$ is identical with Ezra 1^{1-3}, and it is clear that the separation into two books at this point is quite artificial. The purpose of the Books of Ezra and Nehemiah is to give some account of the work of these two men, and the Chronicler (for we assume that whoever compiled the Books of Chronicles also compiled Ezra and Nehemiah) had at his disposal the personal memoirs of the two men. There is, however, strong reason to suppose that, contrary to the Chronicler's account, Nehemiah preceded Ezra. Ezra was a contemporary of the high priest Johanan, the grandson of Eliashib, whilst the latter was a contemporary of Nehemiah. According to the Chronicler, Nehemiah came to Jerusalem in the twentieth year of Artaxerxes, whilst Ezra came in the seventh year of Artaxerxes; but it appears that the historian was not careful to distinguish between Artaxerxes I and Artaxerxes II. We conclude that Nehemiah arrived in Jerusalem in the twentieth year of Artaxerxes I, i.e. 444 B C, whilst Ezra did not arrive in Judah until 397 B C—the seventh year of Artaxerxes II.

NOTE. A connected account of the period from the time of Darius I (*c.* 520 B C) to the time of Ezra (*c.* 397 B C) is obtained by reading the text in the following order: Ezra 4^{1-23}, Neh 1–2^{4}, 6–7^{4}, 11^{1-2}, 5, 13^{4-30}, Ezra 7, 9–10^{16}, Neh 8.

PASSAGES FOR STUDY

Ezra 4^{1-23}—*A Summary of Events from 537 to 444* B C

This chapter gives an account of the hindrances which the Jews suffered at the hands of the Samaritans ('adversaries', verse 1; 'people of the land', verse 4) as they endeavoured to restore the Temple and the city of Jerusalem. Verses 1–5 refer to the difficulties encountered by the first group of exiles who returned during the reign of Cyrus. As Darius was favourably disposed towards the Jews the restoration of the Temple was completed during his reign in 516 B C.

Verse 6. When Xerxes I (Ahaseurus 486–464 B C) succeeded to the throne of Persia the Samaritans renewed their accusations against the Jews and so halted the work of rebuilding the city. The details of the accusation are not given, but it is probable that any building that the Jews undertook was represented to the Persians as being fortifications preparatory to rebellion (cf. the letter to Artaxerxes, Ezra 4^{11-16}). From the remainder of the chapter we learn that when Xerxes was succeeded by Artaxerxes (464 B C) the Jews began to repair the walls of Jerusalem. This again provoked their opponents to complain to the Persian authorities with the result that building operations were suspended and the walls partly demolished.

Nehemiah 1–2^{4}—*The Building of the Wall*

This account of the repairs to the wall of Jerusalem, which were undertaken after Nehemiah had taken up his post as governor, comes from Nehemiah's own memoirs. In spite of the royal support which Nehemiah enjoyed, he suffered much opposition from Sanballat, the governor of Samaria, who even threatened to attack Jerusalem. Nehemiah posted guards at all the vulnerable points and so the building work proceeded. The wall was completed in fifty-two days.

Nehemiah 6–7^{4}, 11^{1-2}—*Enemies and Plots*

This passage gives a vivid account of the attempts which were made against Nehemiah's life or reputation. Sanballat proposed a meeting ostensibly to settle their differences, but Nehemiah was not deceived and declined the four-times-repeated invitation. His enemies then tried to alarm him by saying that rumours were circulating to the effect that he was about to proclaim himself king in Jerusalem. Had such rumours come to the ears of the Persians Nehemiah's position could have been very difficult. However, he refused to be intimidated by this device of his enemies.

An attempt was then made to destroy his reputation. Under the pretext that a plot against his life had been uncovered, he was encouraged to take refuge in the Holy of Holies, and so lay himself open to the double charge of cowardice and of entering the most holy place.

The cryptic note at the end of Chapter 6 (verses 17–19) indicates that many of the upper class in Judah had no desire to break with the Samaritans so that Nehemiah not only had to deal with enemies outside the city but also with foes within.

The defence of the city was something of a problem. Its population was relatively small and not all the inhabitants were loyal to Nehemiah. However, he was aided by his brother Hanani and a loyal captain, Hananiah to whom he entrusted the defence of the city (7^{1-4}).

The brief note in 11^{1-2} tells how Nehemiah repopulated the almost deserted city. It is clear that it was not a popular place of residence so that it was necessary to compel people chosen by lot to move into the city. The ones who *volunteered* to take up residence in Jerusalem receive special commendation (11^{2}).

Nehemiah 5—*Distress and Exploitation*

We have already suggested that this chapter describes a situation which may have arisen towards the close of Nehemiah's first period as governor. The distress may have been caused by a failure of the harvest. The exploitation of the less fortunate people by their more fortunate neighbours called forth Nehemiah's strong condemnation and equally vigorous action.

Nehemiah 13—*Second Period as Governor*

This has already been dealt with in the introduction and needs no further comment.

Ezra 7—*Ezra receives a Commission from Artaxerxes II*

The bulk of this chapter comprises the letter which Ezra received from the king authorizing him to go to Jerusalem in order to regulate the religious life of the community in accordance with 'the law of your

God' (verse 14). The provisions of the letter are another illustration of the liberal policy which the Persian kings adopted towards the subject people. Any Jews who wished were free to accompany Ezra; state funds were made available for the provision of sacrifices for the Temple. In addition the Temple personnel were exempted from taxes (verse 24).

Ezra 9–10[16]—*The Reform*

In his second term as governor, Nehemiah had forbidden the Jews to marry foreign women. This law had ceased to be observed. Ezra's measure was much more drastic; he decreed the divorce of foreign wives.

Nehemiah 8—*The Reading of the Law*

This public reading of the Law was begun on the first day of the seventh month, and a fortnight later there was a celebration of the Feast of Booths. The audience consisted not merely of men and women, but presumably children also, provided they were old enough to understand what was being read ('those who could understand', verse 3).

NOTE. Verse 9. Since Nehemiah was not a contemporary of Ezra, the reference to him in verse 9a ('And Nehemiah, who was governor') must be omitted as an error on the part of the Chronicler.

JONAH

Both Nehemiah and Ezra had realized that there was a real danger that the small Jewish community, which had been established in the province of Judah, might become merged with the surrounding people and so lose its identity. Consequently they had tried to put a 'fence' round the community by forbidding mixed marriages and by insisting on the strict observance of the Law. From the time of Ezra the Jews became increasingly a people of the Law. Ezra had formally introduced the Law at a public gathering in Jerusalem, and had given such explanation of its details as seemed necessary. This set the pattern for Judaism. Following Ezra there was a succession of 'scribes', that is students of the Law, whose business was to relate its provisions to the conduct of everyday life. From this time onwards the faithful Jew was one who strove to fulfil the Law in all its details. Such an attitude very naturally led to a sharp distinction between Jew and Gentile, although it always remained possible for the Gentile, who was willing to submit to the Law, to be admitted to the community of faithful Jews.

Whilst the possibility always remained open for Gentiles to adopt the Jewish faith and so become a part of the people of the Law, very few Jews had any sense of missionary responsibility towards the heathen world about them. The dominant attitude was one which emphasized the great distinction between Jew and Gentile, and which prompted the faithful Jew to separate himself as much as possible from the foreigner. There were some Jews, especially during the Greek period (see below), who adopted foreign ways of life; for such the faithful Jew had nothing but contempt.

In spite of this strong current which favoured an exclusive and separatist attitude, there was a minority in the community who were conscious of the Jews' missionary responsibility. This sense of mission receives expression in the Book of Jonah. This book is included among the prophets, though it is quite different from the other prophetical writings in that it is a story about a prophet and not a record of his teachings. The author uses the story as a vehicle to proclaim his own conviction concerning Israel's missionary task, 'The message lies in the story, and in what God said to Jonah, rather than in what Jonah was commanded to say to the Ninevites'.[1] The historical Jonah ben Amittai, a native of Gath Hepher in Galilee, lived in the eighth century B C and prophesied during the reign of Jeroboam II, whom he had evidently encouraged in his efforts to extend his kingdom (2 K 14^{25-7}). It seems that for Jonah the destruction of Israel's enemies was to be equated with the will of God.

In the Book of Jonah we have a work of fiction probably composed during the late Persian period, after the time of Ezra. The author chose Jonah as his chief character because the historical Jonah typified that dominant element in the Jewish community which despised and hated the Gentile world, and believed that it was destined by God for destruction. The author himself belonged to that minority which believed that God had a concern for the heathen world; that it should be given an opportunity to repent and be saved from destruction; and that Israel should be His agent in preaching repentance to the heathen.

PASSAGES FOR STUDY

Jonah 1–$2^{1, 10}$—*No Escape from God*

Jonah is bidden to pronounce doom on Nineveh (cf. 3^4), but he is reluctant to take even this stern message lest the Ninevites should repent and the doom be averted. Instead he tries to escape from his task and

[1] G. W. Anderson, *A Critical Introduction to the Old Testament*, p. 153.

from God by taking ship to a distant land. There is, however, no escape from God who pursues him in the storm. The introduction of the storm incident gives the writer an opportunity of stressing the piety and compassion of the heathen sailors who show great concern for the welfare and safety of their passenger. Their attitude towards Jonah contrasts with his hostility towards Nineveh.

Jonah's presence in the ship is discovered to be the reason for the storm, and with considerable reluctance the sailors agree to throw him overboard. But Jonah had not yet carried out the task which had been laid upon him. The storm had prevented him from escaping to Tarshish to avoid his assignment. Now a great fish saves him from drowning and brings him back to land.

Some scholars have thought that the great fish symbolizes Babylon which 'swallowed up' Israel in the exile (cf. Jer $51^{34, 44}$). If this is correct then we see even more clearly that the writer of Jonah is pleading with the restored Israel to fulfil her missionary obligation of being 'a light to the nations' (Isa 49^{6}). So Jonah is bidden a second time to go to Nineveh.

Jonah 3–4—'*Should not I pity?*'

With ill grace Jonah undertakes his mission to Nineveh, and, as he feared, the Ninevites repented and were spared. Only now is it apparent how hardened Jonah's heart had become, for the beautiful description of Yahweh taken from Exodus 34^{6}, 'The LORD, the LORD, a God merciful and gracious, slow to anger, and abounding in steadfast love and faithfulness', turns to bitter irony in his mouth (Jonah 4^{2b}). Jonah has yet to learn the lesson that God hates nothing that He has made, and 'desireth not the death of a sinner, but rather that he may turn from his wickedness and live'. His pity is stirred by the sudden destruction of the miraculous plant which had afforded him welcome shade from the sultry east wind. How much more then must God pity the heathen world which was His creation no less than the chosen people, and in which there were innocent children (persons who do not know their right hand from their left) as well as cattle.

The author could not know whether Israel would heed his message and accept her missionary task. He could only confront his people with this last haunting question: 'And should not I pity Nineveh?' (4^{11}).

II—FROM ALEXANDER THE GREAT TO THE MACCABEAN REVOLT (333–167 B C)

From the time of the Patriarchs to the time of Nehemiah and Ezra, Palestine had either been subject to the great powers of the Near East, or divided into small States enjoying a temporary independence during those periods when the great empires of Egypt or Mesopotamia were weak. With the rise of Alexander the Great a new situation developed in which the Middle East was brought face-to-face with a new culture —that of the Greeks.

This contact of East and West may be traced back to the campaigns of Cyrus and Darius I. We have already met Cyrus as the conqueror of Babylon and liberator of the Jewish exiles. Before conquering Babylon, however, he had already overthrown the more northerly kingdom of Media and had swept into Asia Minor. He conquered the wealthy State of Lydia which was ruled by the fabulous king Croesus, and then reduced the Greek colonies of Asia Minor one by one. At his death Cyrus left a vast empire stretching from Asia Minor to the frontiers of India, and from the southern steppes of Russia to Egypt.

When Darius succeeded to the throne, after quelling widespread rebellion, he divided his empire into twenty provinces or satrapies. Then he organized a vast army with the ultimate intention of conquering Greece itself. He did cross into Europe but eventually suffered a defeat at the Battle of Marathon in 490 B C. His successor Xerxes I also attempted in vain to conquer Greece. The Persian army was large but badly organized, but the Greeks would not unite so that neither side was able to inflict a decisive defeat on the other. This uneasy stalemate lasted for about a century until, in 360 B C, Philip of Macedon conquered Thrace and Thessaly. In 338 B C he won a decisive victory over Athens and her allies and so united Greece by force. Two years later Philip was assassinated.

Philip was succeeded by his son Alexander, who resolved to free the Greek city States of Asia Minor from the Persian yoke (even though some of them were not anxious to be set free!). The Persians completely underestimated their foe. A victory at the Battle of Granicus (334 B C) secured Asia Minor for Alexander. He met the Persian forces again at the River Issus (near the modern Alexandretta) in 332 B C, and tore them to pieces with his Macedonian cavalry and Greek infantry. The conquest of Syria, Palestine, and Egypt followed rapidly, then in

331 B C the all-conquering Macedonian swept eastwards carrying all before him as far as the Indus. The great Persian empire had fallen to the conqueror.

Alexander, still a young man, died in Babylon eight years later and the empire was divided between four of his generals. Ptolemy took Egypt and seized Palestine; Seleucus took Babylonia and extended his power over Syria in the west and Persia in the east; the other two seized Asia Minor and Greece respectively. For rather more than a century the Ptolemies maintained control over Palestine, and, as they appear to have continued the liberal policy of the Persians towards their subjects, we may assume that the Jews continued to enjoy religious freedom in Judea (as we may now call the province of Judah).

The capital of the Ptolemaic State was established at Alexandria on the Nile Delta. This city developed rapidly and soon attracted a large colony of Jews who continued to practise their own religion. They were joined by 'proselytes' who, having been attracted by the faith and worship of Judaism, submitted to the ordinances of the Law. These proselytes would be Greek speaking, and probably amongst many of the Jews, Hebrew and Aramaic fell out of use, so that the need arose for a Greek version of the Old Testament. During the course of the third century B C a beginning was made in the work of translating the Scriptures into Greek. The completed translation, now known as the Septuagint, was widely used, especially in New Testament times, amongst Greek-speaking Jews who were dispersed throughout the Roman empire.

Palestine remained a part of the Ptolemaic kingdom until 198 B C when Antiochus III, who had succeeded to the throne of the Seleucid kingdom in 223 B C, obtained possession of the territory. Under this ruler the Seleucid State reached the pinnacle of its power, for before gaining control of Palestine, Antiochus had already added Asia Minor to his kingdom. Unfortunately his presence in Asia Minor brought him face-to-face with the Romans who were by this time steadily extending their rule eastwards. The change of rulers in Palestine did not seriously affect the Jews; in fact to compensate the Judeans for the ravages and misfortunes of war, Antiochus allowed all the inhabitants of Jerusalem, who had been dispersed or enslaved in the war which gave him control of Palestine, to return home, and he also remitted all taxes for three years.

In 190 B C Antiochus' forces were heavily defeated by the Romans in Asia Minor and henceforth the Romans tended to support the

Ptolemies against the Seleucids to the embarrassment of the latter. The difficulties which faced the Seleucid State led to a hardening towards the subject peoples during the reign of Antiochus IV (Epiphanes) (175–163 BC). In an effort to bolster up his tottering kingdom, this ruler embarked on a policy of unification by suppressing the religions and customs of the subject peoples, and by compelling them to adopt the Greek mode of life and worship. This process of Hellenization had, of course, been going on since the time of Alexander the Great, and many folk had been attracted by, and had voluntarily adopted, the Greek way of life. Thus even before Antiochus attempted to stamp out the Jewish religion in Judea many Jews had already abandoned the manners and customs of their fathers. Others, however, who called themselves the 'Hasidim' (i.e. the devout or pious ones) stuck faithfully to the Law and scrupulously observed its teaching. This cleavage amongst the Jews was not a division between the laity and the clergy, for some of the priests were favourable to the introduction of Greek culture into Judea. The high priest Jason (who had already adopted the Greek form of the Hebrew name 'Joshua') sought permission from Antiochus to introduce a Greek sports arena, or gymnasium, into Jerusalem. He then decreed that the Temple sacrifice should cease and that and his family who eventually led the rebellion against Antiochus.

Matters came to a head in 168 BC when Antiochus, compelled by the Romans to abandon an offensive which he had launched against Egypt, ordered one of his leading officers to attack and pillage Jerusalem. He then decreed that the Temple sacrifice should cease and that the Sabbath should no longer be observed. In addition the Jews were forbidden to circumcise their children; and pagan altars, on which swine's flesh was sacrificed, were set up throughout the land (cf. 1 Macc $1^{41\,\mathrm{ff}}$, Dan 11^{31}). A year later an image of Zeus ('the abomination that makes desolate'—Dan 11^{31}) was set up in the Temple.

Antiochus sent his officers throughout the land to punish by death any who had circumcised their children and also to compel all Jews to sacrifice at the pagan altars. When one such officer arrived at the village of Modein he was met by a priest Mattathias who not only refused to offer the sacrifice, but slew a Jew, who was about to sacrifice, and also the enforcement officer. Mattathias and his four sons then took to the wilderness where they quickly formed an army of all who were willing to defy the Seleucids, and defend by force their right to obey their

2 The Books of the Maccabees in the Apocrypha should be consulted for further details.

ancient Law. Not long afterwards Mattathias died and the leadership fell to his second son Judas who was nicknamed 'Maccabaeus' or 'The Hammer'. The name was well earned, for with comparatively small forces he successfully resisted and defeated much larger Syrian armies. Three years later he had virtually freed Judea from Syrian control. A Syrian garrison remained in Jerusalem, but Judas was able to confine this to the citadel in one sector of the city, whilst he freed the Temple and fortified the area around it. The pagan altar and the image of Zeus were removed from the Temple, a new altar was built and the Temple rededicated in 164 B C.

Some months later Judas was able to send his elder brother Simon with an army into Galilee in defence of the Jews living in the north, whilst he, along with his youngest brother Jonathan, led an army against the Syrians in Gilead. As a result of these two campaigns many of the Jews from these areas were taken back to the comparative security of Judea.

Antiochus IV died at about this time and was succeeded by his eight-year-old son Antiochus V. The government of Syria and Palestine fell to the regent Lysias who launched a full-scale offensive against the rebels. This was so successful that Judas was ultimately driven back to the small fortified Temple area in Jerusalem. At this crucial moment a rival of Lysias made an attempt to seize power and the latter had to come to terms with Judas. The treaty, which was concluded, guaranteed religious freedom to the Jews. The 'Hasidim' who had supported Judas now considered that, with the restoration of their rights, the aims of the revolt had been achieved. Judas, however, now wished to attain complete political independence, and, although the 'Hasidim' withdrew their support, he continued the struggle against the Syrians. This went on with varying success for the next thirty-five years, during which period Judas was killed in battle (160 B C), Jonathan was murdered (143 B C), and Simon assassinated (134 B C). However, by 128 B C Judea was being ruled by Simon's son, John Hyrcanus, who was both king and high priest. Once again there was an independent Jewish State.

THE APOCALYPTIC LITERATURE

The Old Testament, according to the order of the books in the English versions, closes with the prophecy of Malachi. This fact has given rise to the erroneous notion that the period from Malachi to New Testament times, a period of more than four centuries, was a time of silence. The division of the books in the Hebrew Bible is a better guide to the true state of affairs. The third part of the canon—'The Writings'—containing such books as Chronicles, Ezra, and Nehemiah, which carry the history down to the beginning of the fourth century, could not have been completed until some time during that century at the earliest.

In addition both individual and national experience posed problems which demanded solutions. Why do the righteous suffer? What is the meaning of the rise and fall of empires? The great prophets had spoken of a time when Israel would be restored to her land and enjoy the blessings of the Messianic kingdom (Jer 29^{10}, 25^{12}, 24^{5-6}), but the restoration had brought neither independence nor the golden age, so the non-fulfilment of prophecy posed yet another problem. These last two problems were the particular concern of a succession of writers who flourished between about 200 B C and A D 100. The body of literature which they left is known as 'Apocalyptic' literature. The corresponding noun 'Apocalypse' means 'revelation', and in their writings the authors claimed to be making known special revelations which they had received from God. The apocalyptic writers were the direct successors of the prophets, but whereas the prophets spoke their messages which were subsequently written down, the apocalyptists wrote theirs and later published them under the names of the great heroes of the past. There are two examples of such literature in the Bible, the Book of Daniel and the Revelation of John. The New Testament apocalypse (Revelation) is, exceptionally, published under the name of its author. Outside the Bible there are many apocalyptic writings such as *The Book of Enoch, The Testament of the Twelve Patriarchs,* etc.

THE BOOK OF DANIEL

The Book of Daniel falls into two distinct sections. The first section, Chapters 1–6, consists of stories about Daniel or the three Jewish youths, Shadrach, Meshach, and Abednego. The remainder of the book purports to be written by Daniel and is an account of a series of visions or dreams experienced by him. The events described are set in the reigns of Nebuchadnezzar, Belshazzar, and Darius the Mede. On closer examination of the book it becomes evident that it could not belong to this early period, for the author is clearly less well informed about the Babylonian and early Persian period than he is of the Seleucid era. Thus he speaks of Nebuchadnezzar's seven years of madness (4^{28-37}) and in this seems to have confused him with the later Babylonian king Nabonidus. The writer also appears to assume that there was a period when the Jews were subject to the Medes under a king,

'Darius the Mede', whereas in fact the Babylonian empire was followed immediately by the Persian, and he must have assumed, incorrectly, that Darius the Great (who followed Cyrus) was a Median king.

By contrast the conflict between the Seleucids and the Ptolemies, and the details of the measures taken by Antiochus IV against the Jews are accurately described in Daniel 11. Since 'the abomination which makes desolate' (11^{31}) was still in existence, the book must be dated during the latter part of the reign of Antiochus IV, but before the rededication of the Temple, i.e. sometime between 168 and 164 BC. The author was probably one of the Hasidim, and his purpose in publishing this work during this critical period of persecution was twofold. In relating the stories of Daniel and his friends in the first section of the book he is setting before his people the example of these four faithful Jews who refused to adopt the manner of life and the religion of their captors, even if refusal should mean death (cf. especially Dan 3^{17-18}). This section of the book is thus a call to all faithful Jews to resist to the uttermost Antiochus' policy of Hellenization.

In the second part of the book the author expresses his conviction that in spite of appearances God is in control of His world. The present period of persecution is the darkness which precedes the dawn; it is the final hour of the night which began, for his people, with the fall of Jerusalem. So he begins his review of history at that point. Since that time the Jews have been subject to the dominion of four world empires—the Babylonian, the Median, the Persian, and finally the Greek. The last is the most terrible of all—this is the fourth 'beast, which was different from the rest, exceedingly terrible, with its teeth of iron and claws of bronze; and which devoured and broke in pieces and stamped the residue with its feet' (Dan 7^{19}). But this empire will pass like the others, and then 'the kingdom and the dominion and the greatness of the kingdoms under the whole heaven shall be given to the people of the saints of the Most High' (Dan 7^{27}). The author 'recognized constantly that all earthly power exists only at the sufferance of the Almighty'.[3]

In one particular the teaching of the apocalyptic writers marked an advance on that of the prophets and prepared the way for Christianity. For it is in these writings that we find definite teaching on the possibility of resurrection. By the time that Daniel was written this had become an accepted article of faith so that the author only refers to it quite incidentally (Dan 12^{12}).

[3] C. G. Howie, *Ezekiel and Daniel*, p. 97.

PASSAGES FOR STUDY

Daniel 1—*Daniel and his Friends*

This story would have special relevance during the reign of Antiochus IV when the Jews were being compelled to eat 'unclean' food. The parallel between Daniel and his friends and the persecuted Jews for whom the author was writing is not exact, for the former were not being *compelled* to eat 'unclean' food. However, to refuse the food provided by the king himself might be taken as an affront to the king who would doubtless take revenge on his insolent subjects as well as on the steward. The faith of the young men was justified when they were found not to have suffered as a result of their austere, self-imposed diet, for not only were they 'fatter in flesh than all the youths who ate the king's, rich food' (1^{15}), but 'God gave them learning and skill in all letters and wisdom' (1^{17}).

Daniel 3—*The Fiery Furnace*

The motive for telling this story is obvious. Though ostensibly writing about Nebuchadnezzar and the great image which he caused to be set up at Dura, the author is in reality alluding to Antiochus and the image of Zeus which he had set up in the Temple. Furthermore the author has no illusions as to the possible outcome of resistance, but even if it means death, the blasphemous claims of Antiochus must be resisted. In verses 17 and 18 the author's thought reaches a high-water mark when he expresses his conviction that God is to be served, not because He will necessarily keep His faithful people from tribulation, but simply because He is God. But verse 25, with its added thought that God is to be found with His servants in the midst of their tribulation, must be read in conjunction with verses 17 and 18.

Daniel 6—*The Lion's Den*

Not only had Antiochus set up an image of Zeus in the Temple, but it appears that he took rather more literally than some kings the usual claim of Oriental monarchs to be divine. This is indicated by his title 'Epiphanes' which means 'manifest', i.e. 'God manifest', which his detractors changed into 'Epimanes', i.e. 'madman'.

This familiar story of the lion's den was intended to enhearten those faithful Jews who refused to pay divine honours to the king. Daniel knowing full well what would be the consequences of his faithfulness to God (verse 10), nevertheless quite openly continued his regular practice of daily prayer. In the story, the enemies of Daniel are high-ranking State officials who are jealous of the favour which he enjoys with the king. Darius himself is portrayed in a very favourable light and is represented as being genuinely sorry for the consequences, which he had not foreseen, of the decree which he had been enveigled into signing.

Taken as a whole, however, the story was told to encourage resistance to the measures of Antiochus with the assurance that God was able even 'to stop the mouths of lions' (Heb 11^{33}).

Daniel 7—*The Four Beasts*

Using somewhat bizarre symbolism, whose meaning is not difficult to unravel, the author reviews the course of history from Nebuchadnezzar to Antiochus IV. According to his scheme of history there had been four empires or kingdoms, the Babylonian, the Median, the Persian, and the Greek, these are the four great beasts which came out of the sea (verse 3). The sea here does not refer to any particular sea, but is rather a symbolic expression. To the Hebrew mind the sea was evil, and symbolized all that was evil (hence in the Book of Revelation there is the promise that there shall be no more sea—Rev 21^{1}). These four kingdoms were evil in their origin.

The author is primarily interested in the fourth beast, and the little horn which is 'the real centre of gravity in this chapter'[4] The horns were the rulers of the kingdom, the little horn was Antiochus Epiphanes, who even at the very time that the book was being written was 'speaking great things' (verse 8). In his arrogance and pride he was defying God Himself (verse 25), but in spite of the present evil times the author held fast to his belief in the sovereignty of God. Antiochus may blaspheme against God and rampage against the 'saints of the Most High' but he is already under judgement.

The judgement is described in graphic symbolism (verses 9–14, 26–7), which owes something of its inspiration to the chariot vision of Ezekiel. In contrast to the indescribable beast arraigned before Him, God (the Ancient of Days) clothed in a garment of purest white and 'Whose white hair proclaims that This was the God of all ages',[5] is seated on His throne. Then judgement is pronounced against the beast, and for the saints of the Most High to whom the kingdom was given (verse 27).

[4] C. G. Howie, *Ezekiel and Daniel*, p. 120. [5] Ibid., p. 121.

This chapter may serve as an introduction to one of the key themes of the book—the writer's unshakable belief in the sovereignty of God for 'he recognized constantly that all earthly power exists only at the sufferance of the Almighty'.[6] However the beast may rage his time is limited; though he 'shall wear out the saints of the Most High' it is only 'for a time, two times, and half a time' (i.e. three and a half years) (verse 25).

The following passages in which the sovereignty of God is emphasized should also be noted 2^{20-3}, $4^{3, 34-5}$, 5^{20-3}, 6^{26-7}.

NOTE. 'a son of man' (verse 13). A comparison of verses 13–14, where the kingdom is given to the 'son of man' with verse 22 and verse 27 where the kingdom is given to the 'saints of the Most High' suggests that the term 'son of man' is used here to designate the faithful remnant or the Hasidim.

Daniel 11^{21-45}—*The Reign of Antiochus IV*

This chapter sketches the history of the Ptolemaic and Seleucid kingdoms from the death of Alexander to Antiochus IV. The former is the mighty king of verse 3 whose kingdom is broken into four parts at his death (verse 4). The career of Antiochus IV is described in some detail in the verses selected for study. He is the 'contemptible person' who had usurped the throne from an older brother (verse 21). Antiochus' campaigns against Egypt are described in verses 25–6 and 29–30. The Kittim in verse 30 are the Romans whose intervention forced Antiochus to withdraw from Egypt. He then intensified his efforts to Hellenize his kingdom, and the Jews who resisted were subject to terrible persecution (verse 33) which provoked the Maccabean revolt. This latter the author describes as 'the little help' (verse 34) which those who resist are receiving; but he sees all too clearly that this was in part a political movement which had attracted its proportion of opportunists: ('Many shall join themselves to them with flattery' —verse 34). The ultimate hope for the persecuted saints was God Himself.

The chapter closes with a prediction of the downfall of Antiochus (verses 40–5). In fact the end of the tyrant was not long delayed but it did not come in the manner anticipated by the writer, for he died whilst on a campaign in the east of his dominions.

6 C. G. Howie, *Ezekiel and Daniel*, p. 97.

Daniel 12—*Resurrection*

Though he had confidently predicted the downfall of Antiochus, the author was still living amidst the fires of persecution. The ultimate issue, he was convinced, was in God's hand, but what of the present, and what of the faithful ones who were dying in the great tribulation? In this final chapter he endeavours to pierce through the gloom and terror of the present to find a message of hope for his people. These terrors are a prelude to deliverance (verse 1) and as for those who have died, there is a resurrection either to everlasting life or to punishment. The author of Daniel would surely have approved our Lord's words to His disciples: 'Do not be anxious. . . . Fear not little flock, for it is your Father's good pleasure to give you the kingdom' (Lk 12[22, 32]). For he too had continually insisted that the everlasting kingdom would be God's gift to the faithful ones, and his doctrine of the resurrection meant that not even death could take this gift from them.

CHAPTER TWELVE

AN OUTLINE OF OLD TESTAMENT THEOLOGY

I—THE IDEA OF GOD

THE EXISTENCE of God is taken for granted in the Old Testament. It is true that 'the fool' of Psalm 14[1] (and 53[1]) appears to deny His existence, but the remainder of the psalm makes it clear that the fool is not so much denying God's existence as ignoring Him, and so the fools 'are corrupt, they do abominable deeds' (Ps 14[1b]). The basis of Old Testament faith is that God cannot be ignored. It is assumed that He exists and furthermore that He is not some remote 'First Cause', but that He is living and active in the midst of His people. God is sometimes called 'the living God', and in using this name the Old Testament expresses in vivid language the fact that God is a Person, and even more, One who can only be ignored at man's peril, as the following passages show. 'For who is there of all flesh, that has heard the voice of the living God speaking out of the midst of the fire, as we have, and has still lived?' (Deut 5[26]; cf. Josh 3[10], 1 S 17[26, 36], 2 K 19[4, 6]). But as the 'living God' (Ps 84[2]) He is also powerful to succour those who appeal to Him (Ps 84[9, 11–12]). A similar notion is conveyed by the phrase, 'As the LORD liveth', so that when Elijah announces the impending drought with these words, he is saying that Yahweh Himself is the surety that the drought will really come. There is perhaps here also a contrast between Yahweh and Baal, the fertility god. The hot, rainless summer was a sign that the god was dead, even more a prolonged drought would signify the death of Baal. But Yahweh is the living God; the drought is not a sign of His impotence, it is the instrument of His judgement on Ahab and Jezebel.

The Names of God

Various names are used for God in the Old Testament, the commonest being God (Heb. *Elohim*, sometimes *El*), The LORD (*Yahweh*), The LORD of Hosts (*Yahweh Sebaoth*), and God Almighty (*El Shaddai*).

God (*Elohim*)

The Hebrew noun 'Elohim' is a plural form and occasionally means 'gods' but only when referring to pagan deities. The word was the common Semitic word meaning 'god', but unless the contrary is obvious from the context it always refers in the Old Testament to the God of Israel. The origin of the word is obscure, it is, however, known that the supreme Canaanite god was called 'El'. This fact has been held to suggest that the word '*El*' or '*Elohim*' emphasizes the power of God.

LORD (*Yahweh*)

This is the personal name of the God of Israel. But a name in the ancient world concealed the character of its bearer, so it is natural that we should ask what we can learn about the character of the God of Israel from His name 'Yahweh'. This name is derived from the verb '*hawah*' (or '*hayah*', cf. *RSV* marginal note to Exodus 3^{15}) which means 'to be' or 'to exist', so that the difficult verse Exodus 3^{14} gives a clue to the meaning of the name 'Yahweh'. Yahweh is the One who was, and is, and will be. 'Since the name is the expression of the living God, it must make evident one of the aspects of that life; "El" expresses life in its power, "Yahweh" expresses life in its continuance and its actuality.' [1] In the name 'Yahweh' we have an expression of the eternity of the God of Israel; this is emphasized above all by Deutero-Isaiah: 'I am He, I am the first, I will also be the last' (Isa 48^{12}; cf. 14^{4}).

LORD of Hosts (*Yahweh Sebaoth*)

The name 'LORD of Hosts', is found most frequently in the prophets, especially Isaiah, Jeremiah, and Zechariah. This may be taken as an assertion, on the part of the prophets, of the Lordship of Yahweh over all other powers and in particular over the supposed power of the heavenly hosts (i.e. the heavenly bodies) which were worshipped by the Assyrians and Babylonians. Thus the name was at once a proclamation of the universal dominion of Yahweh, and a protest against the cult of the stars (Amos 5^{26-7}, Jer $44^{24\,ff}$). (A fuller form of the name 'Yahweh, God of Hosts' is also used occasionally (cf. Hos 12^{5}, Amos 3^{13}, 6^{14}).)

God Almighty (*El Shaddai*)

According to Exodus 6^{3} this was the name by which Yahweh revealed Himself to the Patriarchs. The meaning of the word '*Shaddai*' is uncertain, though in so far as the usual translation 'Almighty' lays stress on the majesty of God it probably represents the intention of the original. If, as some scholars suppose, the word '*Shaddai*' is derived

[1] E. Jacob, *Theology of the Old Testament*, p. 51.

from an Assyrian word '*schadu*' (=mountain),[2] the name *El Shaddai* would then mean the 'mountain God', and then perhaps because of His very remoteness the name came to mean 'God Almighty'.

This brief study of four important names used of God in the Old Testament may be summed up by saying that they express His Omnipotence and Eternity.

The Attributes of God

The attributes of God may conveniently be discussed by studying some of the key words and ideas which are used by the Old Testament writers to describe His character.

God is Holy

Holiness is *the* characteristic of God; to say that God is holy is to say that He is God. The word translated 'holy' ('*qadosh*' in Hebrew) means 'separate'. Thus God can be described as 'holy' because He is distinct from man and from the world which He has created. His existence is an *independent existence*, whereas the world and man depend for their existence on God, theirs is a *dependent existence*. Since God is a free agent, in fact the only completely free agent, He is under no obligation to make Himself known to man. If He chooses to disclose Himself this must be regarded as a gracious act on His part (cf. Gen 18^{17}). The proper attitude of man before this self-existent, independent God is one of reverence and awe. (The biblical term is the 'fear of the LORD'; cf. Prov 1^{7}). Abraham describes himself as 'dust and ashes' in the presence of Yahweh (Gen 18^{27}, etc.); at Bethel Jacob confesses 'how awesome is this place' (Gen 28^{17}), but perhaps nowhere is the gulf which separates God and man set forth more dramatically than in Exodus 19^{10-25}. Elaborate precautions must be taken to ensure that the Israelites are kept at a proper distance from this overpowering and majestic God.

The Holiness of God invokes fear

But this is not all that there is to say about God's holiness. He bridges the gap. He calls Abraham from Ur; He calls the Hebrews from bondage in Egypt to be His people, and He calls them to be holy and binds them to Himself with a covenant. But holiness is what God is, and whereas in its earliest usage the word describes the 'separateness' of

[2] L. Koehler, *Old Testament Theology*, p. 242, note 44; E. Jacob, *Theology of the Old Testament*, p. 46, note 3.

God, through the teaching of the prophets God's holiness is seen to embrace His righteousness, and mercy, and faithfulness. Isaiah's Temple vision teaches him that there is mercy in God's holiness. Though he stands trembling before Him expecting to be destroyed he is in fact sanctified (Isa 6). The sin which separates him from God is forgiven and taken away. Isaiah seems to have been the first person, perhaps as a result of this experience, to use the title 'Holy One' or 'Holy One of Israel' for God. This description still conveys the sense of 'otherness' which the word 'holy' suggested from the first, but in the teaching of Isaiah and of the later prophets, to whom we owe the second part of the Book of Isaiah (Ch 40–66), the Holy One is also the Righteous One (5^{16}), who will uphold the remnant (10^{20}; cf. 17^{7-8}), and support the meek (29^{19}). This twofold aspect of 'holiness', suggesting on the one hand the 'otherness' of God and on the other His active concern for man, is summed up in the words of a post-exilic prophet: 'For thus says the high and lofty One who inhabits eternity, whose name is Holy: "I dwell in the high and holy place, and also with him who is of a contrite and humble spirit"' (Isa 57^{15}).

God is Righteous

Righteousness (Hebrew, '*tsedeq*' and '*tsedaqah*') means primarily conformity to some standard. When God is described as 'righteous' or 'just', this must not be taken to imply that He conforms to some standard other than Himself, but rather that His behaviour and attitude is always consistent. It is just because he believes that God is dependable that Jeremiah can say in his distress and perplexity: 'Righteous art thou, O LORD, when I complain to thee; yet I would plead my case before thee' (Jer 12^{1}). The righteousness of both God and man are made manifest in their activity. Man is righteous when he conforms to the standard revealed by God's activity. God's righteousness was revealed above all in His concern for the welfare of His people, shown by their deliverance from Egypt, and their establishment in the promised land, but shown also by the activities of the prophets who declared His judgement on His people, for the purpose of this judgement was to persuade His rebellious children to turn and return to Him. God's righteousness was shown in His concern for the oppressed—the widows, the orphans, and the meek (Ps 10^{14-18}, Isa 30^{18}).

The eighth-century prophets condemned the social injustice in their midst because it did not conform to God's 'righteousness'. Amos's plea for 'righteousness' and 'justice' (Amos 5^{24}) is a plea that Israel should order her behaviour in conformity with God's will, which is the standard of righteousness.

Since God's righteousness and justice are concerned with man's true welfare, and not with punishment except as a means of salvation, it is not surprising that among the later writers righteousness becomes almost synonymous with grace and salvation. Thus the writer of Micah 7^{9-10} (thought by some scholars to be a post-exilic passage) acknowledges himself to be a sinner and yet waits confidently, though penitently, for God's judgement which will be 'the grace which will put an end to' his sin [3] (cf. also Isa $45^{22\,ff}$).

God is Faithful

Micah 7^{20} describes God's dependability: 'Thou wilt show faithfulness to Jacob, and steadfast love to Abraham.' The two words 'faithfulness' (Hebrew, '*'emeth*') and 'steadfast love' (Hebrew, '*chesed*') often occur together as a description of God's reliability (cf. Ps 25^{10}, 40^{11}, $61^{7,}$ 138^{2}).

'*'emeth*' is derived from a verb which means 'to sustain', or 'support' and so is used metaphorically to mean 'to be trustworthy' or 'to be sure'. Thus the noun '*'emeth*' describes God's trustworthiness.

'*chesed*' is a word of wider meaning and is difficult to translate adequately. The older English versions rendered it by 'mercy' or 'lovingkindness', but these translations do not convey the idea of 'steadfastness' and 'loyalty' which is implied by '*chesed*'. The loyalty which God shows is His loyalty to His people with whom He entered into a covenant relation. He had promised 'I will be your God' and this promise was guaranteed by His faithfulness (*'emeth*) and steadfastness (*chesed*). But the covenant was a two-sided relationship, and God's loyalty (*chesed*) ought to be matched by Israel's, instead the latter was 'like a morning cloud, like the dew that goes early away' (Hos 6^{4}—in this verse 'love'='*chesed*'; it is Israel's failure in loyalty that Hosea is condemning). Yahweh's loyalty remained and Hosea came to understand, in the light of his own domestic tragedy, that Yahweh's loyalty to the covenant was not dependent on Israel's loyalty. Yahweh was loyal to His covenant because He also loved Israel; His steadfastness is a steadfast love (cf. Hos 2^{19-20}, Jer 3^{12}, merciful=plenteous in steadfast love; Isa 54^{7-8}). The latter passage couples with the thought of steadfast love that of eternal duration. The forsaking and wrath were but temporary, but the steadfast love endures: 'but with everlasting love I will have compassion on you'.

[3] E. Jacob, *Theology of the Old Testament*, p. 101.

The Love of God

The Old Testament found the answer to the question 'Why did Yahweh choose Israel?' in His love for Israel. The Hebrew word for this love, which has been called 'Election Love'[4] to distinguish it from the 'steadfast love' (*chesed*) described above, is '*'ahabh*'. When used in a secular context the word describes 'the overwhelming force of passion between men and women'.[5] It is characteristic of such love that it neither requires nor can have any *a priori* reason or justification for its existence. This love is its own sufficient reason. God's love for Israel is of this nature. Deuteronomy is at pains to emphasize that there was no reason why God should love Israel, except His own determination to do so (cf. Deut 7^{7-8}, 9^{4-5}). This is made abundantly clear in one passage: Deuteronomy 10^{14-15}. The writer is amazed that the Sovereign LORD of all creation should love Israel. The word translated 'yet' (verse 15) is used to introduce 'what is contrary to expectation'.[6]

Hosea understood better than any other writer the depth of this unconditional, inextinguishable love of God. The poet who wrote the Song of Songs had sung of the love of a man for his beloved, 'for love is strong as death' (Song of Songs 8^{6}). If this were true of human love, how much more of divine love? Hosea's own love for Gomer is a striking illustration of God's unmerited love for Israel. 'Go again, love a woman who is beloved of a paramour and is an adultress; even as the LORD loves the people of Israel, though they turn to other gods and love cakes of raisins' (Hos 3^{1}). The prophet's love for Gomer had brought heartache and misery to him, but had not destroyed his love; so he dares to portray God Himself 'as suffering and bewildered in the face of the lovelessness of His people' (Hos 11^{8}, 6^{4}).[7] Fierce threats alternate with expressions of love towards Israel, but this only serves to illuminate the intensity of that divine love which is 'unmerited and free' and which triumphs in the end. 'I will love them freely' (Hos 14^{4}; and cf. Hos 11^{9}).

II—GOD AND ISRAEL

Election

'When Israel was a child, I loved him,
and out of Egypt I called my son' (Hos 11^{1}).

[4] Cf. N. H. Snaith, *Distinctive Ideas of the Old Testament*, ch. 6.
[5] W. Eichrodt, *Theology of the Old Testament*, p. 250.
[6] N. H. Snaith, *Distinctive Ideas of the Old Testament*, p. 135.
[7] W. Eichrodt, *Theology of the Old Testament*, p. 253.

With these words Hosea recalls one of the basic convictions of the Old Testament: that Israel stood in a special relation to Yahweh. Israel was, by Yahweh's free choice, His chosen people. Hosea connects the call of Israel with the event of the Exodus, and he is not alone in interpreting that great historic event as Yahweh's intervention on behalf of a people whom He had chosen 'out of all the nations of the earth to be the vessel of revelation'.[8] Amos places the same significance on the Exodus (Amos 3^{1-2}) but the fullest statement of the election of Israel is to be found in Deuteronomy. The ground of Israel's election is Yahweh's love for her (Deut 7^{7-8}); of His own free will Yahweh has 'chosen you to be a people for His own possession, out of all the peoples that are on the face of the earth' (Deut 7^{6}; cf. also Ex 19^{3b-6}—a passage attributed by many scholars to the Deuteronomic editor of Exodus).

The Old Testament writers are not forgetful that the people of God are also the servants of God. In the eighth century BC Amos had already hinted that election meant responsibility as well as privilege. 'You only have I known of all the families of the earth; therefore I will punish you for all your iniquities' (Amos 3^{2}). It was left to Deutero-Isaiah to underline the equation of election with service. In many passages belonging to the first period of his ministry (see above pp. 203 ff) the prophet addresses Israel both as 'servant' and as 'chosen' (cf. Isa 41^{8-9}, 42^{19}, 43^{10}, 44^{1-2}, 45^{4}). The term 'servant' (or better, 'slave') carries a twofold implication. On the one hand the 'slave' belongs to his master, and can look to him for protection. Hence just because Israel is Yahweh's servant she can appeal to Him for succour in time of distress (Ps $79^{2\,ff}$, $89^{49\,ff}$, etc.). On the other hand a servant has duties to perform for his master; in Israel's case it was the duty of rendering loving obedience to Yahweh (cf. especially Deut 10^{12-22}).

The Remnant

We saw (pp. 170 ff), when discussing the teaching of Isaiah, how that prophet realized that the continuance of God's people lay in the survival of a godly remnant even though the nation as a whole were doomed to destruction. The idea of the remnant receives the fullest treatment at the hands of Isaiah, but it runs through the Old Testament like a scarlet thread. The pattern is set in the Yahwist's introduction to the account of the Flood (Gen 6^{5-8}). In symbolic language the author had described the entry and rapid spread of sin throughout mankind, and had pronounced Yahweh's doom on His creation. In this crisis

[8] S. H. Hooke, *Alpha and Omega*, p. 18.

Noah is spared because he had 'found favour in the eyes of the LORD' (Gen 6^{8}). Noah and his family form a remnant saved from the general destruction, and this is a pattern which is repeated throughout the history of Israel.

It is only a remnant of those who came out of Egypt which is allowed to enter Canaan. The refusal of the Israelites to go into Canaan from the wilderness (Num 13) brought them under judgement, only Caleb 'because he has a different spirit and has followed me fully, I will bring into the land into which he went, and his descendants shall possess it' (Num 14^{24}). Already there are the beginnings of the distinction between the true Israel, that minority which is faithful to Yahweh, and the Israel 'after the flesh' (cf. Rom 9^{6-7}). Even in the critical days of Jezebel's persecution, Elijah receives the assurance that he is not alone; he is not the only champion, and that a disillusioned one, of Yahweh, but there is a faithful remnant, 'seven thousand in Israel, all the knees that have not bowed to Baal, and every mouth that has not kissed him' (1 K 19^{18}).

When Isaiah found that his message was falling on deaf ears he realized that the future lay not with the nation ('Israel after the flesh') but with the poor despised remnant (see above, pp. 171 f). Henceforth the future will lay with this remnant (Zeph 3^{12-13}).

The folly of the descendants of Josiah brought Judah to destruction, but neither this national disaster nor the exile which followed could destroy the true Israel. In the teaching of Jeremiah and Ezekiel we are led to recognize the remnant among those who have been taken to Babylon—they are the good figs of whom it can be said 'they shall return to me with their whole heart' (Jer 24^{7}; and cf. Isa 10^{21}, Ezk 11^{14-20}).

With the return from exile, the remnant is found once again in the homeland. Whilst we may deplore the extreme measures adopted by Ezra to preserve the purity of the Jewish community, we must also recognize that it was this Jewish community which produced the Hasidim, that faithful remnant which resisted Antiochus Epiphanes and suffered martyrdom at his hands.

We meet the remnant again in the Gospels. 'Now there was a man in Jerusalem whose name was Simeon, and this man was righteous and devout, looking for the consolation of Israel' (Lk 2^{25}). Amid the grandeur of Herod's Temple, which was so soon to be razed to the ground, the Old Testament story of the remnant reaches its climax.

Simeon, the representative of that godly remnant who 'were looking for the redemption of Jerusalem' (Lk 2^{38}), took the infant Christ in his arms and gave thanks to God. 'His song gathers up the longings of patriarchs and prophets.'[9]

> 'Lord now lettest thou thy servant depart in peace;
> according to thy word.
> For mine eyes have seen thy salvation;
> Which thou has prepared before the face of all people;
> To be a light to lighten the Gentiles, and to be the
> glory of thy people Israel.'
> (Lk 2^{29-32}, Book of Common Prayer)

III—THE MESSIANIC HOPE

'Now when John heard in prison about the deeds of the Christ, he sent word by his disciples and said to him, "Are you he who is to come, or shall we look for another?" And Jesus answered them, "Go and tell John what you hear and see: the blind receive their sight and the lame walk, lepers are cleansed and the deaf hear, and the dead are raised up, and the poor have good news preached to them"' (Mt $11^{2\,\text{ff}}$). John's question reminds us of the eager longing among many of his contemporaries for the advent of Messiah—'He who is to come'. Jesus's answer was not a direct 'Yes' or 'No', but by quoting phrases from various parts of the prophecy of Isaiah (29^{18-19}, 35^{5-6}, 61^{1-2}) He drew John's attention once again to some of the Old Testament expressions of hope and aspirations for the future, and invited him to compare these with such reports of His ministry as his disciples had brought to him.

In this section we shall endeavour to trace the origin and growth of this Messianic hope. The word 'Messiah', like its Greek translation, 'Christ' has, since New Testament times become, for Christians at any rate, another name for Jesus, but originally it had no reference to Him. It is a Hebrew word meaning simply 'The Anointed One'. Both persons and things could be anointed; the anointing ceremony was performed by a priest who poured or smeared sweet-smelling oil over the person or thing to be anointed. But 'The Anointed' or 'The LORD's Anointed' (i.e. The Messiah) could only be one person in ancient Israel—the king. The climax of the coronation ceremony by which a

[9] 'The Scapegoat and the Countenance', by a Religious of the Society of the Sacred Cross, p. 45.

man was made king, was the anointing by the priest (cf. 1 K 1$^{34, 39}$, 2 K 11^{12}), so that it would probably be better to speak of consecrating the king rather than crowning him. The king then belonged to Yahweh in a special way; his person was sacrosanct. Thus when David had Saul in his power and could easily have slain him, he contented himself with cutting off a piece of his robe. Even then his conscience smote him: 'The LORD forbid that I should do this thing to my lord, the LORD's anointed, to put forth my hand against him, seeing he is the LORD's anointed' (1 S 24^{6}; cf. 1 S 26$^{9-11, 23}$, 2 S 1$^{14 \text{ ff}}$).

In consequence of his anointing, the king stood in a special relation to Yahweh. The nature of this relationship and the resulting benefits which the nation expected to enjoy are described in certain of the psalms (e.g. Ps 2, 72, 110, 132, and possibly others) which were used at the consecration ceremony. In Psalm 2^{7} and Psalm 72^{1} the king is called 'the son', and the first reference makes it clear that this means 'the son of Yahweh'. The Psalmists are using here a form of expression common to the Ancient Near East. The Pharaohs actually claimed to be divine, so that they could be called 'the god' or even 'the good god'. The Mesopotamian rulers, whilst not claiming to be divine, did regard themselves as the adopted sons of their gods. Indeed the expression used in Psalm 2^{7} of the Israelite king—'You are my son'—was the regular formula of adoption. The kings of Judah (all of whom were descendants of David) were thus regarded as the adopted sons of Yahweh.[10] Whilst this did not imply that they were regarded as divine, it did mean that they were especially endowed by Yahweh to rule over His people, and to ensure their welfare in every sphere of life.

Psalm 72 opens with the prayer that God would give His justice and righteousness to the king. Thus endowed he would then rule the kingdom in accordance with the will of Yahweh; and in particular the poor, the needy, the weak, and the oppressed would find in him their champion (verses 2 ff, 12–14). For the nation as a whole there would be an era of prosperity (verse 3), with abundance of grain and flourishing cities (verse 16) and the overthrow and subjugation of enemies (verses 2–11).

We turn now to other passages which speak of the equipment of the king and the hopes which were placed in him. Just as the consecration of a king was a time when expectations of peace and prosperity were high, so similar expectations of a new order were expressed at the birth of a royal child. The birth of such a child is greeted in a well-known

[10] This may be true of the kings of Israel also.

passage in Isaiah (9^{2-7}), where there is an allusion in verse 2 to the Syro-Ephraimite invasion of Judah, a time when the people 'walked in darkness'. But the birth of the child (perhaps Hezekiah) gives grounds for renewed hope, for when in due course the child comes to the throne there will be an era of 'peace', 'justice', and 'righteousness' (verse 7). In anticipation of the consecration ceremony the prophet already announces the names (verse 6) which the child would then receive in addition to his personal name. These 'throne' names describe the equipment which the king must have in order to rule over God's people with 'justice' and 'righteousness'. 'The first and last of these names are immediately intelligible to us: to rule over the land and the nation in war and peace, to have the right counsel in every situation, and to carry it into effect, to secure 'peace' and 'happiness' by victory in war and by prudent and just government were always the tasks of kings in ancient Israel.'[11] The other two names 'Mighty God' (or Divine Hero), and 'Everlasting Father' appear to imply the divinity of the king; but as it is unlikely that the Hebrews ever regarded their kings as divine these names probably mean no more than that the king was equipped by Yahweh for his tasks. The names were in any case borrowed from Egyptian or Canaanite sources and originally did signify that the rulers were divine. These pagan associations were dropped when the titles were used by the prophet, for *his* final word is: 'The zeal of the LORD of Hosts will do this.' The king is only king by the grace of God.

This latter point becomes still more clear in another passage (Isa 11^{1-9}) which describes the king and his beneficent rule. The wisdom and understanding and all the virtues which make the king a worthy ruler are gifts from Yahweh. 'The Spirit of the LORD shall rest upon him.' In consequence the poor and meek are protected, while the wicked are held in check. Furthermore the peace which will come when a truly righteous king sits on the throne of David will extend to the whole of nature. As in the garden of Eden, when all the animals under the dominion of Adam were at peace with one another, so they will be once again when this ideal king exercises his rule (verses 6–9).

We have seen from the enthronement psalms that the accession of each new king gave rise to ever-renewed hopes that the expctations of peace and prosperity, so glowingly described in Psalm 72, would be realized. Similar hopes were expressed in almost identical terms at the accession of Assyrian and Babylonian kings and these hopes were as little realized in Judah as in Babylon. Of course some kings approxi-

[11] S. Mowinckel, *He That Cometh*, p. 105.

mated more closely than others to the ideal king of the psalms and the prophecies. Certainly in popular imagination, and not without reason, David came close to the ideal and so could be described as 'a king after Yahweh's own heart'. At the other extreme we recall Jeremiah's rebuke of Jehoiakim (Jer 22^{13-19}) who had 'eyes and heart only for your dishonest gain, for shedding innocent blood, and for practising oppression and violence'.

In spite of the hopes that were expressed either at the birth of a royal child or at the consecration of each new king, the peace and prosperity of the kingdom was not assured. It must have seemed to be the final denial of all expectations when Jerusalem fell to the Babylonians in 586 BC and the king was taken 'bound in fetters' to Babylon.

> 'The breath of our nostrils, the LORD's anointed, was taken in their pits,
> He of whom we said, "Under his shadow we shall live [i.e. flourish] among the nations" ' (Lam 4^{20}).

Thus did one poet express the dismay of many people when the king in whom they had hoped was carried off.

However, the collapse of the kingdom did not mean that Yahweh's purposes had been defeated. The prophets Jeremiah and Ezekiel, who taught that the exile was a divine judgement on the people of God, also looked forward to a restoration. Deutero-Isaiah even promised a triumphal return across the desert to Jerusalem, until he realized that the true destiny of Israel was to be a missionary people to the Gentiles. He glimpsed the truth that the kingdom which was to be established was not a political one, but the rule of Yahweh among all nations.

The confusion and widespread rebellion, which broke out throughout the Persian empire when Darius came to the throne, seemed to Haggai and Zechariah to be a sign that the time had come for the kingdom of Judah to be re-established. The grandson of Jehoiachin was already exercising rule as governor of the Persian province of Judah, and now these two prophets hailed him in language which would only have been addressed to the king in pre-exilic days. His very name appeared to bear a special significance—he was Zerub-babel—i.e. the 'shoot' from Babylon; twice Zechariah calls him the 'Branch' (3^{8}, 6^{12}). This cryptic description means that Zerubbabel was considered to be the legitimate descendant of the house of David. Zechariah associated with the anticipated reign of Zerubbabel all the blessings which, in times past, had been promised at the beginning of each new reign (Zech 8^{1-8}). Once again hopes had been pinned on a historical personage. However, Darius did not lose control of his empire, but Zerubbabel disappeared and the expectations which had been aroused by the two prophets were disappointed.

The passages from the prophets which we have examined above (Isa 9^{2-7}, 11^{1-9}; Zech 3^{8}, 6^{12}, 8^{1-8}, to which we could add Hag 2^{23}) were uttered in times of distress, and linked the promise of deliverance from affliction with some person actually present, such as Zerubbabel or the royal child of Isaiah's prophecies. So long as the monarchy existed hope could always be placed in each succeeding king, even if that hope always turned out to be misplaced. In fact the ideal of kingship, such as we find for example in Psalm 72, was at best only partially realized even to the end of the monarchy. In the case of kings such as Jehoiakim it was not realized at all. How then did this hope survive this continual frustration? We have already had a hint of the answer in one of the earliest of these prophecies (Isa 9^{2-7}); from verse 7 we learn that the ultimate hope is in Yahweh. When it became clear that the kingdom would not be restored under Zerubbabel, then the belief that Yahweh Himself would restore the kingdom became increasingly insistent. Among the passages in which this teaching is to be found we may cite Jeremiah 23^{1-6} and 30^{18-21} as typical. Many scholars believe that they are post-exilic. From these we learn that it is Yahweh Himself who gathers the scattered remnant (23^{3}), and restores 'the fortunes of the tents of Jacob' (30^{18}). No longer will the welfare (peace) of the people depend on the king, but on Yahweh (30^{18-20}, 23^{3}). The kingdom will then be the kingdom of Yahweh, and He will set over the kingdom 'shepherds' (i.e. a succession of rulers) who will care for the people. The ruler of the future will be raised up by Yahweh (23^{5-6}), he will be righteous and hence will ensure the continued welfare of the people; he will also act as mediator between Yahweh and the people—'I will make him draw near and he shall approach me. . . . And you shall be my people and I will be your God' (30^{21-2}). Another post-exilic passage (Zech 9^{9-10}) adds some details to the picture of the Messianic king who will rule in Yahweh's kingdom. This portrait of the king is in striking contrast to the kings pictured in the enthronement psalms. This one comes in peace and to bring peace to all nations, *he* is 'humble and riding on an ass'; *they* were ruthless warriors breaking their enemies 'with a rod of iron' (Ps 2^{8-9}, 72^{9}). This passage (Zech 9^{9-10}) dates from the Greek period and 'the prophet is describing the Messianic king in deliberate contrast to the martial rulers of his own age'.[12]

The post-exilic prophets were content to express their faith in Yahweh's purpose for His people, which had been once for all guaranteed by the covenant, by pointing to a future kingdom which He would establish and which would be ruled by His Anointed.

How then would Yahweh establish His kingly rule? From the exile Deutero-Isaiah gives an answer in his teaching on the Suffering Servant (see above, Ch 10). Yahweh's rule will be established by His Servant (Isa 42^{1-4}) as he brings justice to the nations, but at the cost of misunderstanding, suffering and death (contrast Ps 72^{7-14}). But the Servant's triumph is assured and he receives at the last kingly status. In spite of this element in the teaching about the Servant, the concept of victory through suffering on the one hand, and the reign of the Messianic king on the other, were too dissimilar for them to be connected in Old Testament thought. It remained for Jesus, who discarded all ideas of victory by force (contrast Ps 2^{9}, but compare Zech 9^{9-10}) to realize in His Person the ideal of a suffering Messiah. Hence He could answer John the Baptist by quoting Messianic prophecies: 'If it is by the Spirit that I cast out demons, then the kingdom of God has come upon you' (Mt 12^{28}). By the Spirit of God He establishes the kingdom, by the same Spirit He is Lord of it.

IV—THE PROBLEM OF SUFFERING

One of the problems which perplexed men in Old Testament times was to understand why the righteous should suffer. The old belief, which is expressed in many parts of the Old Testament, is that suffering is a punishment for sin. The unrighteous man or nation will be punished by suffering; one who is seen to suffer cannot be righteous. This is 'the simple and thorough-going theory that righteousness brings to individuals and to people material reward, and that evil brings material loss and penalty'.[13] This theory is implied in the following psalms: 1, 112, 128, and is worked out in great detail in Deuteronomy 28 (cf. also Lev 26). It provided an explanation of the chequered course of Israel's history. National apostasy brought national disaster, but obedience to Yahweh was rewarded by prosperity or deliverance from the national enemies. This is seen very clearly in the Book of Judges where the

12 J. Lindblom, *Prophecy in Ancient Israel*, p. 419.
13 O. S. Rankin, *Israel's Wisdom Literature*, p. 77.

periods of oppression are attributed to the fact 'that the people of Israel did what was evil in the sight of the LORD' (cf. Jdg 2^{18-23}, 2^{11}, 3^{12}, 4^{1}, 6^{1}, etc.); it is also the basis on which the editors of the Books of Kings pass judgement on the rulers of Israel and Judah. The theory is pushed to extreme lengths in the Books of Chronicles where every misfortune is duly related to some sin or disobedience, real or imagined.

But the most cruel conclusion which could be drawn from this theory was that great suffering was evidence of great sin, whether the sufferer was known to be a sinner or not. Driven thus to its logical conclusion the simple theory of rewards for the good and punishment for the wicked was seen to be at variance with experience. The unjust, the unscrupulous and the oppressors were often seen to be the prosperous ones; the righteous were often the ones who suffered, whether at the hands of the oppressors or from sickness or other misfortune. Habakkuk's question must have troubled the minds of many who had been taught that God prospered the righteous and punished the wicked—'Thou who art of purer eyes than to behold evil and canst not look on wrong, why dost Thou look [i.e. with apparent favour] on faithless men, and art silent when the wicked swallows up the man more righteous than he?' (Hab 1^{13}; cf. Jer 12^{1-2}). So far was prosperity and well-being from being the reward of one who strove to obey Yahweh, that this anguished cry was wrung from the lips of Jeremiah: 'O Yahweh Thou hast enticed me, and I let myself be enticed. . . . I have become a laughing stock all day long, everyone mocks me' (Jer 20^{7}).[14] He has seen the 'way of the wicked prosper' (12^{1}) but for himself there was loneliness, persecution, and humiliation (15^{15}, 16^{2}, 20^{2}). Yet though obedience brings this nightmare of suffering he must continue to obey; to refrain from speaking was even more intolerable than his present suffering (20^{9}). There is little wonder that he cried: 'Why did I come forth from the womb to see toil and sorrow, and spend my days in shame?' (20^{18}).

In his perplexity Jeremiah cries out 'why'—'why is my pain unceasing, my wound incurable?' (15^{18}), and then in his torment he reproaches Yahweh for enticing and deceiving him. 'Wilt Thou be to me like a deceitful brook, like waters that fail?' So he dares to question Yahweh's integrity and this 'fearful revolt of the prophet Jeremiah is the forerunner of the Book of Job, and of Psalm 73'.[15] For the problem

[14] J. Lindblom, *Prophecy in Ancient Israel*, p. 195, writes: 'The Hebrew which I have translated "entice" means "deceive", "seduce", "bewitch", i.e. persuade without rational arguments.'

[15] L. Koehler, *Old Testament Theology*, p. 97.

of the suffering of the righteous man, which almost overwhelms Jeremiah, is the theme of the Book of Job and of the 73rd Psalm.

THE BOOK OF JOB

The Book of Job consists of a prose introduction (Ch 1 and 2) which sets the stage for the main poetical portion of the book (Ch 3 to 42^{6}); finally there is a brief prose conclusion (42^{7-17}). The book belongs to a type of literature called the Wisdom literature. Writing of this kind was well known in the Ancient Near East; examples considerably older than Job are known from ancient Egypt, other examples in the Old Testament are Proverbs, Ecclesiastes and certain psalms.[16] A common feature of all this literature, regardless of the nationality of the authors, is its concern with problems of daily life. Thus the Book of Proverbs gives advice for right conduct which was as applicable in Egypt as in Israel, and it is probable that some of the 'proverbs' owe their inspiration to similar proverbial sayings which had been current in Egypt centuries before they were known in Israel. In like manner 'in Babylonia, as in Israel, the suffering of the pious was a religious problem'.[17] It is not surprising then that, when the story of Job was told to focus attention on this problem, the characters in the story are not Israelites. Job is simply introduced as a wealthy sheik whose home was the 'land of Uz'—somewhere to the east of Palestine, perhaps in the land of Edom. Superficially the story belongs to the age of the Patriarchs, but a study of the language and contents of the book point to a date about 450 B C for its composition. It is likely that the author used a 'familiar story of a righteous man overwhelmed with misfortune' [18] to serve as the basis for his discussion of the problem of the suffering of the righteous.

The prose prologue of the book (Ch 1 and 2) gives a brief picture of the prosperity and happiness of Job before calamity befell him. He was blessed with a large family and great wealth; in character he was pronounced by Yahweh Himself to be 'blameless and upright' ($1^{1,8}$, 2^{3}). Then in a short space of time he was first deprived of his family and his wealth, and then he was struck down with some loathsome and painful disease. The problem which had tormented Jeremiah is brought into sharpest focus in this brief, vivid introduction to Job.

16 The following extra-canonical books fall into this category: *The Wisdom of Jesus ben Sirach, The Wisdom of Solomon, The Sayings of the Fathers.*

17 O. S. Rankin, *Israel's Wisdom Literature*, p. 5.

18 A. S. Peake, 'Job', *Century Bible*, p. 4.

The man, acknowledged by God Himself to be blameless, is brought to the verge of despair by his misfortune and suffering. But Job, blameless even in his dire extremity, does not curse God and so find in death a way out of his misery, but turning to the friends who had come to console him, he asks 'Why?'

The major portion of the book consists of the dialogue between Job and his friends. Racked by pain, and unable to find any reason for his suffering, Job curses the day on which he was born; it would have been better if he had never been born, and even now the oblivion of death would be preferable to the unending torment he is called upon to endure (Ch 3). In the succeeding chapters he is addressed in turn by Eliphaz, Bildad, and Zophar, and to each speech Job makes an answer. The friends, however, can offer no explanation of Job's suffering except to suggest, according to the current theory, that Job must, in spite of appearances, have committed grave sins. This is no consolation to Job, nor indeed is it an answer to his question, for though he is willing to admit that he may have transgressed he cannot recall any instances and begs his friends 'teach me and I will be silent, make me understand how I have erred' (6^{24}). But the platitudinous generalities concerning the fate of the unrighteous do not convince Job, who maintains that he is innocent; 'there is no violence in my hands, and my prayer is pure' (16^{17}). Finding neither comfort nor explanation in his friends' words Job turns to God, though even God appears to be his enemy (19^{6-12}). But the conviction has been growing that, though God seems to be his opponent, striking him down without cause, He will ultimately vindicate him. There is a hint of this in 16^{18-19}. The thought in these verses is that after his death, his blood poured out on the ground will cry out for vengeance (cf. Gen 4^{10}), and his avenger will be God Himself. The 'vengeance' in this case is to be understood figuratively to mean the re-establishment of Job's character as a righteous man. This hint that God will ultimately vindicate Job is the prelude to the great affirmation of 19^{25-6}:

> 'For I know that my Redeemer lives,
>   and at last He will stand upon the earth;
> And after my skin has been thus destroyed,
>   then from my flesh I shall see God,
> Whom I shall see on my side,
>   and my eyes shall behold, and not another.'

This thought is far removed from the ideas with which the friends are familiar, and so the debate continues. In his final speech (Ch 22) Eliphaz roundly accuses Job of specific crimes. The friends have nothing new to add to the assertion they made at the beginning of the debate, that Job's suffering is a proof of his sin. This section of the book concludes with a speech by Job (Ch 29–31). First he reviews the course of his life until the misfortune overtook him (Ch 29). Formerly he was a man of prosperity and integrity, respected and honoured by young and old, by the nobles as well as the common people. Then he contemplates his present state, emaciated by his disease, mocked and scorned even by the most disreputable of his neighbours (Ch 30). Finally (in answer to Eliphaz's accusations?) he names specific sins, and by implication challenges his accusers to show that he had been guilty of any of them. Confident to the last of his innocence he is willing to give 'an account of all my life' (31^{37}) to any adversary, whether man or God.

Chapters 32 to 37—speeches by Elihu who appears now for the first time—are generally regarded as being a later addition to the book. In Chapter 31 (verse 35) Job had pleaded for an answer from Yahweh, but in the present arrangement of the book this answer is delayed until Chapter 38. This might be understandable if Elihu contributed anything significant to the debate, but 'nothing new is added . . . though he dwells more fully on the disciplinary aspect of suffering (Ch 33), a thought first suggested by Eliphaz (5^{17})'.[19]

The climax of the book is Yahweh's answer to Job in Chapters 38 and 39. (It is probable that the descriptions of Behemoth and Leviathan in Chapters 40 and 41 are a later addition.) Superficially there seems to be no answer here to Job's problem. There is a parade of Yahweh's superior knowledge and His omnipotence, the effect being to crush Job into silence. But more is intended than a mere display of divine might; if it is true that all creation was brought into being and is prevented from lapsing again into chaos by the might of Yahweh, it is also true that He cares moment by moment for the world He has called into being. It is this vision of the omnipotent and yet gracious God which is granted to Job. The One who had seemed to be his Enemy is not only his Vindicator but his Friend.

> 'I had heard of Thee by the hearing of the ear,
> but now my eye sees Thee' (42^{5}).

[19] J. Patterson, *The Wisdom of Israel*, p. 43.

The prose epilogue to the book (42^{7-17}) shows Job restored to his former state of prosperity and health. This might seem to be an anti-climax, but for the writer it was not sufficient that Job should know himself to be vindicated, but that by these material signs his neighbours should also see that he was indeed, as he had continually protested, a truly righteous man. It was not enough that justice be done, but justice must be seen to be done.

PASSAGES FOR STUDY

Job 1–2—*Job is deprived of wealth and health*

In this chapter the writer describes briefly how misfortune overtook Job. The reader is also permitted to know the reason why the disaster befell the admittedly righteous man, though Job himself is kept in ignorance throughout. The chapter falls into six sections.

1^{1-5}—This thumbnail sketch portrays a man of manifest integrity and considerable prosperity. But though Job is described as 'the greatest of the sons of the east' his manner appears to be completely free from ostentation. His chief concern is to keep both himself and his family free from sin. Three times it is said of him that he 'was blameless and upright, one who feared God and turned away from evil' ($1^{1,8}$, 2^{3}).

1^{6-12}—The reader is now transported to the court of heaven where the heavenly beings (sons of God) who serve Yahweh are gathered to report to Him or to receive His commands. The function of the Satan (i.e. the adversary) was not to tempt men to do wrong, but rather to oppose or test them, as in this case he is permitted to test Job's character by afflicting him. (In later writings and by New Testament times Satan was regarded as God's opponent who sought to tempt men away from allegiance to Him.) Satan's job as a tester of man had made him sceptical, so he cynically suggests that Job's piety has been bought by the prosperity with which Yahweh has surrounded him. But Yahweh is sure of Job's integrity and permits Satan to test him.

1^{13-22}—With a few rapid strokes the author shows one calamity after another hitting Job in quick succession. In one day he loses property and family. Job had received the messengers, who brought the tragic news, sitting, but when the last sorry tale had been told, with an almost terrifying dignity he rose, solemnly rent his outer garment, and shaved his head—the usual outward signs of mourning. Then, prostrating himself, he worshipped Yahweh confessing his utter dependence on Him: 'Naked I came from my mother's womb, and naked shall I return; the LORD gave and the LORD has taken away; blessed be the name of the LORD' (verse 21).

2^{1-6}—Once again the reader is taken to the court of heaven and hears Yahweh commending Job. He had come through the first trial and had vindicated Yahweh's confidence in him. Satan now proposes a further test. Let Job be smitten with a terrible disease and he will curse God.

2^{7-10}—The scene changes. We see Job, stricken with a loathsome and painful disease, sitting on the ash-heap outside the village wearily scraping himself with a piece of broken pottery in an effort to allay the intolerable itching. Even in this extremity he will not curse God, rejecting his wife's suggestion as impious. Though he later regards death as preferable to the unrelieved suffering which he is called on to endure, he will not seek this escape by uttering blasphemy. Satan has been proved in the wrong, Yahweh's confidence in Job is well founded.

2^{11-13}—Three friends hearing of Job's plight arrange to visit him in order to console him. They were so appalled at the change which disease had wrought in him that they are struck dumb. Flinging dust on their heads as a sign of their distress they sit with him in silent sympathy for seven days. 'When grief is so crushing, what form but silence can sympathy take?'[20]

NOTE—There is implicit in this introductory section of Job one explanation of the purpose of suffering, i.e. that it may sometimes be permitted in order to test character. This thought does not seem to be developed elsewhere in the book, and as Job is never permitted to realize this possibility it cannot be regarded as a solution of his problem.

Job 15^{20-35}, 18^{5-21}—*The Traditional Teaching*

These two passages, from speeches by Eliphaz and Bildad, illustrate the viewpoint of the three friends who are convinced that Job's suffering can only be accounted for by some secret and heinous sin. In the early stages of the debate they do not accuse Job directly of sin, but they point out repeatedly that misfortune, misery, and suffering is the certain fate of the wicked. In the second of the passages (18^{5-21}) the similarity of the fate of the wicked—'by disease his skin is consumed'—'he has no offspring'—to the misfortune which had overtaken Job is

20 A. S. Peake, 'Job', *Century Bible*, p. 68.

obvious. It is clear that Bildad is hinting that Job too must be a great sinner.

Job 16^{18-19}, 19^{23-7}—*A Ray of Hope*

We have already noted (p. 254) that, dissatisfied by his friends' explanation of his suffering, Job turns from them to God. The awful tension in Job's soul is revealed in the chapters in which these two short passages occur, for in both cases in the verses which precede the passages Job is driven to regard God as his enemy (16^{6-17}, 19^{2-22}). At the same time he cannot forget that, before this monstrous calamity overtook him, he had rejoiced in God's friendship. Now his old trust in God enables him to pierce this dark night of suffering and catch a glimpse of the 'smiling face' 'behind a frowning providence'.[21] It is not that he hopes for a reversal of his plight; his cry in verse 16^{18}, 'O earth, cover not my blood', shows that he already anticipates that his death cannot be long delayed. But worse than the physical suffering, intense though this has been, is the mental anguish resulting from the knowledge that his integrity has been called in question by friend and enemy alike. Only God can clear his name and the conviction is born within him that He will vindicate His servant (16^{19}).

The second passage expresses much the same thought. Job's assertion of his innocence has been unavailing, his friends remain unconvinced. Perhaps if his plea 'Not guilty' is written in a book or chiselled in rock, later generations may be convinced and his name cleared. Then 'in a sudden burst of faith he utters the great conviction enshrined in these verses' [22]:

> 'For I know that my Redeemer lives,
> and at last He will stand upon the earth;
> and after my skin has been thus destroyed,
> then from my flesh I shall see God,
> Whom I shall see on my side,
> and my eyes shall behold, and not another' (19^{25-7}).

His own desperate protests of innocence will not be necessary, for after his death the One who seemed to be his Adversary will turn out to be his Advocate. Not only so, but Job will see this for himself. In 16^{18-19} he had found consolation in the thought that God would clear his name, though he himself would have passed into oblivion. But here is a better hope; though his vindication will still be after his death he

[21] MHB, No. 503. [22] A. S. Peake, 'Job', *Century Bible*, p. 192.

will then see God arise like a judge (the imagery is taken from the law court) and pronounce him innocent.[23]

Job 38^{1-11}, 42^{1-6}—*Yahweh's Answer*

Job has pleaded that God would speak either to condemn or to acquit him. At last He intervenes in the debate, but as we have already remarked, His answer does not solve Job's problem. Job is, however, led to an understanding both of the omnipotence and the grace of God. This opening section of Yahweh's speech calls for little comment. In a series of word-pictures the writer passes in review the wonders of the world which Yahweh has created and which He continually sustains. Job's conception had been too limited and so he had obscured the purpose of God by words which he had spoken in ignorance. When his ignorance is dispelled he begins to realize that though God's purpose, particularly in permitting suffering, may always remain a mystery, yet he can rely on Him as One who cares, for he has 'seen' Him (42^{5}). 'What Job has seen, i.e. experienced, is just what he had wished to see (19^{27}), viz. that God is not against him or estranged from him; and his wish has been more than fulfilled, for the vision has come to him before death.'[24]

Psalm 73—*The Cry of a Sufferer*

Like Jeremiah, the psalmist has seen the 'way of the wicked prosper'; there is none of the easy optimism of Psalm 1 here, it simply was not true that the wicked were like chaff driven away by the wind (Ps 1^{4}). On the contrary they enjoy good health and material possessions (Ps $73^{4-5,\ 12}$). Their wealth gives them authority which they abuse by oppressing those who come into their power (verse 8). Their success, based on ruthlessness, gives rise to an attitude of mind which sneers and scoffs at everything, even at God Himself (verse 9). Such an arrogant display inevitably attracts a certain type of admirer who becomes convinced that God neither knows nor cares (verses 10–11).

The psalmist had almost succumbed to the temptation to fall in with these admirers and to regard his hitherto virtuous life as being in vain (verses 2, 13–15). However, instead of 'speaking thus' (i.e. like the admirers of the wicked in verse 11) he joined the company of faithful worshippers in the sanctuary. In worship there comes the realization

23 On Job 19^{25-7} see particularly, Peake, 'Job', *Century Bible*, pp. 192 ff., and Driver and Gray 'Job', *ICC*, pp. 171 ff.

24 Driver and Gray, 'Job', *ICC*, p. 372.

that his 'portion' is God (verse 26); the material wealth of the wicked is but a passing glory.

The psalmist does not discover the meaning of his suffering, but he is granted 'the living assurance that God is also near him in those times when his life is veiled in obscurity, and will eventually see to it that everything ends well'.[25] In verse 24b ('And afterwards Thou wilt receive me to glory') there seems to be an indication of a belief in a blessed life after death where the communion with God which the psalmist has experienced in worship will be unbroken. This is the 'portion' which far outweighs the present, but ephemeral, riches of the ungodly. So the psalmist finishes on a note of triumph—'I have made the LORD God my refuge.'

25 A. Weiser, *Psalms*, p. 514.

QUESTIONS

CHAPTER ONE

(1) The Israelites looked upon Palestine as 'a land flowing with milk and honey'. How far do the geography and climate bear out this description?
(2) What do you understand by: 'The Law, The Prophets, and The Writings'?
(3) What is the religious value of the first three chapters of Genesis?

CHAPTER TWO

(1) 'In the wanderings of the Patriarchs the divine purpose was being fulfilled.' Illustrate this from the life of Abraham.
(2) Comment briefly on the following passages: (*a*) Gen 12^{1}, (*b*) Gen 15^{6}, (*c*) Gen 17^{7}, (*d*) Gen 18^{25}, (*e*) Gen 22^{2}.
(3) How can archaeology help us in our study of the Old Testament?

CHAPTER THREE

(1) Show how the character of Jacob was influenced by his religious and other experiences.
(2) 'God's hand . . . in all the confusion of human guilt directs everything to a gracious goal.' Show how the life of Joseph illustrates this truth.
(3) Write a brief account of the historical background to the Patriarchs.

CHAPTER FOUR

(1) Outline the events of the Exodus and the journeyings in the wilderness. Illustrate with a map.
(2) Assess the importance of Moses as a national and spiritual leader.
(3) Comment on the following passages: (*a*) Ex 3^{14}, (*b*) Ex 20^{5}, (*c*) Ex 20^{8}.

CHAPTER FIVE

(1) What conditions did Joshua find in Canaan, and how far was he successful in dealing with them in his invasion?
(2) What lessons were the stories of the Judges intended to teach? Illustrate from the stories of Barak and Gideon.
(3) What part did Samuel play in the history of Israel?

CHAPTER SIX

(1) (*a*) What did Saul achieve as a king? (*b*) Why is his reign described as tragic?
(2) Show how David came to power. In what respect was he a good king?
(3) Describe Solomon's reign and show how his policies led to the division of the kingdom.
(4) Comment on the following verses: (*a*) 1 S 14^{43}, (*b*) 2 S 12^{7}, (*c*) 2 S 12^{23}, (*d*) 1 K 11^{6}.

CHAPTER SEVEN

(1) Write short notes on (*a*) Jeroboam I, (*b*) Ahab, (*c*) Jehu, (*d*) Jeroboam II, (*e*) Ahaz, (*f*) Hezekiah.
(2) What was the role of the prophet in Old Testament times?
(3) Justify the description of Elijah as 'the greatest religious personality since Moses'.
(4) What do we learn from Psalm 51 about the nature of true religion?

CHAPTER EIGHT

(1) Comment on the historical and theological significance of the following quotations from Amos:
(*a*) I am no prophet, nor a prophet's son (7^{14}).
(*b*) You only have I known of all the families of the earth (3^{2}).
(*c*) Hear this word, you cows of Bashan (4^{1}).
(*d*) Come to Bethel, and transgress (4^{4}).
(*e*) Let justice roll down like waters, and righteousness like an ever-flowing stream (5^{24}).
(*f*) Is not the day of the LORD darkness and not light (5^{20}).
(2) Show how Hosea's personal experience led to and coloured his prophetic message.
(3) How do the prophecies of Isaiah (*a*) proclaim judgement, (*b*) offer hope during the two great crises of his period.

CHAPTER NINE

(1) Write a short account of Josiah's reign and show how far his reforms were successful. What was Jeremiah's attitude to the reforms?
(2) (*a*) What is the main teaching of Deuteronomy?
(*b*) Why is it connected with Josiah's reformation?
(3) What abuses and wrong ideas of God's ways were attacked by Jeremiah in his prophecies?
(4) Write notes on the religious significance of the following: (*a*) Jeremiah's call; (*b*) the almond tree, the boiling cauldron, and the broken cisterns; (*c*) the New Covenant.

CHAPTER TEN

(1) Outline the course of events in Jerusalem from the return of the exiles from Babylon to the rebuilding of the Temple.
(2) The year 586 BC 'marked a turning-point in Ezekiel's prophetic career'. Write an essay on this statement.
(3) What is the teaching of Deutero-Isaiah on the nature of God.
(4) Outline Deutero-Isaiah's teaching on the Servant of the LORD.

CHAPTER ELEVEN

(1) Describe the work of Nehemiah.
(2) (*a*) Give a short account of the work of Ezra.
(*b*) Show how the Book of Jonah may be regarded as a protest against the policy of Ezra.
(3) (*a*) In what circumstances was the Book of Daniel written?
(*b*) What were the chief lessons it was intended to teach?

CHAPTER TWELVE

(1) Outline the Old Testament teaching on the nature of God.

(2) Trace the origin and growth of the Messianic hope among the Jews.

(3) What contributions do the Book of Job and Psalm 73 make to the discussion of the problem of the suffering of the righteous man?

Note for Local Preachers 'on Trial' who are using this 'Guide' to prepare for the Connexional Examination in Old Testament.

(a) The Revised Standard Version of the Old Testament is the translation prescribed for the examination.

(b) Candidates normally take six months to prepare for the examination. The 'Guide' has, therefore, been divided into twelve chapters so that each chapter should form the basis for two weeks' study. *Special* attention should be given to the 'Passages for Study' as the examiners attach considerable importance to an accurate knowledge of the Bible itself.

(c) Students taking correspondence courses should send to their tutors each fortnight answers to at least two questions—but more if possible—on each chapter.

The maps and the summary tables (on pages 49, 153, 193, and 215) should be consulted when studying the background material.

Some students, who may prefer to have a general survey of the background before embarking on the detailed study of the prescribed passages, are recommended to read the following sections first: pp. 11–16, 41–54, 68–71, 89–93, 109–11, 116–20, 125–7, 132–45, 194–7, 216–22, 228–31.

SYLLABUS FOR THE CONNEXIONAL LOCAL PREACHERS' EXAMINATION IN OLD TESTAMENT

Ch. 1 Gen 1^{1}–2^{25}, 3; Ps 8, 104, 29.

Ch. 2 Gen 11^{28}–12^{9}, 13, 15, 17^{1-22}, 18^{16-22}, 19^{1-29}, $21^{1-8,}$ 22^{1-19}; Ps 105.

Ch. 3 Gen 25^{19-34}, 27^{1-45}, 28^{10-22}, 29, 32^{3-32}, 37, 39–47; Ps 139.

Ch. 4 Ex 1–4^{23}, 4^{27}–6^{1}, 11^{1-8}, 12^{1-42}, 13^{17}–14^{31}, 19, 20^{1-17}; Deut 5^{6-21};
Ex 31^{18}–32^{35}, 33^{1-23}; Num 13–14; Deut 34; Ps 114.

Ch. 5 Josh 1–6^{27}, 7–8^{29}, 9–11, 24; Jdg 1–3^{6}, 4–8; 1 S 1–4^{22}.

Ch. 6 1 S 11–16^{23}, 17–18^{5}, 28–31; 2 S 1^{19-27}, 2–4, 5–7^{29}, 8, 11–12^{25},
15–19; 1 K 3, 6^{1-18}, 9^{26}–10^{13}, 11^{1-13}; Ps 132.

Ch. 7 1 K 17–19, 21; Ps 51.

Ch. 8 Amos 7^{10-17}, 3^{1}–6^{14}; Hos 8^{1-3}, 1^{2-8}, 3^{1-5}, $2^{2-15, 21-3}$, $4^{1-3, 11-14, 17-19}$,
5^{1}–6^{6}, 11^{1-11}; Isa 6^{1}–9^{7}, 29–31, 1^{2-31}, 5^{1-7}, 6^{11-13}, 10^{20-27}, 14^{32},
$28^{5, 16}$, 37^{32}.

Ch. 9 Deut 6–12^{28}; Jer 1^{4-19}, 2, 11^{1-8}, 11^{18}–12^{6}, 26, 7^{1-15}, 36, 29^{1-15},
37–39^{14}, 42^{1}–43^{7}, 31^{27-34}; Ps 130.

Ch. 10 Ezk 1, 2^{1}–3^{14}, 4^{1-17}, 8, 18, 34, 37^{1-14}; Isa 40, 42^{18}–43^{13}, $44^{9-20,}$
$^{23-8}$, 45^{1-8}, 42^{1-4}, 49^{1-6}, 50^{4-9}, 52^{13}–53^{12}; Ps 22.

Ch. 11 Ezra 4^{1-23}; Neh 1–2, 4, 6–7^{4}; 11^{1-2}, 5, 13; Ezra 7, 9–10^{16}; Neh
8; Jonah 1–$2^{1, 10}$, 3–4; Dan 1, 3, 6, 7, 11^{21-45}, 12.

Ch. 12 Job 1–2; 15^{20-35}, 18^{5-21}, 16^{18-19}, 19^{23-7}, 38^{1-11}, 42^{1-6}; Ps 73, 2, 72.

SUGGESTIONS FOR FURTHER READING

Geography

Teach Yourself Bible Atlas, H. H. Rowley (EUP). (1)
The Land of Palestine, D. Baly (USCL). (1)
The Geography of the Bible, D. Baly.

Archaeology

God's People among the Nations, L. Toombs (USCL). (1)
Documents from Old Testament Times, ed. D. Winton Thomas (Nelson)
Discovering Buried Worlds, A. Parrot (SCM). (1)
Foundations in the Dust, Seton Lloyd (Penguin). (1)
The Archaeology of Palestine, W. F. Albright (Penguin).
The Hittites, O. R. Gurney (Penguin).
Iran, R. Ghirshman (Penguin).
The Pyramids of Egypt, I. S. Edwards (Penguin).
Ur of the Chaldees, Sir Leonard Woolley (Penguin).
A Forgotten Kingdom, Sir Leonard Woolley (Penguin).
Early Anatolia, Seton Lloyd (Penguin).

History

A History of Israel, J. Bright (SCM OT Library).
The History of Israel, M. Noth (A. & C. Black).
The Splendour that was Egypt, Margaret Murray.
The Greatness that was Babylon, H. W. F. Saggs (Sidgwick & Jackson).

The Bible

Peake's Commentary on the Bible (new edition).
Layman's Bible Commentaries (SCM). (1)
Torch Commentaries (SCM). (1)
Epworth Preacher's Commentaries. (1)
A Critical Introduction to the Old Testament, G. W. Anderson (Duckworth). (1)
Introducing the Old Testament, F. Moriarty (Burns & Oates). (1)
Moses, G. von Rad (USCL). (1)
The People of God in the Old Testament, H. J. Kraus (USCL). (1)

When Israel Came Out of Egypt, G. Hebert (SCM). (1)
The Prophets, J. Dheilly (Burns & Oates). (1)
Prophecy and the Prophets, T. H. Robinson (Duckworth). (1)
Prophecy in Ancient Israel, J. Lindblom (Blackwell).
He That Cometh, S. Mowinckel (Blackwell).
The Theology of the Old Testament, E. Jacob (Hodder & Stoughton).
The Theology of the Old Testament, W. Eichrodt (SCM OT Library).
Ancient Israel: Its Life and Institutions, R. de Vaux (Darton, Longman & Todd).
Dictionary of Life in Bible Times, W. Corswant (Hodder & Stoughton). (1)

The books marked (1) are less advanced than the rest.

INDEX OF PASSAGES FOR STUDY

GENERAL INDEX